A Socialist History of the French Revolution

A Socialist History of the French Revolution

Jean Jaurès

Abridged and Translated by Mitchell Abidor
Introduction by Henry Heller

PlutoPress
www.plutobooks.com

First English translation published 2015 by Pluto Press
345 Archway Road, London N6 5AA

www.plutobooks.com

British Library Cataloguing in Publication Data
A catalogue record for this book is available from the British Library

ISBN   978 0 7453 3500 1   Hardback
ISBN   978 1 7837 1287 8   PDF eBook
ISBN   978 1 7837 1289 2   Kindle eBook
ISBN   978 1 7837 1288 5   EPUB eBook

10 9 8 7 6 5 4 3 2 1

Typeset by Stanford DTP Services, Northampton, England
Text design by Melanie Patrick
Simultaneously printed by CPI Antony Rowe, Chippenham, UK
and Edwards Bros in the United States of America

Contents

Introduction by Henry Heller

Jean Jaurès, the leader of the French socialists, was assassinated on the eve of World War I by Raoul Villain, a nationalist fanatic. As war approached, Jaurès, who was the leader of the Socialist Party, fought valiantly to prevent its outbreak, even calling for general strikes to force peace on the French and German governments. He did so in the face of a rising chorus calling for support of the impending war. Many in his own party and likewise socialist leaders in Germany including "the renegade" Karl Kautsky succumbed to these bellicose demands. Jaurès resisted because he believed that war would be a disaster for Europe, the French nation and the prospects for socialism. Jaurès took the same anti-war position as had his hero Maximilien Robespierre, the Jacobin leader during the French Revolution. Prior to the outbreak of war between France and the absolutist regimes in Prussia and Austria, Robespierre had insisted that war could only benefit those who opposed the Revolution.[1]

Jaurès is remembered as a martyr to internationalism and peace as well as a politician, who was able to unite the historically fractious elements of the French left, and the centenary of his assassination on July 31, 1914 was recently commemorated throughout France. Also, Jaurès pioneered the Marxist historiography of the French Revolution. His *Histoire socialiste de la Révolution française* was published as a series of journal articles and then in four volumes (1901–04).[2] This massive account of the Revolution, which was a highly original work of history as well as a literary masterpiece, is almost forgotten today. Its rhetorical and dramatic character is felt by some to be too evocative of a bygone age of epoch narrative. Yet Jaurès's monumental work of over three thousand pages was not only a great

---

1   Jean Jaurès (1968), *Histoire socialiste de la Révolution française*, Albert Soboul (ed.), 7 vols., Paris: Éditions sociales, vol. 2, p. 168.
2   Jean Jaurès (1901–04), *Histoire socialiste de la Révolution française*. 4 vols., Paris: Rouff.

work of literature, it inaugurated the scientific study of the history of the Revolution.

Jaurès's work analyzed the Revolution from the perspective of Karl Marx's materialist interpretation of history which viewed it as a capitalist and bourgeois revolution. The leading academic historian of the Revolution, Alphonse Aulard, had established the principle that history had to be founded on a critical investigation of the primary sources. But he was still writing the history of the Revolution from the perspective of its politics. Jaurès, too, undertook to write history based on a critical investigation of the sources but he combined this approach with a materialist view of history. The freshness of this perspective deeply impressed contemporaries. Paul Lacombe, a contemporary critic who by no means shared Jaurès's politics, nonetheless conveyed his sense of the originality of Jaurès's approach. Commenting on Jaurès's opening chapter, Lacombe noted that:

In this work I have come across a ground-breaking inquiry, in large part original, which is without equivalent among other historians of the Revolution: a preliminary but step-by-step review of the economic conditions in which the stratified classes of society, peasants, workers, petit and big bourgeoisie, major and minor financiers, nobility, clergy, court nobility, etc. lived in 1789. After which in logical order there follows a review of the provinces from the perspective of commerce and industry. In short an exposition of the economic activity of France.[3]

Jaurès's subsequent narrative of the Revolution then unfolds as a study of the successive conflicts between these social groupings in the years that followed, based on the interplay between revolutionary politics and ongoing social and economic crisis. It was the first assertion of what came to be referred to as the "classic" or "Marxist" view of the French Revolution, in which the French people en masse figured as the main actor. Since Jaurès, the Marxist view has been developed by a long line of twentieth-century French historians including Albert Mathiez, Georges Lefebvre, Albert Soboul, Michel Vovelle, Claude Mazauric, and Guy Lemarchand.

---

3   Paul Lacombe (1908), "Les historiens de la Révolution – Jean Jaurès," *Revue de synthèse historique*, Vol. 16, No. 1, pp. 164–5.

All were sympathetic to the Communist or Socialist Parties and saw their work as an intrinsic part of the political and social movement which it was hoped would lead France toward socialism.[4]

In the 1960s and particularly since the failure of the May 1968 revolution, this interpretation came under attack from a counter-movement called "French Revolutionary revisionism." Appearing first in Britain and the United States, this movement sought to deny the fundamental premise of the classical interpretation that the Revolution was bourgeois and capitalist. Without itself being able to articulate an alternative explanation, the new school initiated by the English academic Alfred Cobban sought to debunk the idea that capitalism or a bourgeois class existed prior to the Revolution.[5] In the US, Cobban's skepticism was reinforced by George Taylor of the University of North Carolina, who presented a serious if flawed case against the economic foundations of the Marxist view.[6] In France, revisionist views were supported by François Furet who first took the view that the radical Jacobin Republic aborted the development of constitutional government in France. Subsequently Furet went further, asserting that this derailment of the Revolution had happened not by reason of deep and uncontrollable social forces but as a result of the subversive ideas of fanaticized intellectuals.[7] The parallel with the Bolshevik Revolution was deliberate as Furet, in addition to being a historian, was one of the leading anti-communist intellectuals in France at the height of the Cold War.[8]

Indeed, the spread of revisionism can be understood as part of a political and intellectual reaction against long-standing Marxist cultural hegemony in France and the threat of revolution which stirred anxiety in France but

4   Claude Mazauric (2009), *L'histoire de la Révolution française et la pensée marxiste*, Paris: Presses universitaires de France.

5   Alfred Cobban (1968), *The Social Interpretation of the French Revolution*, Cambridge: Cambridge University Press.

6   George Taylor (1962), "The Paris Bourse on the Eve of the Revolution, 1781–1789," *American Historical Review*, Vol. 73, No. 4, pp. 951–77.

7   François Furet (1978), *Penser la Révolution française*, Paris: Gallimard; François Furet and Denis Richet (1973), *La Révolution française*, Paris: Fayard.

8   Michael Scott Christofferson (2001), "François Furet between History and Journalism, 1958–1965," *French History*, Vol. 15, No. 4, pp. 421–47.

also in Britain, the United States and the rest of the English-speaking world in the 1960s. As such, revisionism was remarkably successful to such a degree that the Marxist interpretation was pronounced dead in the universities of the Anglophone countries. Inspired by Furet, many historians in the United States took the so-called "cultural turn," arguing that the Revolution could be explained by the peculiar political culture of France.[9] Insistence on the peculiarities of French culture had the additional advantage of undercutting the universal significance of the Revolution. French Revolutionary revisionism must therefore be viewed in the context of the post-structuralist movement which became hegemonic in the humanities, especially from the 1970s in the United States. But this reaction in turn can only be understood as part of the capitalist counter-offensive which gained momentum from the 1970s. It took ideological form through postmodernism and neoliberalism and gained force with the collapse of Soviet Communism.

Despite this apparent revisionist triumph, a strong current of Marxist-inspired historiography persisted in France most visible in the works of Michel Vovelle, Guy Lemarchand and Claude Mazauric. Vovelle, occupying the prestigious chair of the French Revolution at the Sorbonne, published a continuing series of monographs and articles which encapsulated the new quantitative and cultural tendencies in history inspired by the *Annales* school while continuing to interpret the Revolution within a Marxist framework.[10] Lemarchand cut his teeth on a materialist study of the decline of the feudal mode of production in the *pays de Caux* (Normandy) which prepared the way for the Revolution. He followed this up with a sweeping panorama of French economic history from the 1760s until the 1830s, demonstrating that a decisive transition from feudalism to capitalism occurred during that period at the center of which lay the crisis of the

9   Michael Scott Christofferson (2013), "Les passeurs de depasseur: les historiens américains de la Revolution francaise et François Furet," in *Passeurs de révolution: actes de la journée d'étude organisée à Rouen, le 14 janvier 2013, par la Société des études robespierristes et le GRHis Université de Rouen*, Jean-Numa Ducange, Michel Biard (eds.), Paris: Société des études robespierristes, pp. 57–68.
10   See notably Vovelle's study of dechristianization: Michel Vovelle (1988), *1793, la Révolution contre l'Église: de la Raison à l'Être Suprême*, Paris: Complexe.

French Revolution.[11] Finally, there is Mazauric who spent over thirty years as a historian of the French Revolution at the University of Rouen. Member of the Communist Party and of its central committee (1979–87) and a trade unionist, there has been no more staunch defender of the classic view of the Revolution. Mazauric through thick and thin has, through his many publications including works on Rousseau, Babeuf, Jacobinism and Marxist thought and the Revolution, combined serious research with an excellent command of Marxist theory and the historiography of the French Revolution.[12]

In the English-speaking world, after many years in which cultural preoccupations have dominated, there are signs of a revival of interest in the relationship between the Revolution and capitalism.[13] Indeed, various anglophone scholars including myself have taken a Marxist approach to the Revolution that has begun to challenge revisionist work.[14] The outbreak of the economic crisis since 2008 will likely only reinforce this trend. But the truth of the matter is that the influence of Jaurès on the study of the Revolution never went away. As a result of Jaurès's influence, in 1903 the National Assembly established a permanent commission to oversee the publication of the economic and social sources of the Revolution. The series of works published under its auspices over many decades greatly expanded knowledge of the economic and social history of the Revolution.[15] Mathiez

---

11   Guy Lemarchand (1989), *La fin du féodalisme dans le pays de Caux: conjuncture économique et démographique et structure sociale dans une région de grande culture de la crise du XVIIe siècle à la stabilisation de la révolution (1640–1795)*, Paris: Comité des Travaux historiques et scientifiques; Guy Lemarchand (2008), *L'économie en France de 1770 à 1830: De la crise de l'ancien régime à la révolution industrielle*, Paris: A. Colin.

12   Claude Mazauric and Julien Louvrier (2008), "Entretiens de Claude Mazauric avec Julien Louvrier," *Cahiers d'histoire: revue d'histoire critique*, Vol. 104, pp. 19–145.

13   Livesey, James (2013), "Capitalism and the French Revolution," in A. Fairfax-Cholmeley and C. Jones (eds.), *New Perspectives on the French Revolution, e-France*, Vol. 4, Reading University, pp. 19–24.

14   Peter McPhee (1989), "The French Revolution, Peasants and Capitalism," *American Historical Review*, Vol. 94, No. 5, pp. 1265–80; Peter McPhee (2002), *The French Revolution 1789–1799*, Oxford: Oxford University Press; Gwynne Lewis (1993), *The French Revolution: Rethinking the Debate*, New York: Routledge; Henry Heller (2006), *The Bourgeois Revolution in France 1789–1815*, New York: Berghan Books.

15   Charles Peyard and Michel Vovelle (eds.) (2002), *Héritages de la Révolution française à la lumière de Jaurès*, Aix-en-Provence: Publications de l'Université de Provence.

republished Jaurès's *Histoire socialiste* in the 1920s[16] and Lefebvre looking back at the historians of the Revolution concluded that he considered Jaurès his only master.[17] And Soboul gave Jaurès's text new life by providing a fresh edition undergirded with an up-to-date scholarly apparatus which makes the work even now an indispensable point of reference.[18] Even Furet expressed his admiration for Jaurès in so far as the latter had conceived of the Revolution as not simply a change in the mode of production but a civilizational transformation.[19] In the light of the ongoing interest in Jaurès and the renewal of interest in the Marxist perspective, it is a stroke of brilliance that Pluto Press has undertaken to publish this selection from Jaurès's *Histoire socialiste* which is at the same time a great historical work and a literary masterwork.[20]

Jaurès was born in 1859 in the Midi in the small city of Castres into a bourgeois family in decline. Young Jean experienced real deprivation as the son of a father who failed as a would-be manufacturer and merchant and was forced to earn his living as a peasant working a 15-acre farm. On the other hand, Jean had the good fortune to have an uncle who became an admiral and Minister of the Navy (1889) and helped him advance himself. Jean's precocious intellect quickly made itself evident in the college of Castres where he received a thorough grounding in the classics. He was rewarded for his brilliance and diligence with admission first to the prestigious *Lycée* Louis-Le-Grand and then to the *École des hautes études* where he came first in the entry exams ahead of the later-celebrated philosopher Henri Bergson. Having himself majored in philosophy, Jaurès returned to the Midi where he taught first at a *lycée* in Albi and then became lecturer at the University of Toulouse. There he made himself known as a critic of

16   Jean Jaurès (1922–24), *Histoire socialiste de la Révolution française* Albert Mathiez (ed.), 8 vols., Paris: Éditions de la Librairie de l'humanite.

17   Jean-Reneé Surrateau (1979), "Georges Lefebvre, disciple de Jaurès," *Annales historiques de la Révolution française*, No. 237, pp. 374–98.

18   Jean Jaurès (1967–73), *Histoire socialiste de la Révolution française*, Albert Soboul (ed.), 7 vols., Paris: Éditions sociales.

19   Christophe Prochasson (2011), "Sur une réception de *l'Histoire socialiste de la Révolution française*: François Furet lecteur de Jean Jaurès," *Cahiers Jaurès*, No. 200, pp. 49–67.

20   A new edition of the complete *History* has been published in France by Éditions sociales.

avant-garde literature for a local radical newspaper *La Dépêche*.[21] In 1885 at the age of 25, he was elected to the National Assembly partly with the help of his uncle. He sat with the Republicans, associating himself with Jules Ferry and other opponents of clerical influence. Having lost his seat in the election of 1889, he returned to teaching at the University of Toulouse where he received his doctorate in philosophy. His secondary thesis was on the origins of German socialism, which he purported to find in Luther, Kant, Fichte and Hegel. He had already begun to read seriously about socialism, familiarizing himself with the first volume of Marx's *Capital*.[22] In 1891, he could affirm that as a left republican he was loyal to both republicanism because it affirmed the rights of man and to socialism because its goal was to submit property to the rights of man.[23]

His involvement in the bitter strike of the miners of Carmaux the next year moved him definitively into the socialist camp. The strike was occasioned by the dismissal of an employee, Jean-Baptiste Calivignac, by a local mining company because of his election as the socialist mayor of Carmaux. The miners considered this dismissal an attack on the right of the workers to take part in politics and the principle of universal suffrage. As the strike continued, the President of the Republic Sadi Carnot, head of a government racked by scandal, nonetheless saw fit to send the army against the strikers to defend the principle of the right to work. In newspaper articles defending the workers, Jaurès accused the government of siding across the board with industrialists and bankers at the expense of citizens. The government was forced to back down while Jaurès, who proclaimed his conversion to socialism, was rewarded by being elected to Parliament as an independent socialist.[24] But then his principled stand in defending Dreyfus—a bourgeois and Jew (something that many on the extreme left rejected, as well as peasants and workers)—cost him his seat in the election of 1898. Jaurès then became co-editor of *La Petite République*, a republican and Dreyfusard journal sustaining the moderate socialist

21   Madeleine Rebérioux (1994), *Jaurès, La parole et l'acte*, Paris: Decouvertes Gallimard, pp. 31–8.

22   Ibid., p. 52.

23   Ibid., p. 48.

24   Ibid., pp. 55–6.

Alexandre Millerand's entering the Cabinet of the Republican Defense of Waldeck-Rousseau.[25] Lenin later would characterize Millerand's action as the first application on a nationwide basis of the disastrous movement to socialist revisionism. But faced with the threat to democracy from the right led by the army and Church during the Dreyfus Affair, Jaurès advocated collaboration with the Radical Party or the liberal and democratic bourgeoisie. He also believed that such an alliance permitted reforms which, if no substitute for revolution, strengthened the working-class movement and necessary unity with the peasants and petty bourgeoisie. The Republic more and more depended on proletarian democracy around which the peasants and petty bourgeoisie were being forced to cluster. The development of socialism would follow as proletarian democracy became the main political force in the Republic.[26]

In 1902, Jaurès was re-elected to the National Assembly and helped to pass the anti-clerical laws in the wake of the Dreyfus Affair. In assuming this position of cooperation with the radical bourgeoisie, Jaurès came into conflict with critics on the left—anarchists, revolutionary Marxists and Syndicalists—who argued that the new society could not be prepared within the framework of the old.[27] But from Jaurès's perspective, the goal of the Paris Commune, the prime example of a revolutionary workers' government, could only have been the establishment of such a democratic republic. Moreover, he argued that the struggle of the left since 1871 had been a political struggle toward the same end. By the beginning of the twentieth century, France had become a republican state and the struggle for socialism had to be defined in these terms. Only by assuming leadership over the democratic republic could the socialists unite the peasants and petty bourgeoisie under socialist leadership and move toward socialism.[28] Nonetheless, in order to become leader of the unified socialist movement or *Section française de l'Internationale ouvrière* (SFIO) [1905], Jaurès had

---

25   Robert Stuart (1992), *Marxism at Work: Ideology, Class and French Socialism during the Third Republic*, Cambridge: Cambridge University Press, pp. 52–3.

26   Gilles Candar (2011), "Jean Jaurès et le réformisme," *Histoire@Politique*, No. 13, p. 32.

27   Ralph Engelman (1973), "The Problem of Jean Jaurès," *Science and Society* , Vol. 37, No. 2, p. 198.

28   Ernest Labrousse (1967), "Preface," in *Histoire socialiste de la Révolution française*, Soboul (ed.), Vol. 1, pp. 10–11.

to back away at least tactically from what seemed to be reformist positions. An engaged and impassioned politician of the left, Jaurès spent his last years prior to 1914 seeking to consolidate the unity of the factionalized left while fighting ultra-nationalism and social reaction.

* * *

The *Histoire socialiste* emerged from this context of struggle for a democratic republic. It was the democratic republic in Jaurès's view which provided the framework for tying together the peasants, petty bourgeoisie and workers through the consolidation of the Socialist Party. It was Jaurès's object in his work to show that the roots of this ongoing movement toward socialism lay in the French Revolution which had laid the foundations of popular republicanism. The *Histoire* was designed to educate politically and historically the party faithful and proletariat and help to unify the still-divided leaders of the socialist movement. Jaurès's envisaged his work as part of a broader editorial project on the history of socialism embracing the nineteenth century, which would draw in intellectual collaborators from the various currents of the socialist movement, including the revolutionary Marxists. His aim was to use this collaboration as a way of facilitating the unification of the socialist movement. In this he was only partially successful.[29] Jaurès brought to the task his gifts as an academic and literary critic as well as his long years of practical involvement in political and social struggle. During the 1890s, he had begun serious historical research on the French Revolution. He read all the main histories of the nineteenth century—Lamartine, Thiers, Tocqueville, Michelet, and Taine—while familiarizing himself with the increasingly specialized research of the new century. More importantly, he immersed himself in the primary sources found in the library of the Chamber of Deputies, Bibliothèque Nationale, Musée Carnavelet, and Archives Nationales.

The inclusion of the word "socialist" in the work's title took positivist historians aback. According to Jaurès, nonetheless, its title accurately described its primary purpose which was to educate politically workers

---

29   Madeleine Rebérioux 1967, "Le livre et l'homme," in *Histoire socialiste de la Révolution française*, Soboul (ed.), Vol. 1, p. 36.

and peasants. Given the price of the volumes, it is doubtful that it could do so directly. Rather its viewpoint was diffused over many years through the influence of socialist public school teachers whose influence on their charges is well known. Furthermore, its intent was to show that the French Revolution was based on the people and thereby announced not merely the establishment of representative democracy but the eventual establishment of a socialist and democratic republic.[30] This position contrasted with the revolutionary Marxists or followers of Jules Guesde (Guesdists) who asserted that socialism could not be established on the basis of bourgeois institutions but only as a result of a revolution against them. Jaurès's revisionism expressed itself through his apparent rejection of the necessity of a revolutionary break. Jaurès made clear that the Revolution took place under the auspices of the bourgeoisie: "The French Revolution indirectly prepared the way for the rule of the proletariat. It created the two indispensable conditions of socialism: democracy and capitalism. But fundamentally it represented the advent of bourgeois rule."[31] Acknowledging the role of the workers in the Revolution, he nonetheless underscored that the working class remained dependent on bourgeois leadership. On the other hand, he emphasized that the people en masse already played an indispensable role opening the way to a future socialism based on economic abundance and a more profound democracy.[32] The republic was founded in revolution and the future of socialism in France depended on the development of a deepening republican democracy. This view is already manifest in his narrative of the Revolution in which there is a clear progression from 1789 until 1794. At the beginning of the Revolution, the people are clearly subordinated within the Third Estate and see the nobility as the common enemy. But as the Revolution unfolds, the people more and more come to a consciousness that the bourgeoisie are their enemies as well. Indeed, through thinkers like Sylvain Maréchal and Gracchus Babeuf, they come to understand that the workers have an

30 Labrousse, "Preface," p. 15.
31 Jaurès, *Histoire socialiste de la Révolution française*, Vol. 1, p. 3.
32 Bruno Antonini (2004), "Jaurès historien de l'avenir: gestation philosophique d'une 'méthode socialiste' dans l'Histoire socialiste de la Révolution française," *Annales historiques de la Révolution française*, Vol. 337, No. 3, pp. 119, 135.

interest which is opposed to those who control property and the means of production.[33] But such views can hardly influence the immediate course of the bourgeois revolution. They can however prepare the future as the great upheavals of the Revolution contain the seeds of future democratic and socialist development.

In terms of research, Jaurès fully absorbed the philological lessons of the increasingly influential positivist history that was consolidating itself in the French universities at the beginning of the twentieth century. The *Histoire socialiste* is both an epic and dramatic narrative that is unapologetically partisan in the rhetorical style of the nineteenth century and a materialist history founded on deep erudition, study of the primary sources and critical analysis. The development of a critical and historical methodology itself was by no means apolitical. It was based on the aspirations of a new generation of academics to create a scientific historical methodology which could establish the case for the democratic republic in the struggle against political and clerical reaction at the time of the Dreyfus Affair. It created a standard for judging the past that was designed to undercut clerical and chauvinist myths and to intellectually reinforce the struggle for a democratic and secular republic.[34] But in Jaurès's hands, this technique became an instrument for comprehending the significance of the events of the Revolution in terms of their meaning, not simply for the present struggle for the Republic but in terms of their potential in building a socialist future.[35]

Histoire begins with an overview of the Old Regime as it approached its crisis. It continues through the overthrow of the old order, the establishment of the Legislative Assembly and the period of the Convention, coming to a conclusion with the fall of the radical republic at Thermidor. Lacombe noted with admiration the sense of coherence and continuity that Jaurès was able to give his monumental work. He associated this talent with Jaurès's capacity to bring apparently disparate political events and currents

---

33   Raymond Huard (1989), "Peuple et classes dans 'L'Histoire Socialiste de la Revolution Francaise' de Jean Jaureès," *La Pensée*, Vol. 267, p. 68.

34   Madeleine Rebérioux (1974), "Jaures et les historiens dreyfusards," *Bulletin d'histoire économique et sociale de la Révolution française*, pp. 19–31.

35   Antonini, "Jaurès historien de l'avenir," pp. 120–21.

together through his oratorical powers.[36] In explaining the Revolution, the great nineteenth-century historian Michelet had placed the stress on the misery of the people. According to the latter, the upheaval was the result of fiscal oppression from above which reached a breaking point. Michelet especially emphasized the role of a regressive system of taxation which exempted the privileged and ground down the people. Jaurès broke new ground in signaling that the rise of the bourgeoisie was the fundamental cause of the Revolution. Of course there was misery, Jaurès acknowledged. But what is striking in the eighteenth century is the growing economic strength and confidence of the bourgeoisie.[37] The Revolution, he was able to document in detail, was more one of hope than misery. Moreover, this advance of the bourgeoisie was registered in both town and countryside including as it did a stratum of well-to-do peasants. On the growing prosperity of the rich peasant farmers, Jaurès pioneered in demonstrating the increasing value of the net agricultural product in relation to rent. This analysis of the rural economy reflected his ability to explain complicated economic matters in a simple and clear style, something which was on view throughout his narrative. Moreover, he had a way of making such economic questions as interesting to readers as dramatic political crises. In stressing the ascent of the bourgeoisie, he perhaps exaggerated the decline of the nobility. Modern research reveals that the fortunes of some lesser nobles declined but overall the nobility more than held their own based on increasing rents.[38]

While the transformation in the countryside was of great importance, the catalyst for the Revolution came from the towns. The urban world of the petty bourgeoisie and the working class was closed to Jaurès at the time he wrote and would have to wait the result of the researches of Soboul and others. Jaurès's focus was rather on the increasingly wealthy and confident urban bourgeoisie of Paris and the other main cities. He begins with the elite of the world of finance and commerce and is particularly aware of the expansion of overseas commerce, especially the colonial trade signaling out the progress of port towns like Bordeaux, Marseilles and Nantes. The

---

36 Lacombe, "Les historiens de la Révolution – Jean Jaurès," p. 168.
37 Labrousse, "Preface," p. 23.
38 Ibid., pp. 17–19.

bourgeoisie of these urban centers was marked not only by their wealth but by their increasing political and cultural maturity. The development of mining, metallurgy, textile manufacturing and construction are taken into account. The launching of a series of impressive real estate projects like the Palais Royale is noted.[39] Stressing the growing economic strength of the bourgeoisie, Jaurès was unaware of the successive economic crises and grain shortages that marked the century nor of the deterioration of the wages of workers, factors which are important to modern interpretations of the Revolution.[40] In Jaurès's account, the Revolution comes at the end of the eighteenth century because the bourgeoisie reached intellectual and social as well as economic maturity. At the same time, the bourgeoisie needed the support of working people and peasantry whose political consciousness was less formed.[41] While France is the focal point of the narrative, Jaurès finds space at the end of his account of the decisive year 1792 to provide the reader a panorama of the effects of the Revolution on Germany, Switzerland and England.[42] Based on his internationalism, he escapes the chauvinism with respect to Germany so typical of his times by providing a sympathetic treatment of that country.[43] His analysis of the crucially important colonial and slavery question is particularly incisive.[44]

In Jaurès's account, collective forces dominate the course of the Revolution but to what degree they determine immediate events is open to question. As Jaurès represents it, in matters political nothing is decided in advance. The collective forces only create certain probabilities and more in the long than in the short term. In the short term, the individual plays an important role. Accordingly human will, moral force and intelligence can affect the outcome of events.[45] This view emerges from Jaurès's personal experience of politics, his study of the Revolution as well as his reading of

---

39   Ibid., pp. 20–21.

40   Ibid., pp. 21–2.

41   Ibid., pp. 23–4.

42   Rebérioux, "Le livre et l'homme," pp. 43–4.

43   Eric Guillet (2010), "Les courbes et les droites. Patience en Allemagne et impatience en France à l'époque révolutionnaire. L'interpretation de Jean Jaurès," *Annales historiques de la Révolution française*, Vol. 360, pp. 8–10.

44   Rebérioux, "Le livre et l'homme," pp. 44–5.

45   Labrousse, "Preface," p. 25.

the classics. Plutarch's *Lives* particularly affected his own view of political action. Political figures need to be understood within the context of their times. Indeed, the dominant political figures are such because they are most characteristically products of their times.[46] Mirabeau, Necker, Barnave, Danton, and Robespierre who figure largely in the narrative were all men of the hour and consequently their decisions mattered. More often than not in his characterizations of these leaders, Jaurès is able to penetrate to their psychological core. During key events such as the overthrow of the monarchy or during the struggle between the Girondins and Jacobins, the actions of individuals are seen as important to the outcome.[47] Jaurès not only highlights these figures in context, he undertakes to judge both the historical significance and the morality of their behavior. His judgments, moreover, achieve a certain impartiality despite his own political commitments. He advances his own view but only in the course of taking seriously and debating the views of others.[48] Once again, his parliamentary experience served him well in this respect.

Despite his attention to political leaders, it is class above all which is historically determinative. It is the mediator between the economy and ideology. It shapes the individual including his manner of living and his feelings.[49] At the same time, Jaurès offers his judgment of particular events, collective attitudes and political responsibilities. The Gironde were revolutionary in terms of their ends but not in their tactics, which became counter-revolutionary. It is the Jacobins who based themselves on Paris and the unity of France that embodied the hope of the Revolution. He expresses disgust at the September Massacres (pp. 113–14) and while he considered the Terror a regrettable necessity, he thought the Law of Prairial which permitted an acceleration of the work of the revolutionary tribunals atrocious and inefficacious. Among the Jacobins, he sides with Robespierre rather than Cambon or Carnot. The latter were administrators while Robespierre was a far-sighted political leader. Historians from Michelet to Aulard had condemned Robespierre as a tyrant and bigot. Jaurès treated

---

46 Jaures 1967, *Histoire socialiste de la Révolution française*, Vol. 1, p. 68.
47 Labrousse, "Preface," pp. 25–6.
48 Lacombe, "Les historiens de la Révolution – Jean Jaurès," p. 171.
49 Labrousse, "Preface," p. 29.

him as a hero, a true reflection of popular attitudes and a product of the times.[50] At the same time he criticized him for his blood-thirsty attitude at the time of the September massacres (pp. 120–2). Significantly, Jaurès accepts the sans-culottes' overthrow of the Girondins, but he condemns revolutions by conspiratorial minorities in the tradition of Blanqui or for that matter Babeuf.[51] Likewise he shows little patience for the demagogy of Marat (pp. 116, 123, 149–50).

*   *   *

As we have seen, the Marxist interpretation of the Revolution put forward by Jaurès has been rejected by the French revolutionary revisionists. But Jaurès's interpretation and its subsequent influence on Marxist historiography has also been attacked from the left. In the 1960s, Daniel Guérin published *La lutte de classes sous la Première République, 1793–1797*, which argued that the French Revolution already witnessed the mobilization of a class-conscious proletariat evident in the radical movement that ran from the *Enragés* and Hébertists to Babeuf.[52] Guérin asserted that while Jaurès acknowledged this in a grudging way, he opposed the left in the Revolution if it did not ultimately subordinate itself to the bourgeois revolution. According to Jaurès, left extremism endangered the bourgeois revolution necessary to the development of the forces of production under capitalism and the institutionalization of democracy without which a socialist future was unthinkable. But according to Guérin, the principle weakness of Jaurès's' work lay

... in its perpetual oscillation between the Marxist conception of the permanent revolution and the social-democratic conception of the bourgeois revolution. From time to time, he does perceive the embryo of the proletarian revolution stirring in the flanks of the bourgeois revolution. But too often he falls in with those who divide history into

---

50   Rebérioux, "Le livre et l'homme," p. 45.
51   Labrousse, "Preface," p. 27.
52   Daniel Guérin (1968), *La lutte de classes sous la Première République, 1793–1797*, 2 vols., Paris: Gallimard.

rigid periods and immobilize it in rigid categories. Having once pinned the label bourgeois on the Grand Revolution he refuses to admit that the proletariat entered into fateful struggle with the bourgeoisie in so far as the two essential conditions for socialism and democracy had not been realized.[53]

In particular, Guérin criticized Jaurès's unconditional endorsement of the inflationary *assignat* as a war measure even though it came at the expense of the mass of the population, and Guérin blamed Jaurès for endorsing the Jacobin demagogic manipulation of the masses while endorsing their suppression when they were mobilized by the left.[54] Protective of his hero Robespierre, Jaurès fails to acknowledge the common bourgeois outlook of Robespierre and the opportunist Danton.[55]

Guérin's' critique of Jaurès excited much criticism from the professional historians who considered themselves his heirs. Guérin was denounced for being schematic and not sufficiently historical. Yet it has to be said that recent scholarship makes clear that Guérin did not invent his criticisms out of thin air. They were rooted in fundamental differences in the Marxist movement of the late nineteenth century, which influenced the perspective of the *Histoire socialiste* and the subsequent Marxist interpretation of the Revolution. As we have seen, Jaurès moved toward socialism without breaking from the radical republican and parliamentary tradition in which he was educated and to which he was deeply attached. A socialism which entailed breaking from the fundamental institutions of the Republic was beyond his ken.[56] This was even more so in that the political fights of the *fin de siècle* entailed defending the Republic against the immediate threat of military dictatorship and clerical reaction as well as against the depredations of advancing capital. Even more decisively, Jaurès was convinced that the assemblage of the coalition of workers, peasants and other petty bourgeoisie into a unified French socialist party could only

---

53   Ibid., vol. 2, p. 412.
54   Ibid., vol. 1, p. 130; Vol. 2, p. 78.
55   Ibid., vol. 1, p. 444.
56   Franco Venturi (1966), *Historiens du XXe siècle: Jaurès, Salvemini, Namier, Maturi, Tarle, et discussion entre historiens italiens et soviétiques*, Geneva: Droz, pp. 6–7.

take place within the political framework of the democratic republic. The *Histoire socialiste* was designed to provide a historical justification for this strategy.

Following publication of the early volumes of Jaurès's work Kautsky—later Lenin's "renegade Kautsky"—sharply criticized Jaurès's political revisionism from the perspective of orthodox Marxism. Kautsky had long warned against the pervasive influence of Jacobinism on French socialism. In other words, he warned against subordinating the politics of the working class to that of the radical bourgeoisie. Encouraged by French revolutionary Marxists led by Guesde, Kautsky had already published a short historical essay which was the first materialist account of the French Revolution which emphasized class struggle and eschewed any romanticism with respect to Robespierre and the Jacobins.[57] Referring to the *Histoire socialiste*, Kautsky accused Jaurès of throwing the proletariat back to the subordinate position it occupied during the French Revolution. Writing in *Die Neue Zeit* in January 1903, Kautsky insisted that there were two proletarian politics one of which was autonomous and the other which sought to subordinate the working class to the bourgeoisie. According to Kautsky, Jaurès was seeking to replace the class struggle by a return to the forms of political thought of the French Revolution. His aspiration was to base socialism on the Declaration of the Right of Man rather than those of orthodox Marxism.[58] The Guesdists applauded Kautsky who at this point still rejected compromise with the bourgeoisie and the illusions of the democratic republic.[59] Likely it was in response to these criticisms that in the introduction to the published first volume, Jaurès admitted that the Revolution was after all a bourgeois revolution and that the Declaration of the Rights of Man, even in the Jacobin version of 1793, above all affirmed the right to property.[60]

The clearest light on this disagreement is found in the work of Neil Davidson, who has examined the development of Marx's conception of

---

57   Bertel Nygaard (2009), "Constructing Marxism: Karl Kautsky and the French Revolution," *History of European Ideas*, Vol. 35, No. 4, pp. 450–64.

58   Jean-Numa Ducange (2010), *Le socialisme et la Révolution française*, Paris: Demopolis, pp. 26, 28.

59   Stuart, *Marxism at Work*, pp. 59, 22, 233.

60   Rebérioux, "Le livre et l'homme," pp. 46–7.

permanent revolution. According to Davidson, Marx rightly took the view that the roots of permanent revolution appeared during the Revolution. The Revolution must be understood as having been both a bourgeois revolution and the beginnings of permanent revolution. For Marx, the Revolution was a great historical event and a precedent for the proletarian revolution. It was an upheaval in which the bourgeoisie undoubtedly assumed power but also one in which the people did begin to mark out their own autonomous development, and, indeed, opposition to the bourgeoisie. On the other hand, Marx perspicaciously added that however uncomfortable the bourgeoisie were made by the actions of the masses during the Revolution the radicalism of the latter ultimately redounded to their benefit. The fundamental need of the proletariat in the future was to achieve an understanding of its independence from those of the bourgeoisie and to give it political expression. This was Marx's understanding of the idea of permanent revolution and its role in the French Revolution.[61]

In this light, Kautsky's criticism, echoed by Guérin, amounts to saying that Jaurès slighted the permanent revolution at the expense of the bourgeois revolution. Moreover he did this in order to favor the politics of revisionism. This was no small matter because it spelled out the difference between a revolutionary and a reformist politics.[62] Moreover this historical perspective fundamentally shaped the subsequent Marxist interpretation of the Revolution. Yet Jaurès's *Histoire socialiste* for all its reformism can still be seen as a work which can inspire revolutionary change, something which the world needs more than ever. It is incontestable that, like Marx, Jaurès saw the Grand Revolution of the bourgeoisie as a great example for the working class to follow. Contrary to Guérin, moreover, Jaurès did not see the Revolution as one piece but rather one in which there could be radicalization or revolution within the Revolution. Thus, he fully endorsed the Jacobin coup against the Girondins based on the mass support of the sans-culottes and of course championed the armed defense of the Revolution. Moreover, he fully approved the subsequent writing of

---

61   Neil Davidson (2012), *How Revolutionary Were the Bourgeois Revolutions?* Chicago, IL: Haymarket Books, pp. 146–8.
62   Geoffrey Kurtz 2006, "A Socialist State of Grace: The Radical Reformism of Jean Jaurès," *New Political Science*, Vol. 28, No. 3, p. 273.

a new and democratic Constitution by the Convention. This deepening of democracy was also important to the further development of class consciousness. It can be concluded that the political perspective of the *Histoire socialiste* leaves room for making a revolutionary rather than an evolutionary break from capitalism. This is important in the light of the wave of radicalism that has spread over much of Latin America in which, echoing the Revolution, armed defense of revolution and the holding of constituent assemblies in Bolivia and Venezuela, for example, are seen as revolutionary steps away from capitalism. Moreover, these unfolding political crises must be seen as part of the ongoing capitalist crisis that marks the new millennium in which further upheavals are in the offing.

Translator's Note

Jean Jaurès's *A Socialist History of the French Revolution* is not only an impressive piece of scholarship and a guide to action, it is also quite massive, a work of several thousand pages in four, six, or eight volumes, depending on the edition. The best that can be done in this volume is to give a small taste of its riches.

The principle guiding the selections was choosing those portions of the *History* that show Jaurès's description and analysis of the key moments, players, and currents of the French Revolution. Interspersed among these chapters are also his disagreements with other scholars of the Revolution, and Jaurès the militant is not shy in taking on professional historians of the event. His independence and lack of dogmatism shine through everywhere.

As was often the case in multi-volume works like this, there are extensive, sometimes pages-long, transcriptions of articles and speeches. I chose to abridge these quotes and once the point of the quoted work has been made I have placed ellipses in brackets. The introductory and explanatory entries to the chapters, all in italics, are either direct quotations or summaries of what Jaurès wrote; in no case have I used the work of other writers. This is Jaurès's vision of the French Revolution and no one else's. Similarly, the comments within the selections, sometimes found in parentheses, sometimes in brackets, are all in Jaurès's original. Unless otherwise noted, the footnotes are all the translator's.

The first edition of the *Socialist History* had chapter heads but no sub-headings, which were added in the 1922 edition compiled by the great Robespierrist Albert Mathiez and carried forward in the later editions edited by Albert Soboul. I have maintained these sub-heads, which help the reader situate herself in the text.

The four original volumes were all given titles based on the government in place at the time of the events, of which there were three. These shifting names of the government appear in the text, and their dates were as follows:

The National Constituent Assembly: July 9, 1789–September 30, 1791 (Volume 1 of the original edition). Referred to by Jaurès as the Constituent Assembly and the National Assembly.

Legislative Assembly: October 1, 1791–September 1792 (Volume 2 of the original edition).

National Convention: September 1792–1794 (Volumes 3 and 4 of the original edition).

I would like to express my thanks to Richard Greeman and Joan Levinson for their assistance in revising the translation, as well as to Francisco Martinez of the New York Public Library. Fernando was virtually my personal librarian, tracking down volumes that I required, and it's safe to say that without him this book might very well not have been possible.

Mitchell Abidor

1

Introduction

Jean Jaurès

We want to recount the events that occurred between 1789 and the end of the nineteenth century from the socialist point of view for the benefit of the common people, workers, and peasants. We view the French Revolution as an immense and admirably fertile event, but we don't see it as something eternally fixed that leaves the historian with nothing else to do but explain its consequences. The French Revolution indirectly prepared the advent of the proletariat. It realized the two essential conditions for socialism: democracy and capitalism. But at its heart it signified the political advent of the bourgeois class.

The economic and political movement, large-scale industry, the growth of the working class in both number and ambition, the uneasiness of the peasants crushed by competition and besieged by industrial and merchant feudalism, and the moral fears of the intellectual bourgeoisie whose delicate sensibilities were offended by a brutal mercantile society—all of this gradually set the scene for a new social crisis, a new and more profound revolution by which the proletariat would seize power in order to transform property and morality. And so it is the march and the interplay of social classes since 1789 that we want to recount. Though it's always somewhat arbitrary to delineate clear borders and divisions in life's uninterrupted and finely shaded progress, we can nevertheless distinguish with a certain amount of precision three periods in the last century in the history of the bourgeois and proletarian classes.

First, during the period 1789–1848, the revolutionary bourgeoisie emerged victorious and established itself. It used the force of the proletariat against royal absolutism and the nobility, but the workers, despite their formidable activity and the decisive role they played in certain events, were only a subordinate power; one might say a historic supporting player. At times, they inspired real horror in the bourgeoisie, but since they lacked a radically different vision of society the proletariat essentially worked for them. The communism of Babeuf and his few disciples was only a sublime convulsion, the final spasm of the revolutionary crisis before the tranquility of the Consulate and the First Empire. Even in 1793 and 1794, the proletariat was intermingled with the Third Estate: they lacked a clear class consciousness and the desire for, or notion of, any other form of property. They hardly went beyond Robespierre's impoverished ideas: a democracy politically sovereign but economically stationary, made up of small peasant owners and an artisanal petite bourgeoisie. They had none of socialism's marvelous life juices, which create wealth, beauty, and joy. On the most terrible days, they burned with a dry flame, a flame of wrath and envy. They were as yet unaware of the beauty, the powerful sweetness of this new ideal.

And yet, bourgeois society had barely begun to establish itself and peacefully function when the socialist idea made its presence felt. In the years between 1800 and 1848, Babeuf was followed by Fourier, Saint-Simon, Proudhon, and Louis Blanc, and then, under Louis-Philippe, the workers' uprisings of Lyon and Paris. The bourgeois revolution had hardly emerged victorious when the workers asked, "Where does our suffering come from and what new revolution must be made?" They saw the reflection of their worn-out faces in the waters of the bourgeois revolution, waters that were at first foaming and wild, then calmer and clearer, and the workers were seized with horror. But despite all the socialist systems and working-class revolts, bourgeois domination remained intact before 1848.

The bourgeoisie didn't believe it possible that power was escaping it and that property was being transformed. Under Louis-Philippe, it had the strength to fight against the nobility and the priesthood as well as against the workers. It crushed the Legitimist uprisings in the West as well as the proletarian revolts of the starving cities. It naively believed, with the pride of Guizot,[1] that it was the culmination of history, that it had

---

1 François Guizot (1787–1874)—politician of the July Monarchy, overthrown by the Revolution of 1848.

historical and philosophical title to irrevocable power, that it synthesized the centuries-long efforts of France, and that it was the social expression of reason. For their part, the proletariat, despite the spasms of poverty and hunger, were not conscious revolutionaries. They barely glimpsed the possibility of a new order. It was primarily among the "intellectual" class that the socialist "utopias" recruited their followers. In any event, the socialist systems were strongly impregnated either with capitalist ideas, like those of Saint-Simon, or petty-bourgeois ideas, like those of Proudhon. The working class needed the revolutionary crisis of 1848 to achieve consciousness of itself, for it to accomplish, as Proudhon said, the final break with other social elements.

The second period, which ran from February 1848 to May 1871, from the provisional government to the bloody repression of the Commune, was troubled and uncertain. It is true that socialism was already asserting itself as a force and an idea, and that the proletariat was asserting itself as a class. The workers' revolutions against the bourgeois order were so threatening that the ruling classes assembled against it all those forces of the bourgeoisie and the landowning farmers frightened by the red specter. But socialist doctrines remained indecisive and confused. In 1848, the communism of Cabet,[2] the mutualism of Proudhon, and the statism of Louis Blanc hopelessly clashed, and the mold of the ideas that should have given the working class form was inconsistent and incomplete. The theoreticians argued over the molten metal that came out of the furnaces, and while they argued reaction, led by the man of December,[3] smashed all of the unformed molds and cooled the metal. Even under the Commune, Blanquists, Marxists, and Proudhonians proposed divergent versions of working-class thought. It's impossible to say just which socialist ideal a victorious Commune would have applied.

What is more, there was confusion and intermingling in both the movement and in ideas. In 1848, the revolution was prepared by the radical democracy as much as, if not more than, by working-class socialism, and during the June days, bourgeois democracy killed the proletariat on the burning paving stones of Paris. In 1871 as well, the Commune grew out of

---

2   Etienne Cabet (1788–1856)—Utopian socialist.
3   Louis-Napoléon Bonaparte, Napoleon III, who seized power on December 2, 1852.

an uprising of the shopkeepers angered by the law on payment of overdue rents and the harshness of the nobles of Versailles, as well as from Paris's patriotic frustration and republican defiance.

The socialist proletariat wasted no time in putting its revolutionary mark on this confusion, and Marx, in his powerful and systematic study of the Commune, was right in saying that for the first time the working class seized power. This was a totally new event, one of incalculable importance, but the proletariat benefited from surprise. The proletariat was the best-organized and most clear-sighted force in the isolated and enflamed capital, but it was not yet capable of bringing all of France over to its side. France belonged to the priests, the big landowners, and the bourgeoisie, of which M. Thiers was the leader. The Commune was like a knife tip, reddened by flames, that shatters against a large, refractory block. The proletarians had made enormous progress between 1848 and 1871. In 1848, the proletariat's participation in power was all but fictitious: Louis Blanc and the worker Albert were stymied in the Provisional Government, and a perfidious bourgeoisie organized against them the swindle of the National Workshops. The socialists platonically conversed at the Luxembourg Palace; they abdicated their role and resigned themselves to being nothing but a powerless debating society. Lacking the strength to act, they resigned themselves to making speeches. And then, when the deceived working class rose up in June, it was crushed before it was able to attain power for a single moment. In 1871, the sons of the fighters of the June uprising[4] held and exercised their power. They weren't a rioting mob; they were the revolution.

The proletarians thus raised to power were then driven from it. But they nevertheless gave new working-class generations signs of hope that were understood. The Commune closed the second period, in which socialism asserted itself as a force of great importance, though it was still vague and shaky. And yet it was the Commune that made the new period possible, the one we are now living through, where socialism is methodically proceeding to the total organization of the working class, to the moral conquest of a reassured peasantry, to the rallying of bourgeois intellectuals

---

4   The June Revolution of 1848.

disenchanted with bourgeois power, and to the total seizure of power in order to establish new ideals and new forms of property.

Confusion is no longer to be feared. There is unity of thought in the working class and the socialist party. Despite conflicts between groups and superficial rivalries, all proletarian forces are united by one direction and working toward the same goals. If the proletariat were to seize power tomorrow, it would immediately use it in a defined and determined way. There would certainly be conflicts between factions: some would want to strengthen and advance the centralized actions of the community, while others would want to ensure the greatest possible autonomy to local groups of workers. In order to regulate the new relations within the nation, those of professional federations, of communes, of local groups, and of individuals, in order to establish both perfect individual freedom and social solidarity, an immense effort in the field of ideas will be required, and given the complexity of the issue there will be disagreements. But despite it all, a common spirit now moves the socialists and the proletariat. Socialism is no longer divided into hostile and powerless sects. It is an ever-stronger, living unity that is strengthening its hold on life. All the great human forces—those of labor, thought, science, art, and even religion (understood as humanity's taking control of the universe)—await their renewal and growth from socialism.

How, through what crises, through which human efforts and what evolution of things has the proletariat grown into the decisive role it will play tomorrow? This is what we socialist militants propose to recount. We know that the economic conditions and the forms of production and property are the very foundation of history. Just as for most people their work is the essential element of their life; just as, for mankind, it is the occupation which is the economic form of individual activity, that in most cases determines habits, ideas, sorrows, joys, and even dreams; in the same way, in every period of history, it is the economic structure of society that determines the political forms, the social customs, and even the general direction of ideas. And so in every period of this tale we will attempt to lay bare the economic basis of human life. We will attempt to follow the movement of property and the evolution of industrial and agricultural techniques. In broad strokes—as is appropriate in a necessarily rough portrait—we will make clear the economic system's influence on governments, literature, and systems.

But we don't forget that Marx—too often simplified by narrow interpreters—never forgot that it is upon men that economic forces act. There is an enormous variety of passions and ideas among men, and the nearly infinite complexity of human life doesn't allow itself to be brutally and mechanically reduced to an economic formula. Even more, even though man is a fragment of mankind, even though he is affected by his environment and is a continuation of his social milieu, he also lives through his senses and intelligence in an environment even more vast than the universe itself.

In the poet's imagination, the light of the stars most distant from and foreign to the human system can only awaken dreams that are in conformity with the general sensibility of his time and the deepest secrets of social life, in the same way that the fog that floats over the prairie is formed by the moon from the earth's invisible dampness. In this sense, even stellar vibrations, however distant and indifferent they might appear, are harmonized and appropriated by the social system and the economic forces that determine them. Goethe, upon entering a factory one day, was seized with disgust for his clothing, whose production required so immense a productive apparatus. And yet, without the industrial growth of the German bourgeoisie, the Germanic world would never have felt or understood the magnificent impatience to live that caused Faust's soul to burst.

Across the semi-mechanical evolution of social and economic forces we will present the dignity of the free spirit, emancipated from humanity by the eternal universe. Even the most intransigent of Marxist theoreticians could not reproach us for this. Marx admirably wrote that until now human societies have been governed only by fate, by the blind actions of economic forms. Institutions and ideas have not been the conscious work of free men, but the reflection in the human mind of unconscious social life. According to Marx, we are still in prehistoric times. Human history will only truly begin when man, finally escaping the tyranny of unconscious forces, governs production by his reason and his will. His intelligence will no longer live under the despotism of economic forms that he created and guides, and he will contemplate the universe with a free and unmediated gaze. Marx presaged a period of full intellectual liberty where human thought, no longer deformed by economic servitude, will not deform the world. But to be sure, Marx doesn't contest the fact that already, in the darkness of this period lacking in consciousness, great men have attained freedom. They are preparing the advent of a fully conscious humanity. It is up to us to grasp these first manifestations of the life of the spirit. They allow us a foretaste of the great, ardent, and free life of communist humanity which, freed from servitude, will take control of the universe through science, action, and dreams. This is like a trembling in the forest, which at first moves only a few leaves, but which foretells the upcoming tempest.

And so our interpretation of history will be both materialist with Marx and mystical with Michelet.[5] It was economic life that was the basis for and the mechanism of human history, but across the successive forms of social life man, a thinking force, aspired to the full life of the mind, the ardent community of the unquiet intelligence, hungry for unity and the wondrous universe. The great mystic of Alexandria[6] said, "The great waves of the sea raised my boat, and I was able to see the sun at the very moment it rose from the waters." In the same way, the vast rising waters of the economic revolution will raise the human boat so that man, that poor fisherman worn out by a long night's work, can salute from the highest point the first glimmer of the growing spirit that will rise above us.

Nor will we disdain, despite our economic interpretation of great human phenomena, the moral value of history. To be sure, we know that for the past century the noble words of Liberty and Humanity have too often served as a cover for a regime of exploitation and oppression. The French Revolution proclaimed the Rights of Man, but the wealthy classes included in these words the rights of the bourgeoisie and capital.

They proclaimed that men were free when property itself was the only form of domination they possessed, but property is the sovereign force that has all others at its disposal. The basis of bourgeois society

---

5   Jules Michelet (1798–1874)—one of the great French historians, and author of a brilliant and influential *History of the French Revolution*.
6   Plotinus.

is thus a monstrous class egoism compounded by hypocrisy. But there were moments when the nascent Revolution united the interests of the revolutionary bourgeoisie with the interests of humanity, and a truly admirable enthusiasm often filled peoples' hearts. And in the midst of the countless conflicts unleashed by bourgeois anarchy, in the struggles of parties and classes, there were many examples of pride, valor, and courage. Rising above the bloody melees we will salute with equal respect all the heroes of the will: we will glorify the bourgeois republicans outlawed in 1851 and the admirable proletarian combatants who fell in June 1848.

But who could reproach us for being particularly attentive to the militant virtues of that insulted proletariat that over the last century so often gave its life for a still vague ideal? It's not only through the force of circumstances that the social revolution will be made; it is by the force of men, by the energy of consciousness and will. History will never exempt men from the need for individual valor and nobility, and the moral value of the communist society of tomorrow will be marked by the moral elevation of the individual consciousness of the militant class of today. Consider all the heroic fighters who, over the past century, had a passion for the idea and a sublime contempt for death as a revolutionary task. We will not mock the men of the Revolution who read Plutarch's *Lives*. It's certain that the great burst of inner energy Plutarch inspired in them did little to change the march of events, but at least the men of the Revolution remained upright in the storm, though their faces were twisted in fear under the lightning bolts of the great storms. Certainly no one would hold it against them if their passion for glory inspired their passion for liberty and their courage in combat.

And so, in this socialist history, which covers the period from the bourgeois revolution to the preparatory period of the proletarian revolution, we will omit no element of human life. We will strive to understand and interpret the fundamental economic evolution that governs societies, the mind's fervent aspiration for complete truth, and the noble exaltation of human consciousness defying suffering, tyranny, and death. The proletariat will free itself and become humanity by pushing the economic movement as far as it can go. The proletariat must thus become fully conscious of the role of economic activity and human grandeur in history. At the risk of shocking our readers by the disparate nature of these great names, it is under the triple inspiration of Marx, Michelet, and Plutarch that we write this modest history, in which each of the militants who collaborates in it will add his own shade of thought, where all will be garbed in the same doctrine and faith.

2

The Causes of the Revolution

The Nobility and Feudalism

Under the *ancien régime* the nation was dominated by the nobles, the Church, and the king. As a result of the development of the French monarchy, the nobility had gradually lost the power it had had during the Middle Ages. They were now only quasi-sovereigns, and the greatest among them, formerly rebellious vassals, were nothing but the first among courtiers. But they still enjoyed great privileges.

Even though considerably reduced and repressed by royal justice, seigneurial justice continued to exist: the judges of the great fiefdoms were among the first dispossessed for the benefit of the royal judges; but in the smaller fiefdoms, in the small noble domains, justice was meted out by seigneurial judges. It is true that in those cases that had no direct relation to feudal rights they limited themselves to gathering information and certifying the existence of a crime, but the fact that they did so was important in itself. They also judged all cases involving feudal rights, and these were so varied, so complex, they were connected by so many tiny roots to the entire system of property and exchange that, in fact, the seigneurial judge had quite extensive powers. Imagine today's justices of the peace having in certain cases the attributes of county courts and one would have an idea of the place, on the eve of the Revolution, of the seigneurial judges.

Humble rural life, with its quotidian events, its petty and irritating conflicts, was almost entirely within their bailiwick and so within the bailiwick of the lords who named them. It can thus be said that the latter were sovereign judges in those feudal disputes to which they were party, and it was thanks to this sovereignty of justice that, particularly in the last third of the eighteenth century, the nobles were able to despoil the population of the countryside of the property of the "communities," what we would today call communal property. We see here how selfish and lacking in foresight the French monarchy was. It had dispossessed the nobles of their higher judges; it had destroyed those wider feudal jurisdictions that opposed the progress of royal power, and in doing so it had served the general interest of the nation as well as its own; but it had only suppressed seigneurial justice at its highest level, where it hampered royal power. It had left it in place at the lowest level, at ground level, where it oppressed and stifled rural life.

In repressing feudal justice, the crown had wanted to both extend its reach and defend itself. It had not for a moment thought to defend the peasantry, and they, in the immediate grip of seigneurial justice, languished like a poor harvest beneath the countless knots of a voracious plant. It would be the hand of the Revolution that would tear up the last roots of feudal justice. [...]

Feudal rights had extended their hold over all natural forces, over everything that grew, moved, or breathed: over the fish-filled rivers, over the flame that burns in the oven and bakes the miserable bread made of a mix of oats and barley, over the wind that turns the windmills, over the wine that spurts from the press, over the voracious game that came out of the forests and the high grass to ravage the vegetable gardens and fields.

The peasants can't take a step on the roads, cross the narrow river over a shaky bridge, buy a measure of cloth in the village market or a pair of wooden shoes without running up against rapacious and troublesome feudalism. And if they want to get around it, or simply defend themselves against new abuses, another form of game, that of the agents of the law attached to the seigneurial judge, the impudent clerks and half-starved bailiffs, attack with sharpened teeth what remains to them of their harvest and their courage.

How easy it is to imagine the anger that builds up in them. And how ready the peasants must be for a general uprising. They lack but one thing: confidence in themselves, the hope to free themselves. But soon the first thunder claps of the Revolution, striking with terror the gilded authorities who maintain privilege, will awaken peasant hopes. It will shake the peasants out of their centuries-long slumber and they will rise up with a terrible cry, and with the ferocious light in their eyes answer the call of the storm of liberty emanating from Paris.

The Monarchy

If the kings of France would have been able to act apart from and against the nobility, if they could simply have been the kings of the bourgeoisie and the peasants, if they had made use of that freedom of action to wrest the countryside from the last vestiges of feudalism and assure the industrial bourgeoisie, merchants, and rentiers of security in labor, scrupulous observation of public contracts, and frugal and strict management of the state's moneys, it is quite probable that the Revolution of 1789 would never have occurred.

Let us imagine the kings of France of the seventeenth and eighteenth centuries possessing the frugal spirit of Frederick II and his father or the firmness of Gustavus II of Sweden and the King of Portugal with regard to the nobles and monks. If we were imagine our ancient monarchy, with its secular might and its nearly sacred prestige, playing a modern role in modern France it would quite likely have led our country up to the eve of the proletarian revolution. It would have become a bourgeois and capitalist monarchy and would only have disappeared with the last of all powers, that of Capital.

But French royalty didn't have the ability to understand events or to be open to renewal, and it was doubtless historically incapable of it.

It was too old and too tied to ancient powers to accommodate itself to the new times.

The Philosophical Spirit

At the end of the eighteenth century two great forces, two revolutionary forces impassioned minds and things and enormously increased the intensity of events. The two forces were these:

On one hand the French nation had reached intellectual maturity, and on the other the French bourgeoisie had reached social maturity. French thought had become conscious of its grandeur and desired to apply its methods of analysis and deduction to all of reality, to society as well as nature. The French bourgeoisie had become conscious of its power, its wealth, its rights, and of its near-infinite possibilities of development. In a word, the bourgeoisie had attained class consciousness while French thought had achieved consciousness of the universe. These were the two luminous resources, the two sources of the fire of the Revolution. It was through them that it was possible, and it was through them that it was great.

M. Taine[1] falsely—I would even say childishly—interpreted the impact of French thought, of what he calls the classical spirit on the Revolution. According to him, the Revolution was completely abstract. Through the empty and vague concepts of equality, humanity, right, popular sovereignty, and progress, it was led to the worst systematic errors and excesses. It was classical culture that deprived French thought of an acute and complex sense of reality; it was this that accustomed the French of the eighteenth century to noble but vain generalizations.

And so, according to him, the revolutionaries were unable to correctly understand the true diversity of conditions and men. They were incapable of seeing the passions, the instincts, the prejudices, the ignorance, and the habits of the 27,000,000 men they suddenly had to govern. They were thus condemned to recklessly overturn social life and individual existences under the pretext of reforming them. According to Taine, it was the narrow classical ideology applied to the conduct of societies that precipitated the Revolution into utopianism, adventures, and violence. M. Taine repeats Napoleon I's dictum against the Revolution: "It was the work of ideologues." But even more than Napoleon, he underestimated its grandeur and power. And his condemnation goes even further: he not only denounces the revolutionary ideology: he denounces the national ideology and the very foundations of the French spirit.

---

1 Hippolyte Taine (1828–93)—historian and philosopher, his *History of the Origins of Contemporary France* posited the slow development of French institutions and demonstrates a hatred for the Revolution, which in his eyes attempted to artificially force that development.

But M. Taine is completely wrong. He understood neither what the classical spirit was nor what the Revolution was. It was he who substituted futile scholasticism and reactionary ideology for precise knowledge and a clear vision.

Far from having been abstract and vain, the French Revolution was the most substantive, the most practical, the most balanced of revolutions history has ever seen. This will be soon be clear to us.

The men of the Revolution had a profound knowledge of reality, a marvelous understanding of the complex difficulties into which they'd been cast. There has never been a program of action that was more extensive, more precise, and wiser than that contained in the *Cahiers* of the Estates General. Never has a program been more fully realized through methods more appropriate and decisive. And as we will see, the French Revolution met all its goals. It accomplished or outlined everything social conditions allowed, all that the new needs demanded, and in the past century nothing has succeeded in Europe and the world except that which has followed the road laid out by the Revolution.

It is on the counter-revolutionary side that we find utopianism and mad and sterile violence. Even the turmoil of the Revolution had a meaning: hidden beneath the revolutionary phraseology were the most substantial conflicts, the most explicit interests. There wasn't a single group, there wasn't a single sect that didn't correspond to a fragment of social life. There was not a phrase, even the most apparently vain, that wasn't dictated by reality and that didn't bear witness to historical necessity. And if M. Taine, whose work reveals an almost incredible ignorance, has so wildly misunderstood the Revolution, what becomes of his theory about the classical spirit and the vertigo of abstraction?

But here again he was completely wrong. In the first case, by resorting to arbitrary abstraction he incorrectly opposed science to what he calls the classical spirit. He sang a magnificent song of praise to science as it developed in the seventeenth and eighteenth centuries. It revealed the structure of the universe, its immensity, the laws of the worlds that interconnectedly move within it. It taught man what the earth was, its location, its form, its dimensions, its movements, and its probable origin.

It began the classification of the countless forms of life, and it taught man himself, until now proudly isolated, that he was part of a long chain of beings; that he was a bud, the highest one, of the immense tree of life. It set out to analyze human society, to discover the secrets of social life, and to break down economic phenomena, the ideas of wealth, rent, value, and production.

In short, from the distant movements of the stars, barely perceptible in the heavens, to the beginnings of new trades in factories, science attempted to understand and develop everything in the same continuous order as that of nature itself. This is what the scientists of the seventeenth and eighteenth centuries did, and science's education of the public would have been ideal if, according to Taine, the classical spirit hadn't accustomed the French to retaining only a few general and summary ideas about immense reality, ready-made for the frivolous schemes of conversation or the fearsome schemes of utopia.

Solid and stable science vanished into thin air in the salons, and then was deformed in the assemblies and clubs. The result of all this were the vanities and follies of the Revolution.

But by what illusory amputation was M. Taine able to separate modern science from the classical spirit? These two forces are not only connected, they are also intermingled. [...]

It would have been agreeable to religious, monarchical, and feudal absolutism if the eighteenth century had limited itself to dull monographs buried in Benedictine archives, and patient, erudite research into the past. It would have been agreeable to all tyrannies and privileges if French thought, as had been the case in the sixteenth century, had continued to play at verbal debauchery and drowned its revolt in the uncertain and troubled waters of Rabelaisian prose. It would have been agreeable to priests, monks, and nobles if the eighteenth century, getting a head start on romanticism, wasted its time in meticulously describing with the purplest prose the old portal of an old church or the old tower of an old chateau.

But classical thought had other things to do. It precisely and angrily noted all the superstitions, all the tyrannies, all the privileges that opposed thought's free growth, the expansion of labor, the dignity of the individual.

For this combat it needed a direct, sober, and strong language. It rejected the excess baggage of sensations, verbal curiosities, and the systematically picturesque that M. Taine wants to impose on it. Alert, passionate, it cast rays of light in all directions and denounced all existing institutions as contrary to nature and reason.

How could it have smashed the old, out of date, and variegated world if it had not appealed to great, simple ideas? Is it by disputing every feudal right, every ecclesiastical pretension, every royal act, like a village lawyer, that classical thought would have been able to wrest France from servitude and routine? An all-encompassing effort was needed: it required a strong light and an ardent appeal to humanity, to nature, to reason.

But classical thought's necessary cult of general ideas in no way excluded precise and profound knowledge of facts or curiosity about details. And this is M. Taine's second error. He failed to see how rich in facts and sensations the noble classical form was.

I don't have the time to discuss his superficial judgment of the literature of the seventeenth century, but how is it possible to contest the eighteenth century's immense effort to document itself? In the historical and social realms, it was the century of memoirs. And how many studies, how much work in the fields of economy and technology! The Academy of Sciences published a magnificent collection of industrial processes and new inventions. Precise, detailed studies and books supported by statistics and figures abound concerning wheat and staple goods. And the economists didn't limit themselves to formulating general theories. In their collection of *Éphémérides*, they noted the daily variations in prices, supplies, and the state of the market. Books and pamphlets proliferated concerning the feudal regime and the peaceful and practical methods of abolishing the feudal rights through a system of redemptions. In the last third of the century, the royal agricultural societies published extremely substantive studies. Factory inspectors sent reports to the government that our modern labor office wouldn't disavow, and we will soon borrow from those of Roland de la Platière, written five years before the Revolution, which are the most precious and detailed documents on the state of industry, the forms of production, and the condition of wage workers.

No century was ever as attentive to life's details and the interactions of all social mechanisms as was the eighteenth to life's details, and no revolution was ever as well prepared as this one was by more serious studies, by richer documentation. One day Mirabeau exclaimed in the Constituent Assembly: "We no longer have the time to work, to study. Fortunately, we have a head start in ideas. Yes, a head start in ideas and acts." Never had thinkers been better provisioned, and M. Taine, who seems to be unaware of the eighteenth century's immense labor of documentation, is mocking us when he reduces the classical spirit to the noble ordering of impoverished abstract ideas.

But all this information and all this generous philosophy would have been in vain if there hadn't been a new social class with an interest in great change and the ability to make it happen.

The Bourgeoisie

This social class is the bourgeoisie, and here one cannot help but be astounded by M. Taine's frivolousness. In his chapters dedicated to "the structure of society" under the *ancien régime*, he quite simply neglects to study and even to mention the bourgeois class. He barely notes in passing that many ruined nobles had sold their lands to the bourgeois, but he nowhere deals with the economic growth of the bourgeoisie over the previous two centuries.

He seems to have seen in the bourgeois movement nothing but an excess of vanity or of foolish philosophical intoxication. The bourgeois of the small cities suffered in their pride the disdain of the nobles. He read Jean-Jacques and became a Jacobin: this, in short, is the Revolution. M. Taine doesn't even seem to suspect the immense development of interests that imposed on the bourgeoisie its revolutionary role and which gave it the strength to fulfill it.

He reasons as if pure philosophical theories could panic and lead an entire people to rise up. And if he views the theses of the *philosophes* as abstract and considers classical thought to be empty, it's because he doesn't see the solid interests of the growing bourgeoisie, which are the foundation and substance of the theories of the thinkers. This so-called "realist" has limited himself to reading books on philosophy. He didn't see life itself. He ignored the immense effort of production, of labor, of savings, of industrial and commercial progress that led the bourgeoisie to be a power of the first order and which forced it to take over the leadership of a society where its interests already occupied so much place and where it could run so many risks. M. Taine truly missed something by not having read Marx, or having pondered over Augustin Thierry.[2] [...]

Economic Life

But the French bourgeoisie was also powerful in 1789 through its commercial and industrial activity. Under the Regency, Louis XV, and Louis XVI, internal commerce had expanded greatly. It's impossible for us to evaluate the figures, but its rapid growth is certain. The condition and wealth of "boutiques" in all small and mid-sized cities struck the admiration of all visitors.

It wasn't without necessity that for more than half a century the crown had developed a 10,000-league network of roads of a width of 42 feet. This network responded to the needs of circulation and cartage. Agriculturalists protested in vain against the disproportionate width of the roads, which decreased the cultivable surface.

In the nascent conflict between the agrarian and mercantile interests, it was commerce, by the very force of its development, that had the final word. In a well-written memorandum by the future member of the Constituent, Dr. Guillotin, in the period preceding the Estates General, the merchants of Paris requested that the king grant large representation to commerce. Guillotin vigorously compared the insignificance, or at least the mediocrity, of commerce in 1614—the year of the last Estates General—with its marvelous activity in 1789.

It was this shift in affairs that, in 1776, made the creation of the discount bank necessary. It was the property of a limited partnership and

---

2   Augustin Thierry (1795–1856)—influential French historian. Jaurès is referring here to Thierry's *Essay on the Formation and progress of the Third Estate*.

opened with funds of 15 million francs divided into 5,000 shares. It was to discount letters of exchange and commerce bills with a term of two to three months at 4 percent and engage in gold sales. It issued circulating currency analogous to that now issued by the Bank of France. In order for such an organization, with all the risks it entailed, to be superimposed on the preexisting commerce of moneychangers and bankers, and for it to have resisted the perpetual forced loans of the Royal Treasury, it had to have responded to a great need on the part of commerce. A central organ of discount and credit had become necessary to the vast operations of the commercial bourgeoisie. [...]

It would be impossible to properly understand the commercial and industrial development of the eighteenth century if we attribute to corporations the essential role they are normally attributed. It is certain that they constituted a hindrance to freedom of industry and commerce. In order to become a master, i.e., a boss, it was necessary to pass a test given by the corporation of established masters. It was sometimes necessary to pay quite high a sum for this, which prevented poor *compagnons* from rising to the level of masters. What is more, each corporation's industry and commerce was carefully determined: such-and-such a corporation could only sell such-and-such a product; such-and-such a category of artisans could only produce such-and-such a category of objects. In this way economic activity was constantly hindered, and in addition, a narrow professional aristocracy, jealous and all but hereditary, was formed.

And in fact, it was more or less only the sons or sons-in-law of established masters who could aspire to master status. It is obvious that this spirit of strict regulation and exclusion was hardly favorable to a great expansion of affairs, and the entrepreneurial genius of capitalism could not accommodate itself to this narrow and out-of-date system. Nevertheless, it should not be thought that initiative was completely suppressed within the corporations: despite the rules and regulations, the spirit of invention and collaboration was ever awake. But above all, it should never be thought that the corporative regime ever functioned completely or rigorously. [...]

Nowhere—or almost nowhere—did the artisans of the countryside and the villages allow themselves to be included in corporate regulations that, in the hands of the crown, had become a means of fiscal extortion. Finally, and above all, the large-scale enterprises, where capitalism's expansion was beginning to make itself felt, escaped these constraints. Large-scale commerce—trade, properly speaking—was too vast and fluid to allow itself to be imprisoned in this way. Since the sixteenth century, large-scale commerce was ordinarily accompanied by banking operations. The trader was at the same time a banker. Through his extensive operations in Europe and the colonies, he was led to perpetual exchange, to the perpetual negotiation of trade.

When dealing with such trade, how can limits be marked off, categories delineated? How can a banker be told he can recover only such-and-such a category of trade relating to the delivery of such-and-such merchandise? Quite naturally, commerce had the same flexibility and variegated nature as the Discount Bank itself. What is more, as exchange increased, as products from the colonies and distant countries reached our ports, the role of large-scale intermediaries, of large-scale brokers developed. [...]

And so the two extremes of economic life escaped the corporate regime. At one end, the rural artisans were protected by their rural isolation against the mandatory professional community, and at the other end, large-scale commerce, by the multiplicity of its forms and the subtlety of its operations, had created another sphere, an entirely new world of movement, boldness, and freedom. It was only in the middle region of economic activity, in the sphere of small urban industry and small and middle commerce, that the corporate regime seriously functioned, and with more elasticity than the letter of the regulations would lead one to believe. And even in this middle region, peaceful and well-regulated, capitalism's entrepreneurial spirit penetrated. [...]

And so, in the final quarter of the eighteenth century, the economic regime was extremely complex. The corporations, briefly abolished by Turgot's famous edict of 1776, were reestablished, and though they didn't fully recover from the blow they'd received, they still bitterly and fiercely defended their existence. The subtle and varied forms of modern capitalism maneuvered in the face of this corporate system. Even more, capitalist subtlety and activity penetrated the interior of the corporations and prepared the way for their imminent dissolution.

Here were the beginnings of capitalist expansion and organization. The framework within which Louis-Philippe's bourgeoisie would establish itself were prepared in the eighteenth century. The bourgeoisie is not only a force for accumulation and wisdom: it is a bold conquering force that partially revolutionized the system of production and exchange before revolutionizing the political system. M. Taine did not even suspect the essential problems, nor did he discern the deep currents of economic life or even for a single instant ask how, with the restrictive system of corporations, the bourgeoisie was able to grow in wealth and daring. He preferred to attribute the French Revolution to Vaugelas's[3] grammar which, in impoverishing the French vocabulary, condemned the country to abstract ideas and utopias.

---

3   Claude Favre de Vaugelas (1585–1650)—grammarian, author of a *Dictionnaire* and *Remarks on the French Language*.

3
July 14, 1789

(The Revolution was in the making in many realms for decades: "For half a century the crown had been ceaselessly threatened by the state of its finances, its budget being almost constantly in a deficit." The country's "financial ills were too profound, too chronic to be cured without touching the tax privileges of the nobility and the clergy."

In the midst of this ferment, the Estates General were convoked, bringing together the representatives of the three orders—the clergy, the nobility, and the Third Estate—meeting on May 4, 1789 for the first time since 1614.

In preparation for this great event, throughout France, Cahiers de Doléances *were written, by individuals, by towns, and by professional and craft bodies, laying out their grievances and the needs that had to be met. The* Cahiers *of the Third Estate demanded that things must be changed, that "the law must be the expression of the general will, that there is no law unless the Nation decides on it, and that the Nation must make its will known by elected assemblies." But they don't call for a complete overturning of affairs: "No cahier says that royal power is suspended until it's been sanctioned by the nation." Indeed, "the cahiers recognize that monarchical power, hereditary from male to male, must be preserved."*

But in these Cahiers *is a central demand: "The vote at the Estates General must be by head and not order ... this is the key to the Revolution." "Voting by orders the clergy and the nobility would have had two votes and the Third Estate only one ... [W]ith voting by head the deputies of the Third Estate were sure not only of balancing the deputies of the clergy and the nobility, but thanks to their cohesion and the divisions within the other orders they would be able to push the majority in the direction of the Revolution."*

When the Estates finally met, the battle began, as the Third Estate stood firm for the vote by head, opposed by the other orders. It was in the course of

this fight that the Third Estate took its Tennis Court Oath on June 20, 1789
to remain in session "until the constitution of the kingdom is established and
consolidated upon a solid foundation." The king, though, was enraged by all
this and sought to establish control by force. The crisis was about to reach its
height.

"The great city prepared for resistance," most particularly the bourgeoisie.
"What is admirable about the revolutionary bourgeoisie of Paris, what clearly
demonstrates the historical legitimacy of its advent as a class, is its absolute
confidence in itself. It's not afraid to be caught between the revolts of the poor
and the king's coup d'état."

"On the morning of July 14 the entire people of Paris, bourgeois, artisans,
and proletarians, prepared for combat ... .")

For several days, the great city had been preparing itself for resistance.
Mirabeau, in demanding the establishment of the bourgeois Guard on
July 8 at the Assembly, was the voice of the revolutionary bourgeoisie of
Paris. The Assembly adjourned, but not Paris, and its initiative would
save the Revolution. We know that the elections took place by district:
the sixty districts had designated 407 second-degree electors who named
the deputies. But after the elections the primary district assemblies hadn't
been dissolved. They continued to meet and the events of the Revolution
resonated and had repercussions in these many vibrant centers. The
revolutionary echo provided by the districts enabled communication
between the Assembly in Versailles and Paris.

The assembly of second-degree electors had continued to meet; even
after May 10, even after the cloture of electoral activities, the 407 [electors
of the Third Estate] had decided to meet in order to maintain relations
with their elected representatives and to keep an eye on events. After
June 25, after the royal session, they assembled on rue Dauphine at the
Museum of Paris, and on June 28 they moved to the great hall of the
Hôtel de Ville. And so, before there was even a municipal law, a Parisian
city government was established through the spontaneous revolutionary
force of Paris, functioning alongside the former government of the city.
Bourgeois and popular action, spread across Paris by the many district
assemblies, was at the same time concentrated in the *Hôtel de Ville* by the

general assembly of electors. A few priests and nobles had joined the 407 electors of the Third Estate.

On June 30, the Assembly of Electors had to deal with the affair of the Abbaye,[1] and on July 6 it sent a deputation to the National Assembly that gave an account of its actions during those grave events:

> The ferment was great at the Palais Royal; it took on the same character among the more than 2,000 citizens who witnessed our deliberations. The night advanced, the people became agitated, and we decided on a decree that, thanks to its just ideas, calmed matters. We declared in it that it was not permitted to doubt the justice of the sovereign; that as soon as the prisoners were returned 24 electors would go to Versailles to appeal to the king ... The night had not yet ended and the prisoners had already been returned to the Abbaye. The crowds had left the Palais Royal and calm rules in Paris.

The president answered with congratulations and the Assembly of Electors, its prestige increased by this popular investiture, took on a larger role and grew more courageous.

On July 10, at the *Hôtel de Ville*, Carra[2] proposed to the electors that they "constitute themselves as the real and active assembly of the Communes of Paris" and that this assembly assume the rights inherent in this, notably the direct and immediate election of the officers of the Commune, the regulating of the wages of municipal magistrates, and the guarding and defense of the city, of its rights and its properties. But the Assembly of Electors felt that the most urgent need was the organization of bourgeois Guards. It postponed Carra's proposal and on July 11 decided that it would call for the immediate establishment of a Parisian armed force.

It was on the afternoon of Sunday, July 12 that Paris learned of Necker's removal from office, causing an outcry. Paris felt that a *coup d'état* was being carried out against it, and Necker's bust, draped in crepe, was carried

---

1   On June 30, 1789, a crowd had entered the Abbaye prison to liberate French Guardsmen who had disobeyed orders.

2   Jean Louis Carra (1742–93)—once a Jacobin, he came to be suspected of royalist sympathies and was guillotined as an enemy of the Revolution.

around the streets. The German regiments of Reinach and Esterhazy were massed on the Place Louis XV. The crowd threw stones at them, and the Germans fired in response. Colonel Lambesc entered the Tuileries Gardens with his dragoons and in the ensuing panic, an old man was knocked down and trampled by the horses. That evening the people went to the theaters and the Opera and demanded that all performances be suspended as a declaration of national mourning. According to the Venetian ambassador, orders were given for houses to put lights in their windows in order to prevent any troop maneuvers or acts of brigandage, and it was amidst this tumult and illumination that Paris awaited the battles of the morrow. At that same moment, the hated toll-gates of the tax farmers were burned.

The people felt that for resistance to be effective it had to be organized. They had two goals: they wanted the bourgeois militias to immediately become a legal institution and they wanted the Assembly of Electors to take the defense of Paris seriously in hand. On July 13, one of the electors, Doctor Guillotin, deputy of Paris, was sent to the Assembly to obtain a decree creating the bourgeois guard of Paris. The revolutionary bourgeoisie of Paris obviously felt it would be stronger in the face of foreign mercenaries if it was the organ of the Nation and the law.

The National Assembly, awakened from its torpor of July 11, raised itself to Paris's height. The prudent and meticulous Mounier,[3] applying against this violated legality the same noble pride as he had in the fight in the Dauphinois, protested against the dismissal of the patriotic minister and cried out: "Never forget that we love the monarchy because of France, and not France because of the monarchy."

Guillotin's motion inviting the Assembly to assist in the formation of a Parisian bourgeois Guard momentarily encountered resistance. Several members of the Assembly were hesitant to arm Paris, as if Paris, in these tragic hours, was not the revolution itself. But Le Chapelier's strong words swept aside the final reservations:

You must first deliberate concerning the enemy and foreign troops besieging a good and faithful people. Blood is flowing, property is not

---

3 Jean-Joseph Mounier (1758–1806)—politician active in his native Dauphiné as a spokesman for the Third Estate.

safe, and the scandal of the rioting Germans is at its height. Only the bourgeois guard can remedy this situation. Experience has taught us that it is the people who must guard the people.

Guillotin, upon his return to Paris, was able to tell the revolutionary bourgeoisie that the Assembly was being organized with the consent of the Nation. At the same time, the districts forced the assembly of electors to form a permanent committee that was a combination of the legal municipality and the new revolutionary municipal government. It consisted of eight members then in place in the city bureau and fourteen members designated by the electors. This committee's mandate was to repel the counter-revolutionary invasion of the German hordes in the pay of the king.

What is admirable about the revolutionary bourgeoisie of Paris at that moment, what demonstrates the historical legitimacy of its advent as a class, is its absolute confidence in itself. It didn't fear being caught between the revolts of the poor and the king's *coup d'état*. A few timid souls vainly pointed out to it the sordid crowd of 9,000 workers in the charity workshops. It was not in the least afraid that this abscess of poverty would burst over it during the revolutionary turmoil. It wasn't afraid to distribute weapons: it knew it was strong enough to supervise their use. It cast aside and disarmed all those who, having no property, provided no guarantee for property, and, on July 14, Bancal des Issarts[4] announced to the National Assembly that the bourgeois militia had disarmed many individuals. In the heart of the revolutionary storm, it gave its militia a bourgeois character and knew that the proletarians who were dragged along in its wake would not complain—they would throw stones at the counter-revolution if they were unable to fire on it. The ambassador of Venice noted how quickly and decisively the Parisian bourgeoisie was able to organize both revolutionary action and bourgeois order.

On the morning of July 14, all of Paris—bourgeois, artisans, and proletarians—prepared for combat. A detachment of dragoons had crossed the faubourg Saint-Antoine and approached the walls of the Bastille. The

4 Jean-Henri Bancal des Issarts (1750–1826)—moderate member of the National Convention.

people had concluded that the Bastille was going to become the center of a great military gathering, the base of operations of a portion of the troops sent against Paris, and that Paris was to be crushed between these troops and those massed on the Champs Elysées. It was this tactical necessity that turned the efforts of the people against the Bastille. The sad, somber castle where so many state prisoners, both commoners and nobles, had suffered, and which, in cutting across the lively faubourg Saint Antoine, seemed to cut off life and joy, was odious to Paris, to all of Paris. Mercier wanted the new roads that were being planned to finally sweep away the hated prison. And in their *Cahiers [des Doléances]* the noble citizens of Paris decided that "His Majesty will be requested to order the demolition of the Bastille." There was no order, no social class that didn't have members deep in its dark dungeons. If the Third Estate and the nobility didn't view the word "liberty" in the same way, at least bourgeois and nobles shared a common hatred for this monument of ministerial despotism. And the people's attack on the Bastille was a revolutionary stroke of genius, for even the nobility of the great city couldn't resist the movement without odiously putting the lie to what it had said and what it had claimed to oppose just yesterday. And so the court was isolated in its *coup d'état*, and it wasn't only the revolution that rose up against the foreign regiments that surrounded the revolution, it was all of Paris.

More than anything, they needed arms. Between 9:00 and 11:00 a.m., a large crowd went to the Invalides, where there was an enormous storehouse of rifles, from which they took 28,000 rifles and five cannons. The Bastille could now be forced. The permanent committee of electors, gathered at the *Hôtel de Ville*, tried to prevent a confrontation. And then, ceding to the irresistible passion of the people, they tried to obtain the capitulation of the fortress by peaceful means. But on the second attempt the negotiators were confronted with gunfire. Was there a misunderstanding? Treason? Governor de Launay would soon pay with his head for this violation of the rules of war. Led by a group of heroes who crossed the moat and cut the chains of the drawbridge, the crowd entered the citadel. Hesitant and divided, the soldiers surrendered. The French guardsmen played a decisive role in the assault. It is difficult to draw up an authentic list of the victors of the Bastille. By the following day countless claims were made. The newspaper *Les Révolutions de Paris* gave a short list of those who particularly distinguished themselves:

> Sieur Arné, grenadier of the French guards, Ressuvelles Company, a native of Dôle in the Franche-Comté. Twenty-six years old, who was the first to seize the governor, fought everywhere with courage, received several light wounds, and was decorated at the *Hôtel de Ville* with the civic crown and the Cross of Saint-Louis worn by Sieur de Launay.
>
> Sieur Hulin, director of the laundry of the queen at La Briche, who had called on the grenadiers of Ressuvelles and the fusiliers of Lubersac to go to the Bastille with three cannons and two others that were soon brought there. This Sieur Hulin was one of the leaders of the action. He exposed himself to danger wherever the need demanded it. He was one of the first to leap on the drawbridge and to enter the Bastille. He was also one of those who took the governor to the *Hôtel de Ville*.
>
> Sieur Élie, officer of the queen's infantry regiment, who intrepidly ran under the enemy's fire to unload carts of manure and set fire to them. This clever ruse marvelously served us. It was also Sieur Élie who received the capitulation and was the first to leap onto the bridge to force the opening of the Bastille, and accompanied by Sieur Tremplement, took the perfidious governor to the Grève.
>
> Sieur Maillard, junior, who carried the flag and placed it in other hands for a moment in order to leap on a plank laid across the moat to receive the capitulation.
>
> Louis Sébastien Cunivier, twelve years old, son of a gardener from Chantilly, was the fifth person to enter the fortress. He ran to the top of the Bazinière tower where the flag was, grabbed it and boldly paraded it around the platform.
>
> Sieur Humbert, living on the *rue de Hurepoix*, who received a dangerous wound.
>
> Sieur Turpin, fusilier of the company of La Blache, Popincourt barracks, commanded the citizens who were the first ones killed between the two bridges. He also received a bullet in his right hand and another in the shoulder.

Sieur Guinaut received two slight wounds and brought the governor's silverware to the *Hôtel de Ville*.

Sieur de la Reynie, a young *litterateur*, conducted himself with courage.

The assembly of representatives of the Commune, having opened an investigation, stated at its August 13 session, "That Messrs. Hulin, Élie, Maillard, Richard du Pin, Humbert, Legry, Ducostel, Georgette, and Marc distinguished themselves in the attack on and conquest of the Bastille," and decreed that it would be recommended to the districts that "they be invited to employ them in a manner worthy of their courage and patriotism, without consideration as to the district they belong to: citizens who have so effectively contributed to the salvation of the capital should be considered as belonging to all districts." Naturally the assembly recommended them for employment as officers in the new National Guard.

As we can see, it was professional soldiers, officers such as Élie, modest industrialists such as Hulin, and petit bourgeois such as Maillard, who led the movement, but the poorest of proletarians did their duty. On that heroic day of the bourgeois revolution, workers' blood was spilled for freedom. Among the hundred fighters killed before the Bastille there were men so poor, so obscure, so humble that for several weeks afterwards their names weren't known. And Loustalot, in *Les Révolutions de Paris*, sobbed over this obscurity that concealed so much sublime devotion: more than thirty left their wives and children in such a state of distress that immediate assistance was necessary.

Twenty months later, in a letter addressed to Marat, the woodworkers denounced the selfishness of the big entrepreneurs who wanted to maintain the benefits of the Revolution, but who had hidden on the days of peril. It is certain that the woodworkers played an active role in the assault on the Bastille; skillful at handling an axe, they were impromptu sappers, or the engineer corps of the Revolution.

We don't find on the list of combatants the rentiers, the capitalists for whom the Revolution, in part, was made. We find middle and petit-bourgeois, law clerks, artisans, and proletarians who delivered the mortal blow to royal despotism on that day. There was no distinction between active and passive citizens under the fortress's deadly fire. Those who didn't pay enough in taxes to be electors were allowed to fight and die for the liberty of all.

The Bastille had treacherously fired on the people, and their reprisal fell on the governor, de Launay, and the merchant provost Flesselles, who was unquestionably in cahoots with the court, having tricked the combatants by promising them rifles and then sending them trunks full of linen. De Launay, despite Hulin's heroic efforts, was killed on the steps of the *Hôtel de Ville*, and the provost Flesselles had his head smashed by a pistol blow as he was being taken to the Palais-Royal to be judged.

In truth, these executions were in a way a continuation of the battle, and there is no reason to be surprised by the explosion of anger of a crowd that had just escaped danger and which had been threatened by hordes of barbarous soldiers.

Two guilty parties were missing: state counselor Foulon, who had been charged with provisioning the army of the *coup d'état*, and his son-in-law, Bertier. On the day of the seizing of the Bastille, a letter from the ministry of war to Bertier had been intercepted and seized by the people. It left no doubt concerning his complicity with the court. A few days later, Foulon, who had spread rumors of his death and had even prepared his own burial, was arrested and decapitated. The immense crowd carried his head on a pike, and Bertier, led behind the grim trophy, was soon killed as well in a cruel, joyful delirium.

It wasn't only what is called the rabble that savored the joy of murder: according to the testimony of Gouy d'Arsy at the National Assembly, a great number of well-dressed citizens and well-to-do bourgeois exulted in this somber and savage procession. It was the revolutionary bourgeoisie that had been directly threatened by the royal soldiery, and there was fear mixed with this sudden ferocity. Nor should we omit the *ancien régime*'s tradition of barbarism. How well our good and great Babeuf understood and felt all this! And what a source of pride it is for us, what a source of hope as well during those inhuman hours of the bourgeois revolution, to read the noble words of humanity and wisdom of the man who created modern communism. He was there as the procession passed, and on July 25, 1789 he wrote to his wife:

I saw the head of the father-in-law pass, with the head of the son-in-law following behind it in the hands of more than 1,000 armed men. Exposed to public view in this way, Foulon made the long walk across the faubourg and *rue Saint Martin*, amidst 200,000 spectators who shouted at him and rejoiced, joined by with the troops of the escort, animated by the sound of the drum. Oh how this joy caused me pain. I was both satisfied and dissatisfied; I said it's all for the better but also unfortunate. I understand that the people should mete out justice; I approve of justice when it is satisfied by the annihilation of the guilty. But can't it not be cruel? Punishments of all kinds—drawing and quartering, torture, the wheel, the stake, the gallows, and executioners—have done so much harm to our morality. The masters, instead of rendering us orderly have made us barbaric, because that is what they themselves are. They reap and will reap what they have sowed, for all of this, my poor little wife, will have horrible after effects; we are only at the beginning.

O leaders of today: think on these words and make sure your laws and morality are as humane as possible, so that you will benefit from this on the inevitable day of revolution!

And you, proletarians, remember that cruelty is a holdover from servitude, for it attests to the fact that the barbarism of the oppressive regime is still present in you.

Remember that in 1789, when the working-class crowd momentarily surrendered itself to a cruel and murderous intoxication that it was the first communist, the first of the proletariat's great emancipators, who had a heavy heart.

The Consequences of the Taking of the Bastille

The impact of the taking of the Bastille was immense. It seemed to all the world's peoples that humanity's jail had fallen. This was more than the Declaration of the Rights of Man; it was the declaration of the people's might in service to human right. It was not only light that reached the oppressed of the universe from Paris, it was hope. And in the millions upon millions of hearts imprisoned in servitude's dark night, liberty's first dawning rose at exactly the same moment.

Paris's victory put a definitive end to the offensive by the crown and the court. Pushed by the queen and the princes, the king had launched an attack against the Assembly and the Revolution at the royal sitting of June 23. He had just marched against Paris and the Revolution during the confused and violent events of July. Rebuffed by all, he retreated to a hypocritically defensive position, and it was he who would now suffer repeated assaults; on October 6, 1791 with the flight to Varennes, again on June 20, 1791[5] and on August 10, 1792.[6] It was the revolutionary people who would go on the offensive. The mainspring of royal power was broken on July 14, or at least it was so damaged that it would never fully recover. A kind of paralysis had already set in on those days of *coup d'état* and aggression.

Neither Besenval nor Marshal de Broglie risked attacking the people from behind while they were investing the Bastille. What were they waiting for and why did they give de Launay the order to hold out instead of going to his assistance?

Clearly a hitherto unknown fear of taking responsibility had gripped these unimaginative men who were accustomed to only one form of peril, and, without obliterating their courage, the vast uprising of an entire people at the very least troubled it. Their instructions must also have been vague. On July 14, Louis XVI answered the envoys of the Assembly that it could not have been the case that the events in Paris were the result of orders given to the troops. What then was the king's plan?

It's possible that in order to assuage his conscience he had systematically refused to foresee the possible course of events. Perhaps he imagined that Paris, subdued by the mere presence of a vast military apparatus, would cease to be the tumultuous rescuer of the Assembly and that the latter, feeling the dead weight of the immobilized capital, would act uncertainly and stumblingly, ready to fall at the least shock.

The king, warned by the events of July 14, learned that he had to take the power of the Revolution into account. He would exercise cunning

---

5   On the night of June 20, 1791, the royal family fled the Tuileries Palace.
6   August 10, 1792 was the date of the popular massacre of the Swiss Guards at the Tuileries.

against it or would call foreign armies against it, but from that day forward he renounced any form of direct aggression, any open offensive.

The Assembly, still having to foil intrigues but no longer having to fear or repel royal force, was able to undertake a fight against another great power of the past, the Church.

At the same time that they liberated the National Assembly, the events of July 14 made the people aware for the first time of their strength and their role in Paris. To be sure, the Assembly was still important. During those stormy days, the Permanent Committee of Electors deputized it, and the Parisian revolution felt itself truly strong and legitimate thanks to its contact with the national revolution.

What is more, the Assembly itself had set a noble example of firmness and even of heroism. Its Tennis Court Oath, its serene and invincible resistance after the sitting of June 23, had electrified the people's hearts, and the most intrepid of Paris's combatants' sole ambition was to show themselves to be worthy of the bourgeois revolutionaries who, without weapons and solely through the force of right and courage, had emerged victorious. It is nonetheless true that on its own and without the assistance of the people of Paris, the National Assembly would have ended up succumbing. And so the Revolution, which until then had had but one base and center, the Assembly, from then on had two coinciding centers: the Assembly and the people of Paris.

A few days after July 14, Sieur Bessin, orator of the faubourg Saint Antoine, appeared at the bar of the Assembly to request financial aid for the workers of the faubourgs whose salaries had been suspended during the three days of agitation. He exclaimed, "Messieurs, you are the saviors of the Fatherland, but you too have saviors." The minutes say that these energetic opening words grabbed the attention of the Assembly, and I fully believe this. There, standing before it, was the very embodiment of the great event of July. Whatever its power, whatever its majesty, it suddenly felt itself under the protectorate of Paris, and perhaps some unease was mixed in with their joy at the recent victory.

But these were barely perceptible niceties, and, when on July 15 the Assembly sent its delegates to the capital to consecrate and legalize the Revolution, they were greeted with enthusiasm and respect by a huge crowd. Mounier, the choleric bourgeois, always suspicious of democracy, was won over by the respectful and cordial fervor of this reception.

Paris was henceforth emancipated, and in the heat of events it was able to write its municipal Constitution before the Assembly was even able to organize the municipal governments through a general law, before it could write the national Constitution.

The former city bureau, whose counter-revolutionary spirit we saw in the person of Provost Flesselles, was swept away. Bailly was named mayor by acclamation and Lafayette was named commanding general of the Parisian bourgeois Guard. With these two names, Paris attached itself to the National Assembly and two greatest memories of liberty: Bailly represented the Tennis Court Oath and Lafayette was the American Revolution.

At the moment when Paris, with its revolutionary and humane instincts, organized itself municipally, it opened its arms to the liberty of the two worlds. Like ramparts that can be seen against the light of deep space, the city's walls were silhouetted against the great light of universal freedom. It was concentric with the human horizon, and one felt that this circle of municipal life would expand until it took in all of humanity. Following Paris's example, countless *communes* would be established throughout France, to govern, fight, and crush any attempt at counter-revolution, and to make up for the failings of the suddenly annihilated or reduced royal executive power. And all these *communes*, born in the same ferment of liberty and need for order, were to join in a federation with Paris. From the first weeks, numerous bourgeois Guards affiliated with the Parisian bourgeois guard, and fraternal messages were sent from all corners of France to the Parisian city government.

It comes as no surprise that one year later the Festival of the Federation should have been celebrated on July 14. For it was on July 14, 1789, that the federation of the *communes* of France was truly born. The same instinct warned every assemblage of citizens and every city at the same time that liberty would be precarious and weak as long as it only rested on the National Assembly, and that it must have as many centers as there were *communes*. Integrated into the daily life of the citizens, animated and renewed by boundless energy, the Revolution would be invincible.

But all these spontaneous and multiform energies had the Assembly as their political center, Paris as their dominant seat, and the Revolution as their ideal center. They were naturally and necessarily federated. These were great days, when in the ardor of combat a clear and crucial idea was felt. The lightning flashes of the storm seemed to melt into the splendid light of a summer's day.

By reviving municipal life, the events of July 14 brought to the foreground of the action a proletariat that had been relegated to the background. To be sure, the workers and the poor were far from seizing municipal power. As we will soon see, they would be excluded from the bourgeois Guard and they would not sit in the district assemblies. For quite some time, Parisian municipal life would continue to be marked by a more narrowly bourgeois character than the central activity of the Assembly. But it was impossible to organize the legal power in Paris, originally of 60, later of 48 districts, without a certain number of these districts and Sections pulsating with popular power and passion. While Robespierre's voice was half stifled and repressed at the National Assembly, Danton's voice resounded in the Cordeliers district. Increasing the number of points of power meant increasing the contact points between power and the people. Despite all legal barriers, this meant increasing the possibilities and occasions for poplar intervention and for tilting the bourgeois revolution, not towards socialism—that idea had not yet been born—but towards democracy. Had there been a complete dispersal, if each *commune* had been a tiny self-contained world, the bourgeois oligarchy would have succeeded in laying hands on all these separate, weak mechanisms.

But when this profusion of local activities was combined with a great general movement that inspired passion in all those involved, then the cohesion and enthusiasm of the actions gradually gave power to the most ardent, the most active, and the most robust. This is why July 14, at the same time that it was a great bourgeois victory, was also a great popular victory. Of course the fighting people's direct participation on that great day did not have immediate consequences for the proletariat. The Revolution's origins were so profoundly bourgeois that a few weeks after July 14, when the National Assembly, freed by the people from the court's attacks, set up the electoral regime and excluded millions of the working poor from the vote, not a single deputy, not even the most democratic of them, remembered that at the Bastille the workers of Paris had conquered the title of active citizens for the poor of France. This immediate participation of the people in the great events of the Revolution seemed a glorious and fearsome accident that could not be allowed to become the rule in the regular workings of a free and ordered society.

And yet it wasn't in vain that from its first steps the bourgeois revolution had to resort to the fierceness of the workers' hearts and the strength of the workers' muscles. When the war against the Vendéens, against the émigrés, and against the foreigners would raise revolutionary tension to its highest point, when alongside the heroic bourgeois the people would guard the gates of the Revolution, they would finally have to be given the rights of the city. Like the slaves of antiquity who conquered their liberty on the battlefield, the proletarians would conquer the right to vote and a few brief hours of political sovereignty on the battlefields of the bourgeois revolution.

Difficult would be the effort and short-lived the victory. But that the proletariat was briefly able to boldly climb the ladder of events to the leadership of the bourgeois revolution—or at least participate in it alongside the most daring bourgeois—was for it a security and a promise for the future. And so it is that we have glimpsed countless fearless workers among the enormous mass that on July 14 invested the Invalides and then the Bastille. They weren't duped when they mounted their assault. Though disarmed the next day by the distrustful bourgeoisie, and then executed on the Champ de Mars two years later, they nonetheless marked the great revolutionary day with their courage and their strength. And thanks to these valiant men there is nothing under the sun today that belongs wholly to the bourgeoisie, not even its Revolution.

The Great Fear

The taking of the Bastille had its greatest impact in the countryside, among the peasants. Since the opening of the Estates General the peasants had been waiting; when would the Assembly consider their sufferings? They followed from afar the fight of the Third Estate against the privileged and the court. If only the Third Estate were to emerge victorious, how quickly we'd bring down the tyranny of the nobles. And so July 14 was decisive. Paris had taken its Bastille; it was left to the peasants to take theirs, all the feudal Bastilles, all those chateaux with their watchtowers, and dovecotes that loomed over the villages and the plains.

Suddenly, like a spring that uncoils, the countryside rose up. And in this great uprising there could be found two distinct and even seemingly contradictory movements. First, there was a movement generated by fear. The obsolete royal authority, which for centuries had sheltered the peasant while squeezing him, seemed to have been shaken. And since it was the only visible form of authority for the people of the countryside, it initially seemed to the peasants that society itself was collapsing and that they were going to be surrendered to brigandage if they didn't defend themselves. It was in this power vacuum that a legend of terror grew: "Here come the brigands! They're coming to burn down the woods, to cut down the wheat. Let's get ready and arm ourselves." From one end of France to the other, the peasants armed themselves and beat the countryside to uncover these much discussed "brigands," who nonetheless could not be found.

This period of panic left a profound and enduring impression on the spirit of the peasants. In the countryside of the south they still speak of "*l'annado de la paou*," the year of fear; one could say that memory has erased all others. But what was the occasion, the immediate and concrete cause of this universal fright? It isn't enough to say that the vast social upheaval, of which the taking of the Bastille was the prologue, disposed spirits to mysterious terrors, and that when a society ends, as when a day ends, vague and terrifying phantoms arise.

This mystical interpretation has prevented people from seeking the true reasons of the phenomenon. Was there a watchword issued by the aristocracy, by counter-revolution seeking to spread fear everywhere? The Assembly seemed to believe this, or at least it attempted to explain the panic in this way.

It said in the Preamble to its Decree of August 10:

The National Assembly, considering that the enemies of the Nation, having lost the hope of preventing public regeneration and the establishment of liberty through violence and despotism, appear to have conceived the criminal plan of reaching the same goal by means of disorder and anarchy; that among other methods, they have, at the same moment and almost on the same day, spread false alarms in the different provinces of the kingdom.

In fact, the movement did not have the suddenness of a conspiracy, and it was the Assembly itself which used the words "almost on the same day."

If this terror had broken out everywhere at the same time as the result of a watchword, they would have ended everywhere on the same date, once their futility had become clear. But I note that at the end of August, the fair at Beaucaire was delayed a few days "from fear of brigands," who may in fact have carried out a significant operation there. So this was not simply a counter-revolutionary maneuver.

Had the peasants frightened themselves? Were the assemblies they formed in villages to march on chateaux and burn feudal property titles perceived from afar as gatherings of brigands? And was the panic a result of reciprocal misunderstandings? This is possible, indeed certain. But it is also certain that alongside this movement of peasant proprietors marching against the nobles to free their land of all feudal impositions, at that moment of universal turbulence there was also a movement of the property-less, of the poor, of vagabonds, of the hungry. In more than one place they organized themselves in bands, crying out that they had the right to eat and live.

Several municipalities advised the National Assembly that on the night of July 25 "brigands had cut down unripened wheat." Even in the north on that date the wheat couldn't have been far from ripe, and those that were called "brigands" operating on behalf of the counter-revolution were probably the hungry, who didn't want to wait for the ripened harvest to fall beneath the sickle of the landlord and then be hidden away in granges.

A few partial movements of this kind sufficed to spread terror in a countryside where the fear of beggars was already chronic. I am prepared to believe that "the Great Fear" was above all the exaggeration of this chronic fright. If we read the *Cahiers* of the rural bailiwicks and parishes, we see the cultivators everywhere complaining of being at the mercy of beggars. They had to house them, feed them, and give them succor. If not, the beggars threatened them, and nothing was easier for them than setting fire to farm buildings and harvests.

The great economic evolution of the second half of the Eighteenth Century, the growth of industry and cities, and the transformation of the rural economy had uprooted many lives. The roads and the countryside were covered with vagabonds, the fear of whom obsessed the cultivators. The latter speak of them with anger, fright, and scorn. Nothing is more poignant than to see the peasants, in the same *Cahiers* where they complain of being oppressed and robbed by lords, and where they demand the right to harvest the grass of the forests for their livestock, denounce the peril presented by the vagabonds and beggars, or, as they said, "the dregs of society."

Below orderly poverty, there was a wandering poverty, and the latter is an object of contempt and terror for the former. We should recall the complaints of the peasant landowners against the masses of gleaners who invaded the newly harvested fields. I wonder if it was not these men and women who, impelled by hunger and excited by the revolutionary ferment, formed themselves into troops and cut the wheat. It was thus that the poorest of each village, the landless, were mixed in with vagabonds and wanderers.

The newspaper *Les Révolutions de Paris*, in its news from the provinces at the beginning of September, said the following:

Letters from Geneva announce that individuals from the neighboring mountains have advanced *en masse* on Ferney. The Geneva garrison, backed by a large number of volunteers, has marched there. Cannons were sent there and the mountaineers fled. The ignorance or rather the stupidity of the people of a few provinces led them to believe that equality and liberty allowed them to share property. It is from this that flowed most of the ravages that desolated our provinces.

It thus appears evident that in the days that followed the upheaval of July 14 there was a rising of the poor. The Revolution would not cease to be haunted by the fear of an "agrarian law."[7]

There is no question that this fear dates from the first days of the Revolution, which were the most tumultuous, the most agitated. We have

---

7   That is, land re-distribution.

almost no precise information on this movement of the rural proletariat. It was in all likelihood purely instinctive: we nowhere find a clear formulation of their aims, and it doesn't seem there were any conscious leaders.

For the most part, it was limited to the nocturnal and furtive pillaging of crops harvested before their time, or else it was simply mingled with the revolutionary movement of peasant property. When the peasants of the regions of Mâcon and Lyon, for example, set the chateaux ablaze and burned the papers of land registry offices, it's impossible for me not to recall that it was often the case that in the *Cahiers* of the parishes "the rich and sterile bourgeois" were named alongside the nobles. And it would doubtless require little for the angry mobs armed with pitchforks that attacked the nobles' chateaux to also go after large-scale bourgeois property.

The bourgeoisie understood the peril in almost all regions, and the bourgeois Guard of the cities hastened to the countryside to contain and repress the peasants. On the days of July 27, 28, and 29, the flames of the chateaux of Loras, Leuze, Comba, Pusignan, and Saint-Priest could be seen from Lyon. The bourgeois Guard marched against the peasants, and when it returned to the city it was attacked with stones and tiles by the workers of La Guillotière, who took the side of the insurgent peasants. It appeared for a moment as if the entire poor proletariat, workers and peasants alike, was going to rise against the old feudal regime and the new bourgeois regime, and that a profound and formidable class struggle, a struggle of all the have-nots against the haves, was going to be substituted for the superficial revolution of bourgeois and peasant property against the privileges of the nobles. Impotent impulses! Confused and vain attempts!

The time wasn't right, and these first unplanned uprisings were symbolized by the furtive night-time thefts of unripe wheat by roaming bands. But there was a moment when the settled peasants, the small landowners, the inhabitants of the villages who had an enclosure, a garden, a bit of a field, felt the movement of the poor simmering below them.

How is it possible to fully commit to the Revolution, how can one attack the feudal Bastilles if one risks being overwhelmed by a mendicant and threatening proletariat?

What's the good of wresting from the lord sheaths of wheat he takes by feudal right if the humble gleaners of yesterday, now today's rebellious harvesters, carry them all away? And will people expose themselves to losing their property in trying to liberate it?

The best thing to do then is to confront the "brigands," to arm oneself, to organize. It was thus that, from one end of France to the other, village councils were formed. And when they realized that there were few if any "brigands," that the proletarians were neither bold enough, conscious enough, nor organized enough to substitute their revolution for the Revolution, they marched lightheartedly against the chateaux and turned against the *ancien régime* the weapons they'd seized in their instinctive fright.

We can see that there was a kind of conservative movement of contraction, of tightening, which was followed by a revolutionary expansion. Under the fear of the unknown and before the uprising of the have-nots, the communities of the villages withdrew into themselves, elected men of whom they were sure, established a militia, and, having thus guaranteed the order of property within the Revolution, attacked the feudal system.

Or rather there were two movements, one conservative and the other revolutionary, that were connected and virtually combined in this prodigious epoch, where enflamed and exalted minds seemed to be all that were needed to solve all problems. In the same way that in Paris the revolutionary bourgeoisie armed the militias against the court's regiments and disarmed the men it considered a threat to property in the threatening days that preceded July 14, in the countryside the rural Third Estate organized itself both to protect peasant property against any aggression and to bring down feudalism.

The new order stood firm against all threats, and this was the sign of its historical legitimacy. But the historian would be guilty of superficiality if he didn't note, beneath the revolution of the bourgeoisie and peasant property that was organized and triumphed in those fertile days of July and August, the profound disquiet and instinctive revolt of those without a scrap of land. Having no property, they didn't see the Revolution as the liberation of property freed of feudal levies. They viewed it as the liberation of man from poverty and hunger. Instinctively, with a ferocious ingenuousness, like the mountaineers of the Alps who descended on Ferney intending to distribute the property left by Voltaire, they thought that the moment had come for all men to enjoy the fruits of the earth, and they peacefully settled themselves into the Revolution as if it were their home. But they collided with the cannons of the bourgeoisie and pitchforks of the peasant landowner and they returned to their poverty, muttering to themselves that they had misunderstood.

The truth is that they understood too soon. History shut the door on these "beggars" and rudely told them: "You'll pass this way again." And in fact they would pass that way again, and the door would one day open, on a day when they will no longer be "beggars," on a day when they will have property of their own. I mean when they will have an idea, when they will carry in their heads the formula for a new world, when they will be peasant socialists.

While the consequences of July 14 unfurled in this way in the countryside, the victorious National Assembly sought equilibrium.

It was at one and the same time saved, enthusiastic, and worried. Necker was recalled. The king, accompanied by a deputation from the Assembly, had been obliged to go to Paris on July 17, and though people might have tried to distinguish between the king and his "evil advisors" and grant him a triumphal reception, it was nonetheless a visit paid to the victor by the vanquished.

Paris was rapidly coming of age and the Assembly sensed the arrival of a friendly and rival power. It huddled a bit nervously around the king, seeking to forget Louis XVI's criminal errors in order to make France forget them. We have here a strange and inappropriate solidarity of the revolutionary Assembly and the king of the *ancien régime*, unwillingly converted to the new regime by the might of the people. Disorders broke out in Saint-Germain; the tax barriers were broken through, and the tax farmer Thomassin, accused of hoarding, was threatened with death. The moderates of the Assembly, on Lally-Tollendal's motion, quickly proposed an address to the Nation against the disturbers of public order, an address which, through its very exaggeration, would have spread panic and worsened the threat. In addition, the movement in Saint-Germain was a continuation of the great movement in Paris. Wouldn't these crooked proceedings disavow the magnificent revolutionary loyalty of the capital?

The Breton deputies protested, as did Robespierre. He immediately exposed the peril that conservative moderation caused the Revolution, still ensnared in intrigues and hatreds.

We must love peace, but we must also love liberty. But is there anything more legitimate than rising up against a horrible conspiracy aimed at destroying the Nation? A riot was caused in Poissy under the pretext of hoarding; Brittany is peaceful as are the provinces; the proclamation would spread alarm there and would cause the loss of confidence. We must do nothing hastily. Who dares to say that the enemies of the state have ceased their intrigues?

What constituted Robespierre's strength and what would assure it for some time, was that desiring the Revolution he accepted its consequences and conditions, and wasn't foolishly or hypocritically troubled by the disorders that the armed resistance to royal arbitrariness necessarily caused.

The Assembly rejected Lally-Tollendal's motion, but it had briefly applauded it, and this wavering revealed that if the Assembly needed the people, it had also begun to fear them. But this fleeting worry didn't yet slow down its momentum, and it was with a magnificent faith in reason that it immediately began the elaboration of the Rights of Man, the preface to the Constitution.

4

National Lands

(The Revolution began to change the political nature of France,

> *... adopting an intermediary system between bourgeois oligarchy and pure democracy. In October and December 1789 it had passed laws regarding voting and eligibility for office. This is the famous distinction between passive citizens, who have the right to the protection of the common law but who aren't admitted to creating the law, and active citizens, the only ones admitted to choose legislators.*

In fact, even within the body of active citizens there were degrees, with those who paid taxes worth three days' wages able to vote in primary assemblies, ten days' worth of labor required for the second degree, which allowed election to the primary assembly, which chose deputies, and finally those in the highest category, eligible for the National Assembly, who paid the equivalent of the "marc d'argent," the silver marc (around 50 livres), and owned property.

Departmental and municipal governments were also established. "It appeared dangerous [to the legislature] to have the ancient provinces as the basis of organization," and so France was divided into 83 départements.

More radical was the setting on foot of municipalities in December 1789, for this system "set in motion ... all the cells, all the fibers of the social organism.":

> *It was the incessant and ever alert actions of these countless municipalities that made up for the inevitable failings of the executive power, maintained order, punished or prevented conspiracies, ensured through its workshops the livelihood of the poor, and strengthened the hold of the Revolution on the country."*

Nevertheless, France's financial woes had not gone away, and the Revolution had to take radical measures to repair the situation.)

The sale of Church lands will, in fact, serve financiers, who will be able to profit from bold speculations; rentiers, whose incomes they will ensure; businessmen and architects, who will profit from countless exchanges and large-scale building works; traders and industrialists, who will gain greater access to landed property; workmen, small business owners, and village artisans who will be granted much-desired fields around their villages and hamlets; country notaries, who will make fruitful use of their money by clever purchases; and finally landowners, who will round out their little domains with a lot wrested from a priory or abbey.

I cannot enter into the details of the failed financial schemes that left the Revolution no other resource than that of nationalizing Church lands. A first bond, issued in the early months, failed because the Assembly lowered the interest rate below the figure set by Necker and desired by the capitalists. The latter feared that if they subscribed at a moderate rate that it would set a precedent that would soon bring about a general conversion of the loan, as well as a reduction of the overall public debt. It was those bond-holders who made the Revolution in order to avoid bankruptcy who hesitated to increase the weight of the debt by a new bond issue: by refusing a new undertaking, they wanted to force the Nation to take decisive measures for the consolidation of their debts.

The path of loans, which Necker had ambitiously taken, was thus closed. Could the gifts of voluntary subscribers be counted on? It would have been childish to hope that feelings of generosity would suffice to sustain the budget of a great monarchy. In any case, giving meant throwing the money away.

Necker was left with two expedients: imposing a horrific tax on revenue, and negotiating with the discount bank. The Constituent Assembly, with a courage that demonstrates the immense value the bourgeoisie placed on saving the Revolution and avoiding bankruptcy, voted the patriotic contribution of a quarter of all revenues. This was an enormous tax, and it was paid in many cities with a noble dispatch.

Marat was virtually the only one to oppose it. He wrote that this tax, instead of being proportional, should have been progressive. Above all, he saw in the fantastic calculations that estimated the annual revenue of France at 15 billion francs, a plot by the Minister, who would procure 3 billion for himself. And to what, according to Marat, would these sums be dedicated? To pay an enormous army for a few years to crush the Revolution. The truth is that this enormous undertaking barely allowed France to hold out without going bankrupt until the alienation of the lands of the clergy began to take effect, for the payment of all the other taxes in many provinces had been halted de facto.

Necker thought of using the credit of the discount bank and he was authorized to issue bank bills. But if these bills weren't secured, their worth would soon fall to zero, and if they were to be kept afloat, what was the security? Mirabeau, who energetically fought against Necker's financial plans, correctly said: "If a security allows the Nation to support paper money issued by the discount bank, why doesn't it directly support the bills it itself issues with this security?" And so Necker's scheme, which in reality consisted in creating indirect *assignats*, was contradictory: it could only lead to directly creating state bills of National *assignats* secured by national wealth. And this wealth could be nothing but the Church's domains.

The Confiscation of Church Lands

As we have already seen, the Constituent Assembly, by abolishing tithes without indemnity struck a blow against the Church's property. But it was a much bolder act to lay hands on its lands. And while the Church only half-heartedly resisted the abolition of its tithes, it would resist the nationalizing of its landed property with fanatical vigor.

How did the Constituent Assembly justify this seizure of the clergy's land?

It asserted that the Church's property did not have the same character as other properties; that the Church had only received its land and buildings in order to fulfill certain functions, notably those of charity and assistance. As a result, once the Nation decided to itself fulfill these functions, it had the right to seize these resources upon assuming this charge.

Finally, in order to round out its legal case, the Constituent proclaimed that the clergy, having ceased to be an Order, could not as such own anything, and that the Nation can always take back the property of a body that only exists through the will of the Nation itself. After the Marquis de La Coste, after Buzot, after Dupont de Nemours, it was the Bishop of Autun, Talleyrand-Périgord, who posed the question with admirable precision and with the authority granted by his post as bishop.

On October 10, 1789 he made his great and celebrated motion from the tribune:

Messieurs: As all of you are aware, for some time the state has been confronting the greatest needs. Extreme methods are needed to meet them.

Normal means are exhausted: the people are squeezed on all sides; the slightest tax increase would be unbearable to them. We mustn't even think of this.

Extraordinary measures were just attempted (the tax of a quarter of the revenue) but they are mainly aimed at this year's extraordinary needs, and measures are needed for the future and for the complete reestablishment of order.

There is one such immense and decisive measure which in my opinion can be allied to a strict respect for property (otherwise I would reject it); this wealth seems to me to be entirely found in ecclesiastical lands.

It's not a matter here of a contribution to state expenditures proportional to that of other landowners; this has never seemed to be a sacrifice. It's a question of a measure of far greater importance for the Nation [...]

What seems certain to me is that the clergy is not a landowner like other landowners, since the property it enjoys and which it can't dispose of, was donated, not in the interest of persons, but for the serving of functions.

What appears to me to be certain is that if the Nation, enjoying a wide influence over all the bodies that exist within it, does not have the right to destroy the entire body of the clergy, since this body is necessary to religion, it can certainly destroy specific elements of this body if it judges them harmful or simply useless, and that this right over their existence necessarily brings with it an extensive right over the disposition of their property.

What is no less certain is that the Nation, from the very fact that it is the protector of the will of the founder, can and even must suppress those benefits that no longer serve a function; that as a result of these principles, it has a right to hand over to useful ministers and to put to the profit of the public interest the revenue of the goods of this nature currently vacant, and to set aside for the same use all those that will later be vacant.

Up to this point there is no difficulty, and nothing that seems too extraordinary, for throughout time we have seen religious communities shut down, rights to benefices suppressed, and ecclesiastical properties returned to their true goal and used as public establishments. And there is no doubt that the National Assembly has the authority needed to decree such operations if the good of the state demands it.

But can it reduce in this way the revenue of the living title holders and dispose of a portion of this revenue?

In the first case, we must take the following fact as the starting point: this question has already been decided through the decree on tithes.

However inviolable the possession of property that is guaranteed you by law might be, it is clear that this law cannot change the nature of the property in guaranteeing it; that when it is a question of ecclesiastical property it can only ensure each current titleholder the enjoyment only of that which was truly granted him by its act of foundation.

But everyone is aware that the founding titles of ecclesiastical properties, as well as the various Church laws that have explained the meaning and spirit of these titles, teach us that only the portion of this property which is necessary for the honest subsistence of the beneficiary belongs to him; that he is nothing but the administrator of the remainder, and that this remainder is actually granted to the unfortunate and for the maintenance of ecclesiastical buildings. Thus, if the Nation carefully ensures each titleholder, whatever the nature of his benefit, this honest subsistence, it will not in any way infringe on his individual property. And if, at the same time, it takes upon itself the administration of the rest, as it unquestionably has the right to do; if it takes upon itself the other obligations attached to this property, such as the upkeep of hospitals, or charity workshops, church repairs, etc; if, above all, it only draws from this property at a moment of general calamity, it seems to me that all the intentions of the founders are fulfilled, and that justice will have been done.

The great dialectical effort and subtlety by which Talleyrand attempted to demonstrate that this great revolutionary expropriation respected property is clear to see. At heart, this decisive measure could be legitimized with a simple phrase: that above all else, a Nation has the right to live, and that when immense wealth has a traditional allocation contrary to new interests and the very life of the Nation, it can and must modify this allocation.

But it is rare that revolutions so clearly avow their principles and seek to use the judicial system in place to justify the very act that overturns the former law.

There is no question but that there was much specious and feeble reasoning in Talleyrand's argument.

Yes, the Nation, the sole perpetual entity, has the right and the duty to see to the execution of the will of the founders, but it is perfectly clear that when, in the centuries of darkness and faith, thousands of men gave their property to the Church for the relief of the poor, they didn't want simply to give to the poor: they wanted to give to them through the hands of the Church and in doing so ensure themselves of reward in a supernatural order that, according to them, the Church administered.

Consequently, when the Nation, seizing the Church's property, dedicated it to the relief of the poor, to works of assistance and education, it was fulfilling only a part of the donors' will. And in truth, how could a great people, after the enlightenment of the Eighteenth Century, be strictly faithful to the ideas of the Middle Ages?

Nationalizing and secularizing Church properties meant not only wresting them from the Church, it meant wresting them from the donors themselves, that is, from the past. Consequently, it was an act of revolutionary expropriation, to a far greater extent than Talleyrand admitted either to himself or others.

But this first speech left a far greater difficulty unresolved.

Talleyrand's reasoning supposed that the totality of secularized Church property would be applied to works of charity, analogous, if not in their inspiration, at least in their material reality, to the works foreseen by the founders. But in fact, it was above all to ensure the payment of state debts, to avoid bankruptcy, that the Revolution was forced to secularize Church property.

It was thus the legion of rentiers, of bourgeois lenders, and of capitalists who, in the collecting of Church revenues, substituted themselves for its original recipients. Church property, both landed and ecclesiastical, served to guarantee credit. This was truly the expropriation of the Middle Ages for the benefit of modern society.

The Civil Constitution of the Clergy

But the National Assembly couldn't limit itself to seizing and distributing the Church's property. It had to organize all of the relations between the new society created by the Revolution and the Church, and we are about to witness the tragic encounter between Christianity and the Revolution. The Constituent Assembly could not wash its hands of ecclesiastical organization.

In the first place, the temporal power of the *ancien régime*, the king, intervened in the functioning of the spiritual power. The pope installed bishops, but it was the king who appointed them. To a large extent, the Revolution substituted the power of the nation for that of the king. It thus had to decide what it would do with that portion of royal power. In the second place, a great number of clerics, bound to the cloister by perpetual vows sanctioned by civil law, addressed the Assembly, asking it to free them of their chains. Finally, upon seizing Church lands, the Constituent, in order to provide a judicial pretext for this magnificent revolutionary expropriation, had committed itself to providing for religious services and the maintenance of ministers. The Constituent was thus firmly engaged in the ecclesiastical question.

The Constituent Assembly didn't think for an instant to resolve this problem by the separation of Church and State. Not for an instant did it think to declare that religion was a matter of private interest and that the State owed the various religious opinions freedom and nothing else. It was at once both so timid as not to break the bond between Church and State, and so bold as to give the Church a Civil Constitution adapted to the new regime and marked with the revolutionary spirit.

When it came to the religious orders, the Constituent Assembly didn't limit itself to abolishing the civil effects linked to perpetual vows by the *ancien régime*. It didn't limit itself to abolishing the "civil death" of clerics and restoring their right to individual ownership, to have testaments, and to inherit. It considered that in themselves and independently of the legal effects linked to them, perpetual vows were an assault on man's freedom, and it pronounced the prohibition of those congregations that solicited or accepted such vows [...].

The Results of Ecclesiastical Reform

Many details of the Civil Constitution of the Clergy seem bizarre, and many historians have said that it failed miserably, but they are mistaken. In the first place, it lasted in its original form until February 21, 1795, that is, for four years, and it was, at least for three years, truly practiced: the electors charged with choosing priests and bishops took their functions seriously, participated without ill will (even the most free-thinking of them) in the religious ceremonies that were part of the electoral procedures, and far from thinking that in doing so they were compromising themselves with the Church, they thought they were acting as good revolutionaries.

But above all, the Civil Constitution lived on, watered down, it is true, and degraded, in the Concordat.[1] There are two major differences between the Concordat and the Civil Constitution, the first being that under the Concordat the Pope's intervention was re-established.

While the Revolution recognized no Pope and calmly asserted popular sovereignty, as much for the electing of magistrates of the Church as for the other magistrates of the Nation, the Concordat was the result of negotiations with the Pope and restored to him the supreme right of canonical installation.

---

1 Pact signed in 1801 between Napoleon and the Papacy, regulating relations between the French State and the Church.

The other difference is that under the regime of the Concordat, the designation of bishops and priests was carried out through executive power and not through universal suffrage.

From a revolutionary point of view, the Concordat is a retreat from the Civil Constitution. The Civil Constitution is far more secular, national, and democratic than the Concordat. It recognizes no foreign power and, in truth, no theocratic power: it is the Nation which, in its absolute sovereignty and under the popular form of elections, names and installs Church officers.

But what remained of the Civil Constitution under the Concordat is the right for a power of revolutionary and secular origin which received its legitimacy, not from the Church, but from the people, to designate bishops and priests. These assemblies of electors where everyone, even Protestants, even Jews, even nonbelievers, worked together to elect bishops, seem strange to us. But is this not also the case under the regime of the Concordat, where ministers of religions, Protestants, deists, or atheists, designate bishops and priests? What is essential is that a power that didn't emanate from the Church and which represented the Rights of Man, that is, a concept absolutely opposed to that of the Church, intervened in the functioning and recruitment of the Church. This is what survived of the Civil Constitution under the Concordat, and it is this that, despite it all, was a serious check on theocracy.

Those who, like us, wish for not only the complete secularization of the state, but for the disappearance of the Church and even of Christianity; those who impatiently await the day when public authority will be freed of all contact with the Church and where individual consciences will be freed of all contact with dogma, might think that the Civil Constitution of the Clergy was a negligible result and a bastard scheme. But the reality is that for its period it was a feat of revolutionary daring, and it was not, as has been said, a precarious enterprise. In fact, under the action of retrograde and clerical forces it did suffer, like most revolutionary institutions, a terrible defeat, and yet there was an intangible revolutionary element in it that was perpetuated.

Why, though, did the Constituent not immediately proclaim the separation of Church and State? Why did it not say that religion was of a strictly private order and that the Nation must neither persecute, support, pay, nor regulate any religion? Why did it not, following the famous Positivist formula, immediately realize the separation of the spiritual and temporal powers? Monsieur Robinet[2] vehemently reproaches the Constituent for this in his substantial studies of the religious movement in Paris during the Revolution.

I confess that there is a maniacal *parti pris* in the Positivist interpretation and criticism of the facts that irritates me: the Constituent is guilty of having not divined and applied Auguste Comte's ideas.

But his thesis of the two powers is historically false and socially absurd. It is false that the first steps of a separation of the spiritual and temporal powers were taken in the Middle Ages by Christian and feudal society.

There is little doubt that on one side there was the Church, bearing only the "holy books" in its hands, and on the other kings and emperors, bearing the scepter and the sword in their hands. Judging things superficially and strictly by their appearance, the Church inspired those who governed but didn't itself govern. This, for Auguste Comte, is the first separation of the spiritual and temporal powers.

But in fact, the Church had deeply penetrated the mechanisms of feudal society and property. In fact, churchmen participated in government as ministers and guided sovereigns. In fact, the Church constantly intervened in the governing of temporal affairs, and is there anyone who is capable of delineating the border between the spiritual and the temporal? Who doesn't see that a temporal power without its own ideas, without its own consciousness, without an autonomous philosophy, would be completely surrendered to the spiritual power, and that this so-called separation of the two powers would result in the horrific absorption of humanity into a theocracy?

If, even during the Middle Ages, humanity was not completely absorbed by the Church it was not because the Church did not have direct rule over temporal interests: it is because the great temporal interests of emperors, kings, and peoples created for themselves a right opposed to that of the Church.

---

2   Jean-François Robinet (1825–99)—Auguste Comte's executor and historian of Danton.

In truth, despite their apparent submission to dogma, the German emperor, King Philippe le Bel, and the nascent nations had a philosophy of life and the universe different from the Pope's, and this philosophy was the basis for their resistance. There is no temporal power that can last if it is not at the same time a spiritual power—that is, if it doesn't have sufficient power and desire to live to express itself in law and to elevate itself to an idea.

Marx's thesis, which demonstrates that there is a distant reflection of the real order of the world in all great legal and religious concepts, is the opposite of Comte's, and is more profound and true.

In any case, far from it being the case that humanity should aim towards the ideal of the separation of the spiritual and the temporal, it is rather their fusion that it should desire.

It is necessary that the lives of all men, up to and including the least detail of their profession, be penetrated with an ideal of justice, science, and beauty, and this ideal, instead of being monopolized and interpreted by a spiritual caste, must be constantly renewed and invigorated by the experience of those who live and act, by the effects of "temporal" activity.

But in truth, how can M. Robinet, how can the Positivists, apropos of the Church of the late Eighteenth Century, speak of "spiritual power" when it no longer represented anything in the realm of ideas? It was the negation of science, the scandal of reason, the monstrous holdover of outdated dogma.

Science and philosophy constituted the spiritual power of the Eighteenth Century. It was Newton, Buffon, and Hume. It was the Constituent itself, when it summarized all of the goals of free thought in the Declaration of the Rights of Man. Who cares if the Positivists, following Auguste Comte, reproach the Constituent and Revolution for having engaged in "metaphysics" in proclaiming the Rights of Man; that they reproach the Revolution, with its haughty assertions that flowed from its will, for its lack of respect for Comtism? We know all too well the advantages reaction can draw from such a denigration of the Revolution by so-called free spirits.

But at least let them not lament the Civil Constitution of the Clergy, the indiscreet intervention of the Constituent in the functioning of the "spiritual power." The Church was an enormous power, hostile in all of its traditions, all of its principles, all of its interests, to the new order of freedom and reason that the Revolution sought to found.

The Constituent tried, to the best of its ability, and without colliding too violently with that fearsome power and the prejudices that protected it, to have the Church become subject to revolutionary discipline. Say that it poorly calculated its efforts, that it was too fearful or daring, that it would have done better to separate immediately and completely: all of this can be argued. But when speaking of that Church lacking in any ideas, please, spare us the theory of "spiritual power." When one day the State breaks with the Church, when the Republic finally implements the separation of Church and State that M. Robinet doesn't forgive the Constituent for not having carried out, they will not do so in order to realize the separation of the temporal and the spiritual in accordance with the Positivist rite. It will be to expunge from the new spiritual power, I mean from a free society organized in accordance with reason, the remnants of the intellectual servitude of the past.

Was the Separation of Church and State Possible?

But if we take the balance of power in 1790 into account, would it have been possible for the Constituent Assembly to have immediately pronounced the separation of Church and State? The question wasn't even posed at that time and in fact didn't exist. Not one legislator, not one publicist, not one thinker or philosopher suggested the separation of Church and State to the Constituent.

M. Robinet, in order to prove that this idea wasn't foreign to the Eighteenth Century and that, as a result, the Constituent could have realized it, is forced to torture the meaning of texts in a barely credible fashion. He takes all the appeals for tolerance that resounded throughout the Eighteenth Century for an invitation to separate the "spiritual and the temporal," and more precisely Church and State [...]

M. Robinet exults in this and writes: "It seems to us that one could not more clearly state nor better grasp the legitimacy, the obligation, the urgency at that moment to separate the Church and the State." And he abuses the Constituent for "subjugating the Church to the State" instead of following Turgot's supposed advice.[3] I think that never has so narrow a spirit of system led to stranger aberrations and a more fundamental misunderstanding of the real meaning of texts. Every *philosophe* demanded that the State not be a persecutor; all of them demanded that it not impose the Catholic religion by force. None of them expressed or even foreshadowed the idea that the State should sever all bonds with the Church. This idea will soon arise from revolutionary experience, but in 1789 and 1790 it was not yet born. And not only did the philosophy of the Eighteenth Century not contain, apart from principles of tolerance, any immediate watchword, any practical formula that the Constituent could apply; it didn't even lay out a general plan of conduct regarding Christianity. It didn't incline them to desire or prepare—even prudently—the disappearance of the habit of Christianity. Perhaps only Diderot, with his expansive and intimate faith in science, with his naturalist pantheism, in which God appears both as a ferment of the forces of nature and the distant term of the evolution of objects (God makes himself, Diderot said: *Deus est in fieri*), perhaps only the great Encyclopedist communicated the desire to be done with the Christian religion. Montesquieu was extremely prudent, in both the religious and political orders.

Even though Voltaire exposed the tragic and blinding foolishness of the Church, of its mysteries, miracles, and dogmas of all of Christianity; even though he published the most sharply anti-Christian fragments of the Testament of Abbé Meslier, he wrote for and wished to write for an elite only. He hoped to force religion to be tolerant, but just as he was frightened at the idea of seeing education spread to the people, to the "laborers," he would unquestionably have been frightened at the idea of "dechristianizing" the masses.

Emancipate the leaders, the cultivated classes, yes; but that didn't mean going as far as shaking the roots of the ancient faith of the people.

Rousseau's position was particularly ambiguous. On the one hand, in *The Social Contract*, he considered Christianity anti-social, because it proposes an object to men, supernatural salvation, which is foreign to relationships

---

3   On the separation of Church and State.

within society. Indeed, he proclaims that the legislator has the right to define "and to impose a civil religion," that is, beliefs in harmony with the fundamental needs of civil society. According to him, this religion must be composed of simple dogmas, like the existence of God and the immortality of the soul, and all those who will not profess this can and must be banished, not as heretics or unbelievers, but as enemies of the social pact of which these simple dogmas are the guarantee.

The practical conclusion the Constituent could have drawn from this part of Rousseau's work would have been a double persecution, against both Christians and atheists. It would have meant the systematic dechristianization of France for the benefit of an official and mandatory deism.

But we must be wary: the politicians hoped that working within the framework of the Revolution the Christian religion would gradually allow the particularity of its dogmas to vanish or be weakened, and that nothing would be left but a kind of deism tinged with evangelical tenderness. In this way, it is Christianity, slowly stripped of its dogmatic rigor through its contact with the Revolution, which, without any shocks, would become the "civil religion" dreamed of by Rousseau.

And so the Civil Constitution of the Clergy, which allowed Catholic belief to survive, but which dipped it in popular suffrage, completely impregnated with revolution, was the true realization of Rousseau's idea.

What is more, Rousseau, in *The Savoyard Vicar* proposed a mixture of rationalist deism and sentimental Christianity: "If Socrates' life and death were those of a sage," the vicar exclaims, "Jesus' life and death were those of a God," and in this vague exaltation strives to cast aside all his doubts about the essential mysteries of the Christian religion.

In truth though, he doesn't succeed, and the vicar is the very type of the priest who, admiring the Gospels, believes himself authorized to continue the exercise of religion without being strictly orthodox. The Savoyard Vicar takes and gives communion without believing in transubstantiation, but he believes that his soul's religious exaltation exempts him from any fixed faith.

This is an example of the sentimental hypocrisy that unquestionably acted on many men of the Revolution. They said that the Revolution could and must be the Savoyard Vicar; that it could and should go to the altar without believing, but with the goal of slowly transforming the traditional faith of the people into a vague deist belief.

Thus, the Civil Constitution of the Clergy was completely in line with *The Savoyard Vicar*, and far from pushing for a violent rupture with the Church, Rousseau, on the contrary suggested a sentimental and slightly false arrangement that allowed for the reconciliation of rationalism with apparent respect for and practice of religion.

And so the policy of separation or dechristianization could not come to the Constituent from the philosophy of the century. The Assembly, where Jansenists and jurists outnumbered the philosophers, was infinitely more preoccupied with wresting the French Church from Roman domination and applying the public law of the Revolution to the religious organization itself than with precipitating the dissolution of Christian belief or of breaking all legal ties between Church and State.

Reason and Faith: Towards a New Equilibrium?

The Constituent hoped that pure reason would gradually free itself from the heteroclite mix of Christianity and revolution which, in 1789, formed the basis of the national consciousness. At that moment what they considered essential (and they were right in this) was that the revolutionary seal be imprinted on the organization of the Church; that the latter not be treated like an institution apart, but be subject to the same rules as all civil institutions.

This being the case, its spiritual primacy was expropriated at the same time as its property. Above all, its mystery was expropriated, for how could the people continue to revere as the interpreters of a spiritual power men they appointed themselves, whom they put in place through their suffrage like any departmental administrator?

The depths of the mystic heavens were closing. Between the vaguely evangelistic rationalism of most of the civil authorities and the administrative and vaguely popular Christianity of the newly elected men, an equilibrium was being established. If we read the speeches given on, Sunday February 6, 1791 at the metropolitan parish church by the president of the electoral assembly, Pastoret, proclaiming Father Poiret the curate of Saint-Sulpice, and then read the new curate's response, we see a harmony in the two speeches that results in the simultaneous disappearance of both reason and faith: "You who fill this space," said Pastoret,

> ... whose calm attitude and respectful silence are a touching homage rendered to religion and the faith, remember that tolerance is the first of all religious virtues, just as it is the first of all civic virtues. Tolerance is nothing but charity. It is a happy day when piety and philosophy embrace under the auspices of the Being who, with a single glance, measures the universe.
>
> And so, love God! Honor the Nation and the king, and cherish your brothers: these are the principles of the Gospels. They waited for the French Constitution and they were its prophetic monument.

This is a strange concept, one that makes the Gospels the precursor of the Rights of Man, an original and incomplete revelation that the Revolution eclipsed! It's the very negation of Christianity that is presented as the sole and eternal source of all Truth.

And the new curate accepts this partitioning between the Gospels and reason:

> It is with the eternal code of the order—the Gospels—in hand that I propose to work to make the parish you confide to me happy. On opening this admirable book I find written there in letters of light, legible and intelligible to the entire universe: "Mortals, learn from the Savior of men to be gentle and humble of heart. On earth you are in society with God and men. Adore your Creator and treat each other as brothers. Love each other, and in doing so you will fulfill Jesus Christ's law. May the perfect patiently suffer the imperfect. Do not do unto others as you would not want them to do unto you.

This is also the first principle of natural justice, the general law, and so obvious that there's no need to vote to have it accepted by all. Nature's unanimous cry proclaims it everywhere:

This, gentlemen, is our Gospel. We will make higher reason the guide of our behavior. If you listen to it closely there will be nothing but sincerity in the commerce of the word, faithfulness in promises, good faith in agreements, modesty in feelings, moderation in proceedings, and a cordial and universal friendship for all those men with whom we live; we will consider ourselves the citizens of the same city, the children of the same father, and the members of the same body, whose fundamental end is to work together for their reciprocal preservation. Has there ever been a more sublime morality?

And so for the preacher the civic bonds that unite the citizens of a city have the same moral force as the religious bonds that unite "the children of the same father." And so the supernatural and mysterious ends that Christianity proposed to men disappear, leaving in their place the earthly and social end of "reciprocal preservation."

And this, according to the priest, is morality's most sublime object. It could be said that he justifies the Gospels by their conformity with the spirit of the Revolution. It is thus the latter that becomes the real measure of the true, is the real Gospel. It is clear that what we have here is a diffuse labor of adulteration and decomposition of the Christian spirit: by accepting so open an intervention of the civil and popular power in his own institution, the priest accepted the veiled intervention of secular thought and rationalism into his dogma. In the face of the revolutionary people, from whom his priestly authority emanated, he naturally and unconsciously sought the ideas that would bring them closer to him. And since, at bottom, the people had not only Christian habits but also revolutionary and humane ideas, the priest arrived at a strange compromise.

I am not saying that this intellectual mixture of Christianity and rationalism is an attractive one: in fact, it is a mediocre and unstable philosophical composite. But it was as much because of the Church's disdain for the *philosophes* as because of its spirit of domination that the people had been held in ignorance and Christian dependency. Even by entering into revolution they could not immediately accede to the pure philosophy of science and reason. As a result, in the realm of religion, this first revolutionary period was necessarily one of compromise. Again, what was essential was that this compromise, though it forced free thought into disagreeable administrative formalities and unpleasant attitudes, did not harm the internal force of reason; on the contrary, by diminishing the passivity and dependency of the masses it interfered with the Church's power over the individual. The 4 million active citizens who yesterday greeted the bishop as the dual incarnation of God and the king now elected that very bishop. The Church assumed the attitude of a candidate before popular suffrage; it was the people who had the final decision, the people who were pope and, through the communication of priestly power, were in a way God.

This exalting of the people is the lowering of the Church, and dogma lost the aura of power that made it a Truth. In any case, having established the Civil Constitution of the Clergy, it would be easier for the people to look the priest in the eye who climbed the pulpit thanks to them. I am convinced that the Civil Constitution, so disdained by certain haughty spirits, played a great role in the intellectual freedom in religious matters of the people of today. It was the first secular accommodation of religion, and it got the people accustomed to the boldness of free thought.

The Church felt the seriousness of the blow, for under the leadership of the Pope it immediately opposed the Civil Constitution. It claimed that the new distribution of dioceses was completely against canon law. It claimed that the Constituent didn't have the right to block appeals to the head of the universal Church. There's no need for us to argue over these claims.

Monsieur Robinet, as a Positivist, takes the side of the leader of the Church. But over the course of its long life the Church accepted too many different constitutions, it adapted itself to too many and too varied political and social conditions for it to be able to oppose to revolutionary novelties the authority of a consistent tradition. The problem can be summed up in one phrase: The Church aspires to domination. It thus declares everything that opposes its domination contrary to its principles, but since it doesn't persist in the face of the inevitable and prefers to evolve rather than disappear it ends up resigning itself to what it can't destroy and readjusting its principles to what is.

If the Revolution had fully triumphed; if political freedom and universal suffrage hadn't descended into imperial despotism; if the elective principle had continued to function; and if the triumph of the Revolution and democracy had given France a vigorous national spirit, the Civil Constitution would have been successfully imposed on the clergy and on the Pope. To be sure, it wouldn't have detached the Universal Church from the France of the Revolution, and it would have limited itself to maintaining the "unity of the faith" between the Holy See and the elected bishops. It is thus not a canonic question that is posed here, but rather a political one. It's a matter of knowing if the Revolution would have the strength to impose itself in all areas and on the Civil Constitution itself.

I sometimes hear "moderate" thinkers regret that the French Revolution created many serious difficulties for itself by giving the clergy a Civil Constitution. But they reason as if it was possible for the Revolution to ignore the existence of a Church that had dominated and molded France for centuries. They reason as if it was possible for the Revolution, by feigning this ignorance, to abolish the profound conflict between Catholic and revolutionary principles. This was not a question where the Revolution could avoid taking sides, one where it didn't encounter the Church along its path.

To speak only of the question of dioceses, at the moment when the Constitution abolished the former provinces and made France uniform, should it have allowed the former dioceses to remain as a memory of the old France superimposed over the lines of the new France, and by doing so keep reaction's hopes alive? From the moment the Nation took power from the king it had to decide what use it would make of the Church's portion of power. Or should it have left the latter to indefinitely be master of all, of its preaching, of schools, and of civil registries?

Again, the dramatic encounter of Christianity and the Revolution couldn't be put off. The Constituent's sole obligation was to handle this encounter so that it offended as little as possible the prejudices of the masses, who would have turned against the Revolution, and also so that in religious matters the people were allowed to exercise the new practices of freedom. This is what, insofar as it was possible, the Civil Constitution provided for. In fact, the Revolution found priests and bishops willing to swear the oath of allegiance for every parish and for every diocese. It was thus able to divide the Church against itself and prevented an uprising by religious fanaticism that would have led to its fall. Finally, as regards its essential work, it gave itself the time to be unattackable and irrevocable. But it is clear that we have just touched on a dangerous force for resistance, the great spring of counter-revolution, and we can sense that as the Revolution advances, there will be a series of tragic and impassioned struggles that will drive the Revolution from the moderate and middle-of-the-road policies of its first days.

("But what would be the use of this bold expropriation if the Revolution couldn't immediately realize the value of Church property? The debt grew with each passing day ... The needs were immediate and so it was necessary that then resources be immediate."

"The rapid sale of Church property would have absorbed a large proportion of the already rare specie ... [And so] a new form of specie, or to be more precise, an equivalent of specie had to be created." And so the assignat, *a kind of promissory note issued by the government, was established: "The Revolution now found within itself, in the value of the property it seized, in the confidence and the affection it inspired, the credit of the nation to the Nation, of the Revolution to the Revolution."*

Speculation in the assignat, *which was initially backed by confiscated Church lands, and not by funds in the treasury, was to plague the Revolution from the moment it was emitted and would give rise to the social movements of 1792–93.)*

5

The Revolutionary "*Journées*"

("Since the disaster of July 14, 1789 the king and the court had renounced an open offensive," but they hadn't admitted defeat for all that, refusing to accept the series of laws adopted on August 4, 1789, which attacked the clergy and the nobility. The king had written to the Archbishop of Arles that "I will never agree to despoil my clergy and my nobility; I will not sanction decrees that despoil them."

Even more, the Assembly had written the Declaration of the Rights of Man and the Citizen, which they wanted included in the new Constitution but which the king also refused to sanction. The Constituent Assembly, in these first months of the Revolution from August to October, "was to be caught between the Machiavellian resistance of the crown and the new revolutionary agitation of Paris." At the Palais-Royal forces loyal to the Duc D'Orleans wavered between "a legalistic and constitutional sprit and revolutionary effervescence," but in any case were hostile to the king. The writings of Jean-Paul Marat kept the people on the alert against the maneuvers of the royals, sharpened their hostility to the royal veto of measures in favor of the bourgeoisie and the workers. In fact, the Crown had been granted a period of six years during which it could veto measures, which "wounded the popular sentiments as a kind of mockery."

"Popular anger grew. The feeling spread that the Revolution was going to be duped . . . .")

Marat and "The People's Friend"

Beneath all this agitation, at unheard-of depths of anger and revolt, Marat's ideas began to have an effect. They were like a dark underground fire of despair and hatred. It was on September 12, 1789 that the *Publiciste de*

Paris began to appear, which a few weeks later became *L'Ami du Peuple*: "The People's Friend." Immediately, the writer astounded his readers with his extraordinary melange of fanaticism and acute realism. Despite what is often said, it isn't true that he constantly sought to enflame suspicion. He reprimanded the people for their thoughtless mistrust almost as much as he did for their blind confidence. In his first issues, he defended M. de Lafayette who had been frivolously accused of conspiracy: "At that moment, when spirits were so open to suspicion, he might well have become the victim of popular enthusiasm had it not been for the wise precautions of M. de Lafayette."—"The news of the freeing of M. de la Salle was received with pleasure by all classes of citizens, except for the little people, whose extreme distrust is only equaled by the blind confidence they sometimes grant their favorites." He praises Lafayette to excess, who refused the indemnity the municipal government offered him for his functions as commanding general of the National Guard: "This generous citizen, whose soul is open only to those sentiments that elevate humanity, rejected the base metal they wanted to pay him with for his devotion to the Fatherland."

Marat didn't want the people's suspicions to vanish or be misdirected. Nor did he want them to exhaust their strength or to compromise the Revolution through uncontrolled violence: "The emissaries [of the aristocrats] scattered among the people are trying to drive them to excesses; they want them to become disgusted with freedom by allowing them to experience only the misfortunes of license."

Marat having thus analyzed the reckless outbursts of passion invited the people to reflect on the maneuvers of the counter-revolution. According to him it had two goals. First, it wanted to lull the people through apparent concessions. The *coup de théâtre* of August 4[1] was skillfully plotted. The aristocrats gave themselves an appearance of generosity and were thus able to evade affirming the decisive principles that would have saved the Revolution.

How could the nobles take credit for sacrifices they agreed to only under the threat of the peasants? "And so?" Marat exclaimed. "It was only by the light of the flames of their burning chateaux that they had the grandeur of

---

1 Date in 1789 when the Constituent Assembly abolished aristocratic privileges.

soul to renounce the privilege of holding men in irons who had recovered their freedom arms in hand."

At the same time that it attempted to dupe the people, the counter-revolution wanted to harass them. It wanted to fluster them with perpetual alarms, exhaust them by imposing endless patrol and guard duty, and it counted on the resulting inevitable lassitude to return the Nation to the servitude that would become the necessary form of repose.

The workers, exalted by the intoxication of liberty, thought this would give them the strength to suffer for the Revolution for a long period of time, but they were wrong: that exaltation fell quickly. "You are clinging to a ghost. Your workshops are deserted, your factories are abandoned, the earnings of workers and masters are gradually decreasing along with the length of the day [due to winter hours]; all of this will add to the shared misery. Legions of domestics put out on the streets will increase the mass of indigents." Fictions had to be abandoned and reality looked in the face: "Let loudmouths mindlessly vaunt the charms of freedom. It is only of any worth to the thinker who doesn't want to crawl and to men called to play a role by their fortune and rank, but it means nothing to the people. What difference to it are Bastilles? It never knew anything about them but their names."

And Marat, expressing class spirit in its narrowest form, added these strange words: "The ardor with which the unfortunate workers exposed their lives to destroy this monument to tyranny, which was only for their oppressors, is an interesting topic for philosophers to reflect upon." Is he saying that the workers of Paris were supposed to be indifferent to any movement whose immediate object wasn't the conquest of bread?

And didn't Marat see that in participating in all forms of revolutionary agitation the proletarians were increasing their future possibilities? But Marat wanted the Revolution to be on the alert against such fleeting enthusiasm: "The only happiness which nine-tenths of citizens can enjoy is abundance, pleasure, and peace." The conclusion to be drawn from this? The Revolution can't be allowed to drag on, for the people will soon collapse with fatigue. And how can things be speeded up? By concentrating revolutionary power.

This idea of a strong power, which the Revolution would realize at the supreme moment of crisis and danger with the Committee of Public Safety, was formulated by Marat in the first hour, in September 1789. Dispersed among too many hands, revolutionary action languishes. France must not be delivered up to either the anarchy of enflamed and blind crowds, or to the anarchy of too numerous assemblies. Marat proposed 1: To constitute a revolutionary jury drawn by lots from among the citizens of the 60 districts, who would carry out in the name of the people—but more accurately than they—the necessary reprisals; and 2: To substitute for the incoherent and often powerless Assembly at the *Hôtel de Ville* a smaller and more determined committee.

Marat bitterly attacked the Assembly of the *Hôtel de Ville*, and probably deep in his sickened heart he, who had been rejected by all the academies, held a grudge against it for counting recognized scholars among its members. He denounced it furiously. He wrote an article burning with rage against Beaumarchais, calling him an intriguer and speculator. He declared that several representatives were suspect because they didn't have a legal domicile, lived in rented rooms, and didn't pay the capitation tax.

He showed as much defiance towards the *"déclassé"* poor as towards the rich. National Guard patrols seized his newspaper from the hands of its sellers. He redoubled his attacks. Cited before the Assembly of the *Hôtel de Ville*, he proudly said, "I am the eye of the people and you are nothing but their little finger."

And he always demanded that just a few upright, vigorous, and quick-witted men should be charged with leading the Revolution to its goal in the space of just a few days. Are we to see the mark of great political sense in the insistent way that, from the beginning of the drama, Marat demanded this violent concentration of powers, this dictatorship of Public Safety to which the Revolution later resorted?

His admirers often called him a prophet, but is it demonstrating great political clairvoyance to demand extreme measures before the state of affairs made them possible, or even conceivable, to a great number of people?

In September and October 1789, Marat's policies would probably have led to a moderate committee, named by the National Assembly. In any case, as long as the king remained in place, and with him the Court, how would an absolute concentration of powers have been possible? Either it would have been handed over to the king, and this meant tyranny, or the king would have been cast from supreme power and been dethroned in fact. Yet Marat, so proud of his intrepid logic, stopped in mid-stream. He didn't dare propose, he didn't even dare predict the abolition of the monarchy, and even spoke of "our good king." This timidity completely undid his system, for it was the coexistence of the Revolution and the royalty of the *ancien régime* that was the true duality of powers.

I believe that Marat's theories caused bewilderment and even scandal among the people. In his papers, he had attacked Mirabeau more than once, and yet on October 7, 1789 the women of the marketplace in Versailles demanded "our little father Mirabeau." *L'Ami du Peuple* did not yet have a firm grip on popular consciousness. And yet it is inconceivable that at least some chords didn't vibrate at the sound of its cries of revolt and despairing anger. Apropos of the proposed distinction between active and passive citizens, the latter excluded from voting because of their poverty, Marat wrote:

The fate of the poor, always repressed, always subjugated, and always oppressed, can never be improved through peaceful means. This is unquestionably a striking proof of wealth's influence on the laws. But laws only have any influence as long as they submit to them. They smashed the yoke of nobility and they will smash that of opulence. The important thing is to enlighten them, to make them aware of their rights, and then the revolution will unfailingly operate without any human power being able to oppose it.

Marat doesn't provide a bold and detailed social conclusion, and he ends with these moderate and evasive lines: "The sole means that remain to the wealthy to save themselves from the blow that is threatening them is to act in good faith by giving the poor a portion of their excess."

But these words would gradually shake the people to their depths and, outside of any system, they would awaken a revolutionary consciousness in the newly formed proletariat.

In order to destroy the privileges of the nobles the plebeians put forth the great, the irresistible argument that all men being equal, they all have the same rights. In order to destroy the prerogatives of the rich, the unfortunate will put forth the same argument. By virtue of what sacred title, they will say, do you claim a right to preserve a wealth that is always obtained through odious means, almost all of it taken from the poor through trickery or violence, almost all of it the fruits of favor, swindles, rascality, plunder, and misappropriation?

Sometimes his words burn with suffering. When the issue arose of military conscription for all citizens Marat exclaimed in the name of the people (in November 1789):

Where is the Fatherland of those who have no property, who have no claim to any employment, who gain nothing from the social pact? Condemned to serve everywhere, if they aren't under the yoke of a master they are under that of their fellow citizens. And whatever revolution might come, their eternal lot is servitude, poverty, and oppression. What could they possibly owe to a state that did nothing but solidify their poverty and tighten their irons? They owe it only hatred and curses. So save the state, you to whom it assures a peaceful and happy fate. Demand nothing of us, for it is enough that cruel fate reduced us to the cruel necessity of living among you.

This is truly the cry of despair of eternal damnation; it's the cry of hatred of those damned to servitude and poverty who don't even have the fierce consolation of being isolated. In their hell they were struck with the sight of the privileged and the happy.

The October *"Journées"*

While a silent ferment was developing in a Paris agitated by the proposals of the Palais-Royal, by the poverty of the people, by the women's repeated petitions, by Marat's desperate rage, and by the conflicts between the democratic and the moderate bourgeoisie, the news spread that a new *coup d'état* was being prepared by the Court. The king was delaying sanctioning the Declaration of the Rights of Man. Mounier had been raised to the presidency of the Assembly by a coalition of moderates and the right, and the troops were again in motion. The Flanders and Montmorency regiments were concentrated in Versailles on flimsy pretexts. A partial turnover of the *corps de grade* was to take place in late September and the new soldiers would be enrolled while the veterans would be retained in order to swell the ranks with soldiers devoted to the king, soldiers who hadn't yet taken the Civic Oath.

A large number of officers in several army regiments had received week-long leaves and had gone to Versailles, where they met up with gentlemen decorated with the Order of Saint Louis. It appeared they were gathering in preparation for a *coup d'état*. The rumor spread that the troops were going to kidnap the king and take him to Metz, where the Marquis de Bouillé commanded troops that were, in part, made up of foreigners. A great fear gripped Paris, and the democrats joined with Loustalot[2] in exclaiming that in order for France to be saved, "a new revolutionary push" was needed. What exactly was the Court's plan? Here again it is possible that it didn't have a firm design and that it wavered, waiting for events to dictate the path to be taken. But the suspicious preparations, the shady intrigues, were not only a crime against the nascent liberty of the Nation; they were also a great blunder, for counter-revolution's threats necessarily united the two bourgeois factions that were beginning to war with each other.

If the Crown had been faithful, if it had observed the Constitution without any reservations and adopted a frankly revolutionary line of conduct, in a matter of months, it would have become the arbitrator between the bourgeois parties. The debate between moderates and democrats had become so bitter, so violent, that the popular party was already drawing up a list of suspects among the officers of the National Guard accused of being spies in service to the Court. But in just a few days the imprudence and incoherence of the aristocrats re-established revolutionary unity. On October 1, a gala dinner for the *gardes du corps*

---

2   Élisée Loustalot (1761–90)—Revolutionary journalist, editor of *Les Révolutions de Paris*. Of fragile health, he died as a result of overwork.

was given in the Opera Hall of the Chateau of Versailles; the princesses, the marquises, and the duchesses circulated through the halls, stimulating royalist enthusiasm. The musicians played the famous air; "Oh Richard, O my king, the universe abandons you."

The queen, leading the dauphin by the hand, appeared amidst applause. The king, who had returned from the hunt, was also taken to the hall where the feast was being held. The wine and feelings of devotion went to peoples' heads and a few *gardes du corps* tore off their tricolor cockades and trampled on them, while the ladies of the court distributed black ones. Lecointre, lieutenant colonel of the National Guard of Versailles, refused to remove the tricolor cockade and was loudly insulted. His presence, as well as that of other officers of his corps, indicates that the Court didn't have a clear plan. But then again, who knows if the latter hadn't hoped to drag along the National Guard embittered by the people's insults, by having them mingle with the *garde du corps*. One of the National Guard officers, a stocky butcher from Versailles, joined with the aristocrats and like them tossed away his tricolor cockade. A counter-revolutionary delirium enflamed their spirits.

The March on Versailles

Suddenly, Paris was in a state of revolution. Citizens were assembling throughout the city. At the foot of the bridges, at the marketplace, meetings were organized. In the faubourg Saint-Antoine, workers rose up en masse to defend freedom. The women of the marketplace formed a procession and entered houses, inviting the women to join with them. Men armed with pikes, rifles, and sickles followed and marched alongside the women.

Every group denounced the perfidy of the Court and the softness of the three hundred members of the Assembly of representatives of Paris. Deliveries of wheat were becoming rare and it was as if all of Paris wanted to flee in order to flee famine. On October 5, it was to the cry of "To Versailles! To Versailles!" that an enormous crowd gathered in front of the *Hôtel de Ville*. The representatives, who had sat until late the previous night, hadn't yet assembled. The women wanted to enter the *Hôtel de Ville* at 9:00 a.m. Chevalier d'Hermnigny, assistant adjutant of the National Guard, formed his men into a square and opposed their bayonets to the women's advance.

Stones were thrown at the National Guard and the latter, in order to avoid a bloody clash, retreated into the *Hôtel de Ville*. The women entered it and Chevalier d'Hermigny asked only that they not allow the men to enter. They agreed to this and the men served as police at the main gate of the *Hôtel de Ville*. But during this time, the small gate that opened onto the arcade was forced, and it was now pointless to guard the main one. An immense crowd of men and women invaded the halls of the *Hôtel de Ville*. The representatives, warned by the tocsin that was rung in all districts, arrived one by one. The people called on them to organize the movement and to save freedom. They refused to deliberate in the midst of all this confusion and around noon, the districts began sending their battalions, "the battalions of order," as they were to be called in 1848; Belleville's, under the leadership of M. de Seine was the first to arrive.

Assisted by the grenadiers of First Battalion of the Saint-Jacques-Hôpital district, they pushed the people back, or at least contained them on the square of the *Hôtel de Ville*. Three battalions of grenadiers, led by Major General Gouvion, entered the *Hôtel de Ville* and evacuated those inside. At noon, it looked like the moderate bourgeoisie was master of Paris. But the women who had entered the *Hôtel de Ville* unarmed came out of it armed: they'd broken open the storerooms where arms and munitions were kept, and though retreating before the grenadiers' bayonets, they took rifles, powder, and cannons. The National Guard, hesitant and flustered, didn't dare disarm them. There were about four thousand women, and they weren't, as reaction said, shrews and whores. They were good and valiant women whose great maternal hearts had suffered for too long from the cries of their poorly nourished children. Some were wealthy and educated, like Marie-Louise Lenoel, married name Chéret, who left an exquisite account of the October *journées* and who, as she tells us herself, "was engaged in a very lucrative business in Passy."

For these women, this was an uprising born of pity. With their sure instincts they had foreseen the maneuvers against the Revolution of the aristocrats and prelates, and they imputed the famine that Paris suffered from and the poverty that gripped the people to these maneuvers. And were they wrong, after all? Was it not, in fact, the silent malaise spread abroad by counter-revolution's perpetual intrigues that paralyzed labor and the transport of wheat during these troubled months? In any case, it is interesting to see how quickly the women of Paris, provoked by injustice and angered by suffering, separated themselves from the clergy. Just a few weeks before the October *journées*, the market-women expanded the number of services and ceremonies in the churches. They seemed to be placing the nascent Revolution under the protection of the Crucified One. From the time of the October *journées*, the treason of the Court and a portion of the clergy abruptly broke these ancient religious bonds, and the women who went to Versailles hitched their cannons to the cry of "Down With the Priests!" Mme Chéret spoke with satisfaction of the terror the arrival of "these good friends" caused "among the believers."

The courageous little feminine troop, having just been driven from the *Hôtel de Ville*, decided to march on Versailles. To command them, they appealed to the volunteers and victors of the Bastille. Hulin, Richard du Pin, and Maillard took the leadership of the movement and the cannons were hoisted onto carriages. On to Versailles!

During this time and despite the presence of the grenadier battalions, the crowd had grown on the square in front of the *Hôtel de Ville* and it impatiently demanded that the entire National Guard follow the women's example and, like them, go to Versailles to crush the conspiracy, save those deputies who were friends of freedom, and wrest the king from the traitors. The people implored the National Guard to remain faithful to the Revolution and to be wary of their officers, who included many aristocrats and enemies of the Fatherland. Several Guardsmen asked—or even ordered—Lafayette to lead them to Versailles. Lafayette, doubtless frightened by the consequences of such an act, refused. "It is astounding," exclaimed a soldier, "that M. de Lafayette wants to command the Commune when it's the Commune that should be commanding him. We all want him to leave." The general answered them that he could only obey a legal order, and that only the representatives of the Commune could give it.

At 4:30 p.m., the latter were still deliberating and, no more than Lafayette, did they dare assume any responsibility. Finally, in the face of the growing anger of the people and the soldiers, Lafayette sent a letter to the representatives telling them it was no longer possible to resist. He sent them an order, while still trying to cover himself:

> The General Assembly of representatives of the Paris Commune, given the circumstances and the people's wishes, as well as the commanding general's statement that he could not refuse them, authorizes or rather orders the commanding general to go to Versailles; recommends that he take the necessary precautions to ensure the safety of the city; and relies on his prudence for any other measures that must be taken.

To be sure, such timorous men were not capable of great acts. Paris had been stirred by the force of popular sentiment, by the energy of its workers and women, and also by the insurrectionary placard of the lawyer Danton calling to arms the turbulent Cordeliers district, in which resided many lawyers and actors of the Comedie-Française who dreamed of playing Brutus, and who gave the Revolution a vigorous and theatrical flavor, which would also be Danton's distinguishing characteristics.

On October 6, it was clear that the Revolution would slip from the hands of the moderate bourgeoisie, which was too weak to lead it.

Lafayette blanched upon receiving the letter authorizing the march on Versailles. He immediately detailed three companies of grenadiers and one of fusiliers with three cannons to form the vanguard. Seven or eight hundred civilians armed with rifles, pikes, and sticks marched two hundred steps ahead of the vanguard.

At 5:07 p.m., the National Guard paraded in three ranks on the *Quai Pelletier*. Lafayette responded to the acclamation with the air of a man who was saying, "Now you got what you want." The parade lasted forty minutes.

During this time the people, convinced that many officers and even many soldiers did not have the right spirit, hunted down all the men in uniform they could find and forced them to join the army on its march. The drums beat and the standards rippled in the breeze: "Go, march, brave citizens. You bear with you the destiny of France. Our hearts follow you:

rescue our king, save our deputies, support the majesty of the Nation. 400,000 hands are ready to applaud you, to avenge you."

(The people are angry with the king and he attempts to calm them down. Jaurès continues that at the palace "he reappeared on the balcony and begged the people, in touching terms, to spare the lives of the threatened gardes du corps. 'To Paris with the king! To Paris with the king!' shouted the crowd. 'Yes, I will return to Paris,' said the king, 'but on the condition that it be with my wife and children'; he knew how unpopular the queen was, and through a kind of contract with the people he placed her under the safeguard of Parisian loyalty. Louis XVI was a soul more complex and difficult to untangle than is usually imagined. Just as he was sometimes duplicitous in his weakness, there was sometimes grandeur in his affability.)

"To Paris with the king!"

"To Paris with the king!" was one of the decisive cries, one of the decisive moments of the Revolution. The drama was now concentrated in the capital. Now the king was in the hands of the people, along with the Assemblies that didn't want to break with him. It was in Paris that the popular forces were massed. It was in Paris, a condensed version of France, that the idea of French unity was most powerful. The king in Paris meant ensuring that the Revolution would be democratic and unitary. *Moderantisme* and federalism might have prevailed had the center of public life and the Revolution been transferred to the provinces: Paris would then be considered dissident, and in order to resist the city's actions, the bourgeois moderates would have allied with the forces of the *ancien régime*, and the French Revolution would have been nothing but a replay of the English Revolution, a revolution of compromises, and not a revolution of energy, logic, and universal upheaval.

The poor women of the people who left Paris the morning of October 5 to go to Versailles and demand bread and who brought back the king played an extraordinary role, in fact, one of the grandest in recorded history: they tied the formidable knot between the Revolution and Paris, and no aristocratic or Girondin hand could untie it; no Prussian, English, or Cossack sword could cut it.

It was on the very same day, October 6, that the king arrived in Paris. He was proceeded by a long procession of women bearing tree branches, probably already tinged with fall colors; cannons were draped with foliage. The king arrived at dusk, around 6 p.m. The houses were illuminated, and in that strange crepuscular mix of splendor and melancholy, the Revolution marched forward, full of enthusiasm and uncertainty. The people acclaimed the king, carried along by the flow of a vast dream-like sea towards the veiled horizon. An ambiguous and bizarre moment, where the Crown's defeat resembled a triumph; where Paris, half-victor, half-dupe, grew intoxicated on its tumultuous joy and forgot the plots of yesterday.

And strangely, this great crisis of the October *journées* seemed to deflate Paris's revolutionary enthusiasm. We are about to enter two years of calm. The Revolution will develop in its depths, with only limited agitation on the surface.

The woes that followed the bad harvest of 1788 and which had been worsened by the uncertainty of the first days of the Revolution, soon eased. Staple goods again arrived and people returned to work. The price of bread fell from four to three sous a pound. The winter of 1789–90 was extremely mild, and in February the weather was so pleasant that masonry work was able to start up again. The factories were active and the newly organized city governments set up public works projects to employ those still out of work. And at the end of 1790, they were able to close most of these workshops and building sites, so great was the economic activity in the country. The fevers of poverty and hunger were thus calmed, and the Revolution could proceed to its organic tasks.

The shock of the October *journées* and the sudden violence that had put the king's life at risk had perturbed the revolutionary bourgeoisie. The Assembly remembered with displeasure that it had been invaded, and if it followed the king to Paris it was in the firm intention of curtailing the activity on the streets through harsh measures. Its still immense revolutionary authority would have allowed it to promulgate martial law without causing popular outcry against it, and in fact it would have no need to apply it for two years. The Jacobin Club would greatly assist the Assembly in controlling the movement by disciplining the revolutionary forces.

6

The Flight to Varennes

(The king, though on the surface accepting the new reality, persisted in attempting to defend his privileges, as did the Church, "and it was the attitude of the Church that would command that of the king." The Assembly had succeeded in obtaining the royal sanction of the Civil Constitution of the Clergy, which required priests to swear loyalty to the Constitution, but the Church remained recalcitrant, and this recalcitrance was a major contributor to the revolt that broke out in the west of France, in Brittany in the Vendée, where nobles, farmers, and the priests who refused to take the vow "began to resort to force." "The emissaries of the nobles spread the watchword from farm to farm and began to organize bands." The king "denounced the war being waged against the Church, throwing fear into the timid fraction of the bourgeoisie, causing it to fear for its property, expanding its army with foreign contingents, covering them with the banner of the monarchy."

The situation was becoming untenable, and Louis XVI and Marie Antoinette had to make a choice: "Four roads were open to them. Either they had to fully and irrevocably accept the Revolution and remain in Paris, giving, by their presence and conduct, the proof of their good faith … This was the wisest choice, but the prejudices and beliefs of the king and queen rendered them unacceptable. Or they could have accepted the Revolution and left Paris, not to be closer to foreign lands but rather to settle in the provinces … and address an appeal to the nation from there … Or the king could remain silent, passively approving events, allowing things to go along, if need be encouraging the extreme parties in the mad hope that the Revolution would exhaust itself through its own excesses and that the worn-out country would fully re-establish the old royal and religious authority … Or else he had to flee, but not to hand himself over to Mirabeau, that is, the Revolution, but to take command of the [royalist] army of Bouillé and dictate conditions to France with the support of foreigners."

On June 20, 1791 he literally chose his road.)

Suddenly, the news struck like a lightning bolt over an Assembly stubbornly determined to reconcile the Revolution and the king: "The king has departed and his flight is clearly the signal for open, violent combat between royal power and the Revolution."

The king had left the Tuileries at 11:00 on the night of June 20, 1791 to go with his family to Montmédy, near the border, where Bouillé[1] was to join him. Count von Fersen[2] had procured a passport in the name of the Baroness de Korff. It was Mme de Tourzel, the children's governess, who played the role of the baroness. The queen, traveling disguised as a governess, was supposed to be Mme Richer; Madame Élisabeth became Rosalie, *demoiselle de compagnie*; and the king was a valet named Durand, in a gray outfit and wig. They were able to leave without being recognized.

They got into the first of their carriages, which Fersen, dressed as a coachman, drove to Bondy. There they took a large cabriolet driven by three young bodyguards wearing the yellow suit of couriers; they were supposed to reach Montmédy via Châlons-sur-Marne and Sainte-Menehould. Fersen, after having left the royals, went straight to Belgium, and he wrote to the Baron de Taube from Mons on June 22 at 11:00 a.m.: "My dear friend, the king, the queen, Madame Élisabeth, the dauphin and Madame [the dauphin's young sister] left Paris at midnight. I accompanied them as far as Bondy without any incidents. I am leaving at this moment to join them." A short while earlier, at 8:00 a.m., he had written to his father:

I have just arrived here, my dear father. The king and all the family fortunately left Paris on the 20th at midnight. I drove them as far as the first post. God willing the rest of their voyage will be just as fortunate. I await Monsieur's arrival at any moment. I will then continue my trip along the border so as to meet the king at Montmédy, if he has the good fortune to arrive there.

---

1   François Claude de Bouillé (1739–1800)—political figure under the monarchy and fiercely loyal to the king and queen, he was named general-in-chief of the army of Meuse and Sarre-et-Moselle in 1790.
2   Axel de Fersen (1755–1810)—Swedish noble living in Paris and notorious as Marie Antoinette's lover.

How was this flight of the king and his entire family possible? They left by a service stairway that gave onto the Cour des Princes and, mixing with the large number of people that were leaving the chateau at that hour, weren't recognized. But why weren't they more closely guarded? For weeks and even months, there had been no lack of warnings. I've already noted Marat's amazingly precise warnings at the end of March and early April, and he hadn't let up since. In truth, as much as I've searched in the collection of *L'Ami du Peuple* for the "furious" article Louis Blanc[3] wrote of, I've been unable to locate it. In any case, it can't be from those final few weeks since, according to Louis Blanc it contains these words: "Parisians, foolish Parisians, I am tired of repeating this to you: bring the king and the dauphin back within your walls." But in May and June, they were in Paris, and I wonder if what Louis Blanc calls an article by Marat, without giving the date, is not simply a more or less accurate summary of several different articles, and particularly an article of April 20: "O Parisians, you will be the executioners of three million of your brothers if you are foolish enough to allow him to stray from your walls." [...]

The Attitude of the Assembly

The news of the king's flight led the Assembly to again find the great spirit, at one and the same time revolutionary and bourgeois, of its early days. It controlled its emotions and deliberated with a solemn and nearly grandiose calm. It had two main concerns: it wanted to reassure the country and also prevent any despair among the revolutionaries. The confidence it demonstrated in the Revolution at that moment was swiftly communicated to the entire nation.

The Assembly immediately summoned the ministers and decreed that every order it issued in the absence of the king would have force of law, without any need for royal sanction. In doing so it seized sovereign authority, and one might say that it filled in for the Crown. At the same time, the Constituent worked at calming popular upset and maintaining

---

3   Louis Blanc (1811–82)—socialist political figure as well as author of a 15-volume history of the Revolution.

the primacy of the bourgeoisie during the crisis. In order to do this, it first had to cover for Lafayette, of whom the people were violently suspicious. He was accused of being an accomplice in the king's flight either through treason or negligence. His situation was momentarily threatening. Cries arose from all the worksites of Paris where the workers were assembled, echoing Marat's sensational article.

Lafayette discredited or suppressed meant the moderate bourgeoisie losing its military chief; it meant first the streets, and soon perhaps power itself turned over to the angered proletarians. Barnave,[4] who in this great crisis was the bourgeoisie's true leader, understood the peril and, in answer to Reubell's insinuations,[5] hastened to defend Lafayette:

Let me put a halt to the speaker and the doubts he appears to want to spread. The object that should concern us at this time is saving the government, is assembling all our forces and attaching popular confidence to those who truly deserve it. I ask that the Assembly not allow the speaker's speech to continue and that he not be allowed to raise pernicious doubts against men who have always demonstrated their patriotism. There are circumstances in which it is easy to cast suspicions on the sentiments of the best of citizens. (*Calm is re-established.*) Here are men against whom these unfortunate circumstances could give rise to a mistrust that I profoundly believe, that I will swear in the face of the entire Nation, that they haven't deserved. (*Applause.*) Monsieur Lafayette deserves our entire confidence. It is essential to the Nation that it be preserved and that it clearly be shown him. (*Applause from the spectators' gallery.*)

Barnave had long been, and just the day before had still been, Lafayette's enemy. And so his plea appeared as generous as it was adroit, and put an end to the people's mistrust. In his *Introduction to the French Revolution*, that is, in his memoirs, Barnave wrote, in speaking of the crisis of unpopularity

---

4 Antoine Barnave (1761–93)—politician and publicist sympathetic to the royal family.
5 Jean-François Reubell (1747–1807), a former Jacobin and later Feuillant—moderate—deputy, had asked if it wasn't true that the order had been given not to allow the King to go out after midnight, and that if he had been able to do so "that points to something suspicious."

he traversed before June 21: "Fortunately, a few weeks didn't suffice to completely undo my influence, and whatever care my enemies took to deprive me of this scandalous popularity, on June 21 I still had enough left to save Lafayette." And it was in actuality the entire bourgeois regime he intended to save against both the Court and the people. With a bold clarity he declared this on June 21 from the tribune of the Assembly:

I remind all good citizens what truly matters under the current circumstances. It is that in this place where the *res publica* speaks and acts that it be able to do so freely; that it enjoy the greatest calm and the firmest unity; and that all its actions, surrendered to the prudence of the representatives of the Nation, not be influenced by causes which, however popular they might appear, are nothing but the result of foreign influence. [This is quite true.]

Messieurs, force is required in Paris, but so is calm. Force is required, but it must be motivated by one sole will, and that will must be yours. The moment it is believed it can be influenced, authority, which you are the sole depositories of and which you must answer for, is in danger. The true danger at this time resides in these extraordinary circumstances where turmoil is incited by persons for whom patriotism is far from being their sentiment, for whom public safety is far from being their object.

It is essential that all those men who are truly friends of the Fatherland, that all those who have interests in common with it, that those who became the saviors of France and Paris on the July 14 that made the Revolution, assemble again and be ready to march.

You will recall that at that time the initial impulse was given by a class little given to reflection, easily led, and that disorders were the effect. The next day thinking men, landowners, citizens truly attached to the Fatherland armed themselves. The disorders then ceased and were succeeded by truly civic acts, and France was saved. This is the path we must follow. I thus request that the National Assembly vote a resolution by which it orders all citizens of Paris to be armed and ready, but to remain in the deepest silence, to remain immobile and in a state of expectation until such time as the representatives of the Nation need to set them in motion for the maintenance of public order or for the defense of the Fatherland.

This meant placing the leadership of events in the hands of the Assembly. It meant casting suspicion on those who might attempt to encourage the people to go as far as overthrowing the monarchy. It meant proclaiming that the leadership of the new world belonged to the property-owning elite, considered the only "thinking" part. Reubell attempted in vain to respond; he was interrupted as soon as he began to speak, and it should be noted that neither Pétion,[6] nor Robespierre, nor any of the democrats of the far left attempted to protest against Barnave's so-bourgeois words.

It can be said that the Revolution, threatened with a sudden peril, retreated to its center, the moderate bourgeoisie. It can also be said that the Constituent Assembly's bold and confident action, seizing all power, sending the order throughout France to arrest the king, and ordering all public functionaries to take a new oath to the Nation and the law, rallied everyone around it. Enthusiastic addresses reached it from all over. Municipal governments and directorates throughout France told it that far from wearing down their courage, the peril electrified them. And all over France as well, without the word "republic" ever being mentioned, republican sentiment began to emerge.

I've already quoted the admirable words of the municipal government of Nantes: "The king has departed; the Nation remains." Among many other addresses, we must note that of the city of Givet: "The king has departed, and good citizens will say, fine, this event is not in the least discouraging. The National Assembly will replace him in all regards, and if the Crown was a reward, its immortal labors have earned it the right to it."

It was the royalty of the elected Assembly, i.e., the Nation itself, which replaced the fragile and treasonous royalty of the Capets. The workingmen of the public workshops, whose dissolution the Assembly had just decreed, presented themselves at the bar, not to cast recriminations, but to assure the Assembly of their devotion to the Fatherland and the law. According to the transcript: "In their name one of them takes the oath of fidelity

---

6 Jerome Pétion (1756–94)—member of the Gironde. He committed suicide while attempting to avoid arrest by the Convention after fomenting a revolt against it in Normandy.

to the Nation. He makes a respectful speech on the decree that fixed the ending of the charity workshops, and requests the report of this decree. He swears that in any case they will never be unfaithful to their vow." And so, adherence was universal.

At the moment of his flight, the king had left a sealed letter for Laporte, the intendant of the civil list. This letter was handed over to the Minister of Justice Duport-Dutertre. It was a declaration of the king to all Frenchmen in which he lamented at length the encroachments on royal authority of the National Assembly. He asserted that he was never free and he complains of the insufficiency of the civil list (fixed at 25 million francs), and of the inadequacy of the fitting-out of the Tuileries Palace. He ended this dull and vulgar declaration with the complicated and confused announcement of a constitutional change:

Frenchmen, and especially you Parisians, you residents of a city that the ancestors of His Majesty called the good city of Paris, beware of the suggestions and lies of your false friends. Come back to your king. He will always be your father, your best friend. What pleasure he will have in forgetting all personal insults and in finding himself again in your midst when a Constitution, freely accepted by him, will ensure that our holy religion is respected; that the government shall be established on a firm footing and in a manner useful to the Nation; that the property and estate of each shall no longer be troubled; that the laws shall not be broken with impunity; and that, finally, liberty shall be placed on firm and unshakeable foundations.

This was counter-revolution. The Assembly listened to this deplorable document in scornful silence. But the problem that was before it had been openly posed, or rather made clear: what attitude was it going to take towards this king who deserted his post and repudiated in its totality a Constitution whose principal sections he had already sanctioned? The Assembly understood that it couldn't allow the royal protest to go unanswered, and it composed an address to the French people. In this address it applied itself to avoiding the irreparable and vigorously refuting

Louis XVI's allegations, without placing itself in the position of having to pronounce his removal.

It began by expressing the hypothesis that Louis XVI might well have been kidnapped. It was Démeunier who, at the sitting of June 22, read the draft address to the French:

> A great crime has just been committed. The National Assembly was reaching the end of its long labors. The Constitution was completed, the storms of the Revolution were about to cease, and through a single crime the enemies of the public good wanted to sacrifice the entire Nation to their vengeance. The king and the royal family were kidnapped on the night of the 20–21 of this month. (*Murmurs.*)

Roederer violently interrupted: "That's false: he deserted his post in a cowardly fashion."

Démeunier continued: "I ask that the Assembly attentively listen to me until I finish. The Constitutional Committee wrote its draft address as circumstances dictated: perhaps after having heard it in its entirety the protest that was just made will have been answered."

The address, in fact, after that careful reservation, calculated to allow for all future possibilities, was extremely rigorous and severe:

> Public freedom shall be sustained. The conspirators and slaves will learn to know the intrepidity of the founders of French liberty, and before the Nation we solemnly commit ourselves to avenge the law or die. (*Applause.*) France wants to be free and it will be free. It is sought to make the Revolution go backwards. It shall not go backwards.

And Démeunier, recalling all of the king's vows of fidelity to the Constitution, exclaimed:

> If one fine day the king failed to protest that he had been dragged along by conspirators, people would have denounced his breach of faith to the world.

Congratulatory addresses and thanks have arrived from all parts of the kingdom. It is said that it is the work of conspirators, yes, unquestionably, of twenty-four million conspirators. (*Lively applause.*) We're condemned for not having submitted the Constitution for the king's refusal. But royalty is only established for the people, and if great nations are forced to sustain it, it is because it is the safeguard of their happiness. The Constitution grants it its prerogatives and its true character. Your representatives would be criminal if they'd sacrificed 24 million citizens to the interests of one sole man.

The capital can serve as a model for the rest of France. The king's departure didn't cause any great upset and, what causes our enemies to despair is that it continues to enjoy perfect tranquility. (*Lively applause.*)

There are crimes against great nations that only generosity can allow them to forget. The French people were proud in their servitude; they will demonstrate the virtues and heroism of liberty. Let the enemies of the Constitution know this: if the territory of this empire is to be enslaved anew then the Nation must be destroyed. Let despotism undertake such an enterprise if it wishes: it will be vanquished or, after its horrific victory, it will find only ruins. (*Lively applause.*)

The sounds of the "Marseillaise" can already be heard in these words. But at the same time, with an extreme political prudence, the Assembly reserved the right to either certify that the king had been forced to do what he did or to appeal to the generosity of the Nation regarding this great crime. It recalled a great people's need of monarchy in the very document that indicted the counter-revolutionary royalty.

The Arrest of the King

But at that same sitting of June 22, 1792, a half an hour after the reading of Démeunier's address, shouts outside announced the arrival of a courier. The transcript notes that the words "The king has been captured! The king has been captured!" could be made out in the din. The deputies hurriedly returned to the hall, a great agitation reigned in the Assembly, and two couriers entered amidst applause, handing a packet to the president. The king had, in fact, been captured. These were letters from the municipal officers of Sainte-Menehould announcing that the king had been recognized and that Drouet was in pursuit of the carriages: "It is 3:00 a.m. and they haven't yet returned." But letters from Châlons and Clermont announced that the king had been arrested in Varennes.

In vain the king attempted to touch the municipal council of Varennes. In vain the detachment of hussars, posted in Varennes by Bouillé, had been invited to kidnap the king. A large gathering of people had forced the hussars to retreat, and the king was brought back to Paris. The Assembly immediately ordered that Bouillé be arrested. It ordered that the king be brought back under the protection of the National Guard, and that all possible precautions be taken to ensure his life. It dispatched three commissioners—Pétion, Latour-Maubourg, and Barnave—to meet the royal family.

Upon learning of the king's arrest, the moderates of the Assembly congratulated themselves for not having spoken a single irrevocable word. They no longer had to fear a counter-revolutionary movement organized and led by the king with the support of foreigners. They considered ending the crisis quietly, without abolishing royalty and even without replacing the king.

From Barnave's prudent language at the sitting of June 21, that is, in the heat of the news of the flight, it is clear that this was the solution he leaned towards. It is possible, as his adversaries said, that he was fascinated by the queen's beauty and moved by her sufferings during the voyage, when he escorted her. But it was with a political goal; it was, as he had the habit of saying, to "finish off the Revolution" that he advised all his friends to clear the king of all blame and restore him to power.

In his memoirs he explained his conduct and analyzed the general mood, as he viewed it:

The Assembly didn't surrender itself to that precipitation, to that flood of desperate measures that demonstrate nothing but weakness. Rather it provided for everything, and no important measure was omitted. So when, two days after his disappearance, it was learned that the king had been arrested in Varennes, at that moment the long labor of calumny was promptly effaced, and confidence rapidly returned to those who, deep in their hearts, knew his sincerity, his devotion, and his inflexible courage [...] I was one of the three commissioners appointed to accompany him on his return to Paris, an epoch forever engraved in my memory and which provided so many pretexts for slander but which, in engraving this memorable example of misfortune upon my imagination, unquestionably served to help me bear up under my own.

In order to judge if this famous voyage changed anything in my personal dispositions it suffices to examine my conduct and see if what preceded it and what followed it are in accord. Both before and after the voyage to Varennes I didn't believe that that unexpected event struck a blow at the Constitution [...]

What Barnave doesn't add is that, upon the return of the king, he became his advisor and he suggested, or even wrote for him, the clever responses the king gave the Assembly's commissioners charged with interrogating him. The agitation among the people and at the clubs was great. But the moderates of the Assembly were determined not to open up the door to the unknown by bringing the king up on charges. It was on July 13 that the order of the day of the Assembly called for the report of the committees relating to the escape of the king and the royal family. The Constitutional Committee declared that the king was inviolable; that the Constitution hadn't foreseen the crime of flight in sufficient detail; that in any case, if the king could be incriminated, the stability that the legislators had intended to give the crown by maintaining the monarchy would be constantly at the mercy of accusers; that ministers must always be responsible for the acts of the king; or, if the king acted without the ministers' knowledge, it was the advisors, the inspirers of the illegal act, who, through a necessary fiction, would be the primary culprits.

It was in this way that the committees decided to try Bouillé and to clear the king of blame. Barnave did better than summarize all these juridical arguments. In a long and skillful speech, he appealed to the conservative instincts of the revolutionaries of the Assembly. At bottom, he asked two questions: do you want to substitute the republic for the monarchy? Do you want to incite a new revolution?

The facts have been thoroughly established. But I take them as a whole and I say: today, any change would be fatal; any prolongation of the Revolution would be disastrous. I place the question here and it is here that it bears the mark of the national interest. Are we going to end the Revolution? Are we going to begin it anew? (*Repeated applause.*) If you once defy the Constitution, what is the point where will you stop, and more importantly, where will our successors stop?

A great evil is done us when this revolutionary movement, which destroyed all that had to be destroyed, and which led us to the point where we had to stop is perpetuated. Consider, *Messieurs*, consider what will happen after you. You have done what was good for liberty, for equality. No arbitrary power was spared, no usurpation of egoism or property has escaped. You made all men equal before civil and political law; you took back, you returned to the state everything that was taken from it. The result of this is this great truth, that if the Revolution takes one more step it can't do so without danger. It's that in the line of liberty the first act that would follow would be the destruction of royalty; it's that in the line of equality the first act that might follow would be the destruction of property. (*Applause.*)

The question was well posed, and from the point of view of the bourgeois Revolution, Barnave would have been right if it would have been possible to believe that the king was now resigned to the Revolution and that he wouldn't attempt to fight it again in his fashion. This was the decisive point, and it appears that the democrats of the far left should have focused their efforts on this point. They really only had one thing to say: experience had demonstrated that after so many solemn and broken vows Louis XVI and the Revolution could not live together.

The Massacre on the Champ de Mars

(*Even at this time when the king had shown his true colors, there was hesitation concerning what was the proper action to take: "It was republican and democratic theses that had to be opposed to the monarchical, but the extreme left didn't dare to." Should the king be put on trial? Should a republic be declared? The philosophical debates over these issues went on; the Assembly refused to move towards these solutions, but "at the Cordeliers and the Jacobins angry voices called for the judging of the king ... At the Cordeliers and the Jacobins the idea gained strength that a petition should be drawn up calling for the Assembly to reverse its own decision," which placed the blame for the king's flight on his allies and not on the king himself "and quietly prepared to return power to him on the condition that he accept a revised version of the Constitution."*

"The Assembly wanted to impose silence and treat those who protested as conspirators. At its sitting of July 16 it called the municipal officers, the public prosecutors and the ministers to the bar, giving them the order to vigorously repress any agitation ... Several deputies complained that ... the municipality had lacked firmness. Disastrous reproaches that unquestionably greatly contributed to the next day's events.")

The Cordeliers had, in fact, decided to take a more strongly worded petition to the Champ de Mars. The Jacobins, invaded the previous evening by a flood of demonstrators from the Palais-Royal, had adjourned without taking a decision. But the people, growing ever more agitated, went in large numbers to the Champ de Mars. All afternoon, the petition was filled with signatures. It said:

On the Altar of the Fatherland, July 17, the Year III [of the Revolution]
Representatives of the Nation:
You are reaching the term of your labors. Successors, all of them elected by the people, are soon going to walk in your footsteps without encountering the obstacles presented to us by the deputies of the two privileged orders, the enemies of all the principles of sacred equality. A great crime is being committed: Louis XVI fled, shamelessly abandoning his post. The empire is a hair's breadth from anarchy. Citizens arrested him in Varennes and he was brought back to Paris.
The people of this capital strongly request that you not decide the fate of the culprit without having heard the wishes of the 83 other *départements.*

You temporize.

A great number of addresses arrive at the Assembly. Every part of the empire simultaneously demands that the king be judged. You, *messieurs*, already determined that he was innocent and inviolable by declaring in yesterday's decree that when it is completed the constitutional charter will be presented to him once it is completed.

Legislators, this was not the will of the people, and we had thought that your greatest glory, that your duty consisted in being the organs of the public will.

There is no doubt, *messieurs*, that you were led to this decision by the drove of refractory deputies who previously protested against any kind of Constitution. But *messieurs*, representatives of a generous and confident people, remember that the 230 protestors [the deputies of the right who had declared, after the arrest of the king, that they would no longer participate in the deliberations] no longer played a role in the National Assembly; that the decree is thus null and void in both form and substance. Null and void, in fact, because it is contrary to the wishes of the sovereign; null and void in form because it was brought by 290 individuals not qualified to do so.

These considerations, all of them aiming at the general good and the desire to avoid the anarchy to which the lack of harmony between the representatives and the represented would expose us, demands that we ask you, in the name of all of France, to reconsider this decree; to take into consideration that Louis XVI's crime is proven; to see that the king abdicated and that you receive his abdication and convoke a new constituent power to proceed in a truly national fashion to judge the culprit and especially to organizing a new executive power.

For the first time since the events of October 1789, the most ardent portion of the people rose up against a decision of the Assembly. In October, when it was feared that the Assembly gave the king absolute veto power, the democrats had also said that its decision was null and void because the representatives of the nobility and the clergy, who formed half the Assembly, didn't have the right to decide in the name of the Nation. This time it was because the deputies of the right, after having announced that they would no longer vote, had nevertheless taken part in the vote on the inviolability of the king, and the jurists of democracy contested the validity of the vote.

While the petition was being filled with signatures without any disorder or outcry, the municipal government, gathered at the *Hôtel de Ville*, was in a state of turmoil. That morning, two men had been found under the Altar of the Fatherland. They had probably hidden themselves there for dirty-minded purposes, in the hope that women would climb the steps of the altar. When they were discovered, they were killed by the people, who suspected them of having wanted to plant a mine under the altar. The news of this murder reached town hall inflated and deformed. Blood is flowing! The municipal government declared martial law. The red flag, the flag of bourgeois repression, was hung from the windows of the *Hôtel de Ville*. The mayor and Lafayette, at the head of a battalion of the National Guard, marched to the Champ de Mars. They arrived there at nightfall, at around 7:30 or 7:45 p.m. The crowd was large but peaceful. At the arrival of the National Guard, the crowd grew stirred up and angry. Hostile shouts rang out. Down with the red flag! Down with the bayonets! Stones were thrown. According to Bailly's[7] testimony, a pistol was fired and the ball grazed the mayor and pierced the thigh of a dragoon. Either frightened or angered, the National Guard fired without taking the time to issue the three legally mandated warnings.

Bailly assures us that the first shots were fired in the air and no one was wounded. It's strange that men who had enough self-control to fire in the air didn't have enough to wait for the legal warnings. The people, angered by these shots, threw more projectiles, and the National Guard fired. According to the democrats, several hundred men and women fell in what Marat called the "infernal abyss of the Champ de Mars." Bailly, in his report to the Constitutent of July 18, admits to only eleven or twelve deaths and a dozen wounded. In any event, there was a great effusion of blood. Properly speaking, this was not a social battle between the bourgeoisie and the proletariat, for it was a fraction of the bourgeoisie that had written the petition, and the question of property wasn't posed. Nevertheless, it is certain that the wealthy bourgeoisie was on the side of

---

7   Jean Sylvain Bailly (1736–93)—Paris's first mayor, and mayor at the time of these events. Widely condemned by the left of the Revolution.

the National Assembly and the working people were sympathetic to the petitioners. And so that sad day was a starting point of the class struggle, even though bourgeois blood flowed for the Republic at the same time as that of workers.

Great was the astonishment of France and Paris, and great the pain. But it would be wrong to believe that there was general indignation against the municipal government and the Assembly. On the contrary, at that moment, the public sentiment of revolutionary France was more against the petitioners. The Assembly's moral authority was still immense, even among the people. The vigor it had demonstrated in the days that followed the king's flight, the sovereign role it had played, all of this had revived its popularity. It seemed to be the authority that was needed until the day when the Nation would have established another Assembly. And combating its decrees, once they were rendered, seemed an act of great imprudence. What guarantee would be left to the Nation if the revolutionaries themselves attacked the Constitution? Should they not respect even its faults in order to impose respect for it on nobles, on refractory priests, on the court, on émigrés, and on tyrants? And so the courageous and republican vanguard formed by the Cordeliers was quite miserably disavowed, even by the democrats.

7

The Insurrection of August 10, 1792

(Pushed for by the Gironde, war had been declared on the émigrés and the Prussian and Austrian supporters of the king, but the first battles had gone badly: "While marching on Tournai one of Rochambeau's divisions foolishly clashed with the Austrian troops and our soldiers had fled. Believing themselves betrayed they'd killed one of their officers." Priests who had refused to take the constitutional oath were maneuvering, fomenting uprisings. The Legislative Assembly was forced to adopt severe measures against the refractory priests, including the threat of deportation. Jaurès writes: "The Gironde, by the deportation law, struck a heavy blow, but what would the king do? How, having rejected the first anodyne measures passed by the Assembly, could he grant his sanction to a more powerful decree?" These measures "served to make clear the conflict between the crown and the Revolution." The Gironde called for the establishing of a camp of 20,000 men to defend the Revolution, and again the question was posed: what would the king do?

The dispute, the uncertainty couldn't continue indefinitely, and Minister of the Interior Roland, on June 10, 1792 sent a letter to the king placing the issue clearly before him. Jaurès spoke of this letter:

> This wasn't a republican manifesto. On the contrary, Roland proclaims that the Constitution can live on the condition that the king act with a revolutionary spirit; that he cease to stand in the way of the legislative power. But in a measured way he posed a brutal dilemma: "Either the king renounces the exercise of the veto or the Constitution perishes." And in both cases it's a change in the Constitution that the Girondin minister proposes to—or imposes on—the king.

The king responded by removing the Girondin ministers, including Roland:

> The people had the presentiment that the final struggle between the Revolution and the crown was imminent. And as often occurs on the eve of great events,

frightening rumors spread. Paris momentarily believed that the king's guard contemplated the murder of the patriots: suspicious eyes saw a conspirator in every foreigner. In May the emotion was so great, so wide-spread, that for a few days the Assembly had to sit in permanent session and had even issued a decree that the same would hold for the sections. The citizens who went to the section assemblies had thus officially received the charge of guarding freedom and the Fatherland.

Petitions were drawn up in the sections,

... but these petitions had to be supported by a great demonstration of force. They would go en masse on June 20, the anniversary of the Tennis Court Oath, to the Assembly and the Tuileries in order to remind everyone of that great day when royal arbitrariness collided head on with the resoluteness of the representatives.

And on that day the petitioners, after leaving the Assembly, entered the Tuileries:

They still felt a certain amount of respect. They hadn't completely renounced the hope of bringing the king over to the Constitution. And the calm courage that Louis XVI opposed to the anger that surrounded him at that moment of crisis put an end to insults ... Louis XVI, backed against a window, took a red bonnet from a National Guardsman and put it on. He also took a sword from the hands of a woman and waved it in the air. A great cry was issued: "Long Live the Nation!" That flourished sword was the symbol of the valiant and tender Revolution that, though fighting, wanted to love. How many flowers would have decorated the royal sword if it had decided to be the sword of the Revolution? But all of this was just a lie ... The king's life was saved, but a personal duel, a duel to the death had begun between the Revolution and the crown.

For almost immediately the "treasonous crown appealed to the foreigners and breathlessly awaited their arrival to suppress the Constitution." The military threat from the Austrians called on by Louis grew stronger, and on July 4 "the Assembly adopted the procedure of 'the Fatherland in danger,'" calling *citizens to arms and on July 11 threatening death to anyone "wearing a sign of rebellion."*

In the face of these threats, the Paris sections sprang into action, their delegates meeting at the Hôtel de Ville,

> ... *considering themselves the true interpreters of the sovereign, charged with saving France and freedom from the danger that threatened them ... They created and represented a new legality, one revolutionary and bold that stood against the hypocritical, obsolete, and heteroclite disunited legality fashioned by legislative weakness and royal treason.*

The people's anger was heightened when on August 1, the president of the Assembly received a manifesto written by the Duke of Brunswick, and "according to this manifesto, it was for Louis XVI and in his interests that the Emperor of Germany and the King of Prussia were preparing to invade, to crush, to enslave France."

This had all gone too far. The king's treason was too flagrant to be ignored, and in the name of the sections, Pétion denounced the king and began the movement for his removal. Petitions were drawn up and "the Legislative Assembly had fixed August 9 as the date for the debate on the petitions demanding the suspension or removal of the king. But in fixing the date for the debate, it had fixed the date for the insurrection."

And yet the moderates attempted to delay, and

> ... *in the name of the Commission of Twelve Condorcet limited himself to proposing an address to the people on the exercise of the right of sovereignty ... The great problem of removal from office wasn't even posed and the Commission of Twelve said the object of its report was the preliminary measures to be taken before dealing with the question of the removal of the king. Given the general state of tension, any new delay was impossible.)*

The revolutionary gears finally went into motion. The alarm drum was beaten, the tocsin was sounded and on the peaceful night of August 9–10 the people of the faubourgs, grabbing their rifles and hitching their cannons, prepared to deliver combat at dawn. But they weren't motivated by narrow and immediate interests. The workers, the proletarians who were entering combat alongside the boldest elements of the revolutionary bourgeoisie, had no economic demands. Even when they fought against the hoarders and monopolists who had raised the price of sugar and other goods, the workers of Paris had said: "We're not a bunch of women, demanding bonbons. We don't want to leave the Revolution in the hands of a new selfish and oppressive caste."

Above all else, it was full political freedom, it was full democracy that they demanded. This would unquestionably safeguard their interests, their wages, and their very existence. Already in the vast popular movement, in the great agitation of July and August, the Le Chapelier Law[1] had been abrogated and the moderate *feuillantine* bourgeoisie complained on August 7 that the workers were forming assemblies to demand a rise in wages.

The proletarians knew that any praise of national life and of liberty was praise of their strength, and they had a vague premonition of the social changes that were imminent. But their direct and conscious thoughts were for their Fatherland threatened by foreigners, for their freedom betrayed by the king's deceit. They had to bring down the traitorous king in order to more surely repel the foreign kings. The proletarians weren't animated by an explicit and immediate class sentiment.

And yet, while on July 14 and October 5 and 6, it was royal despotism that the united workers and bourgeoisie fought against, on August 10 they fought against both the crown and the segment of the bourgeoisie that had rallied to it. In bringing down the king, they would also be taking their revenge on the bourgeois *moderantistes* who, on the Champ de Mars in July 1791, in order to defend the king, had fired on the people.

The Red Flag

And the red flag, the flag of martial law, the bloody symbol of bourgeois repression, was taken over by the revolutionaries of August 10. They made it the signal for revolt, or rather the emblem of a new power.

---

1   Law promulgated June 14, 1791 banning worker-class associations.

What was the precise moment when the idea occurred to the revolutionary people to appropriate the flag of martial law and turn it against their enemies? It appears that it was some time around June 20. When Chaumette[2] recounts the preparations for June 20 in his memoirs, he shows that the citizens of the faubourgs Saint-Antoine and Saint-Marceau "took pride in being called 'sans-culottes' by the aristocrats in lace," and prepared to go to the king to impose the sanctioning of decrees.

On the other hand, the most ardent and enlightened patriots went to the Cordelier Club and spent nights together planning.

Among others there was a committee where they made a red flag bearing this inscription: "The martial law of the people against the revolt of the court," under which all free men were to rally, all the republicans who had a friend, a son, a relative murdered on the Champ de Mars on July 17, 1791 to avenge.

Carra, recounting the preparations not of June 20 but of August 10, wrote:

It was in the Soleil d'Or cabaret [where the insurrectionary directorate met] that Fournier the American brought us the red flag whose invention I'd proposed and upon which I'd had these words written: "The martial law of the sovereign people against the rebellion of the executive power." It was also to this same cabaret that I brought 500 copies of a poster upon which was written these words: "Those who fire on the people shall be immediately put to death."

And so the idea of appropriating the red flag seems to have occurred to the people before June 20, at the beginning of the period of popular movements against the king. But it seems that on June 20, the red flag was not used, either because there wasn't enough time to prepare a large enough number with the revolutionary inscription, or because Pétion, who sought to legalize the movement of June 20, had had his friends renounce its use. But the idea persisted, and on August 10, the red flag billowed above the revolutionary columns. It signified that it is we the people who are now the law:

---

2 Pierre-Gaspard Chaumette (1763–94)—supporter of Hébert and a spokesman for the sans-culottes.

It is we the people who are now the law. Power now resides in us. And the king, the court, the moderate bourgeoisie, all the traitors who, under the name of Constitutionals, in fact betray the Constitution and the Fatherland, are the ones who are traitors. In resisting the people they resist the true law, and they are the ones against whom we proclaim martial law. We are not rebels. The rebels are in the Tuileries, and in the name of the Fatherland and freedom we turn the banner of legal repression against the seditionists of the court and *moderantisme*.

And so it was more than a symbol of vengeance. It wasn't the banner of reprisals: it was the splendid flag of a new power conscious of its rights, and this is why since then, whenever the proletariat has wanted to affirm its strength and its hopes, it would be the red flag that it would unfurl.

In Lyon, under Louis-Philippe, the workers, ground down by hunger, unfurled the black flag, the flag of poverty and despair. But after February 1848, when the proletarians wanted to illustrate the new revolution with a symbol of their own, they asked the provisional government to adopt the red flag.

It could only burst forth anew like a flame long hidden under the ashes, because the revolutionary tradition of August 10 had remained alive for a half century in the impoverished houses of the faubourgs, passed down from the father's mouth to the son's heart. And Lamartine demonstrated a curious memory lapse when he said to the people assembled before the *Hôtel de Ville*: "All the red flag ever did was circulate around the Champ de Mars dragged in the rivers of the blood of the people."

The people could have answered him with these words: "Yes, but this flag, dyed with the blood of the people on July 17, 1791 led the people against the Tuileries on August 10, 1792. And the splendor of working-class hope is mixed in with the republican victory."

The Tocsin

At around midnight on the night of August 9, the sound of the tocsin and the beating of the drums alerted the legislators scattered around Paris that a great event was in the offing. They hastened to the Assembly, and at midnight the sitting was opened. We might call it a "waiting session." The Assembly was resolved to keep an eye on events but not to intervene directly in the fight between the people and the king.

It was in vain that the ministers, in order to make the Assembly understand its responsibilities, informed the deputies that it was urgent that it take measures to protect the Tuileries chateau and defend the Constitution. They responded that that was a matter for the administrative authorities. It was also in vain that several deputies proposed to their colleagues that they go to see the king, as they'd done on June 20. Choudieu[3] loudly proclaimed that in this hour of danger the true duty of the peoples' representatives was to remain at their posts. The Assembly applauded.

In the meanwhile, the Tuileries laid a trap for Pétion. He was summoned there and the mayor, fearing he'd be seriously compromised if he refused, went to the Tuileries. It is clear that their principal aim was to hold him hostage. Frightened by his long absence, the administrators of the police of the Paris Commune wrote to the Assembly and the latter, in order to save him, called him to its bar. Mandat, who commanded the National Guard and was devoted to the court, didn't dare seize Pétion. The mayor went to the bar of the Assembly and alluded in measured tones to the offensive words that had been addressed to him. He announced that strong defensive measures had been taken by the chateau, sufficient to block any movement. Was it that Pétion wanted to offer the people of Paris a final counsel of prudence? Or provide the Assembly the pretext it needed not to intervene? Or perhaps he wanted the Assembly to authorize him not to reinforce the defenses of the chateau? The general assembly of the sections gathered, at that moment at the *Hôtel de Ville*. And the boldest sections, those of the Théâtre Français and Gravilliers, at around 3:00 or 4:00 a.m. issued the opinion that the authorities in place had to be replaced by new and revolutionary authorities.

Around dawn, when from all the faubourgs, from Saint-Antoine and Saint-Marcel, the militia of *fédérés* and workers formed themselves

---

3   René-Pierrre Choudieu (1761–1838)—a member of the National Assembly and the Convention, he voted for the execution of the king and worked actively to bring down the Gironde.

in columns and marched on the Tuileries, the Assembly of Parisian Sections substituted itself for the legal Commune and organized itself as a revolutionary commune.

This was a daring and perhaps decisive move, for in executing it the fighting people had behind it the support of an organized public force, and this act troubled the general staff of the National Guard and its commander, Mandat, who had been stripped of his office. The revolutionary Commune spread doubt and confusion in the ranks of the enemy. The new Commune immediately issued the following decree, establishing it:

> The assembly of commissioners of the majority of the sections, assembled with plenary powers to save the government, has decided that the first measure demanded for the public good is to seize all the powers that the Commune delegated and to deprive the general staff of the dangerous influence it has had over the fate of liberty until today. It believes that this method could only be employed if the municipality, which in every case can only act in accordance with the established forms, is suspended, and if the mayor and the procurator general continue in their administrative functions.

This was signed by Huguenin as president and Martin as secretary, whom in doing so risked their heads. It was because the authorities in place could not free themselves of legal forms that the sections smashed them. Pétion and Manuel were kept in office, but fearing that Pétion, still tied down by legal forms, would paralyze the people's movement, the revolutionary Commune placed him under house arrest. In doing so, it preserved the freedom of popular action. And it also clearly showed from the beginning of this great day what its true character was. This was not a summoning of the king. It was rather a change in power, and the people installed themselves as sovereigns at the *Hôtel de Ville* in order to drive the sovereignty of treason from the Tuileries.

How would the Legislative Assembly greet this new power, the revolutionary expression of the people's will? It was informed of the events in the *Hôtel de Ville* at around 7:00 a.m. by a whining deputation from the former municipality. But what was to be done? Several deputies proposed repealing the new power as illegal. But the fight around the chateau had already begun, and the proposal failed. The new power acted, decisively, backing the people's efforts. Even before constituting itself as a Commune, the delegates from the sections had obtained from the legal municipality the recall of Mandat, the commander of the National Guard devoted to the king.

In the morning, Mandat, when his presence at the Tuileries would have been most necessary, surrendered to the municipality's order, and upon arriving at the *Hôtel de Ville* he found before him a new power. The revolutionary Commune treated him as a defendant and demanded that he account for the irregular orders he had given to arm the National Guard against the people without the explicit authorization of the mayor. And when the interrogation ended, and he was preparing to hastily return to the Tuileries, the Commune had him arrested.

The King Takes Refuge in the Assembly

The resistance in the Tuileries immediately fell into a state of disorganization. The court lost every legal point of support; the National Guard no longer gave the Swiss Guards or the *gentilshommes* the least assistance. The king became fully aware of this at about 6:00 when he briefly left the palace to review the positions at the Place du Carrousel and the Tuileries Gardens. The artillerymen of the National Guard received him either with a gloomy silence or with shouts of "Long Live the Nation!"

Louis XVI had the stinging, fatal sensation that he stood alone against the people and returned to the chateau in a state of despair. In the meanwhile, the attackers were gradually arriving and began, though at first half-heartedly, to invest the chateau via the Carrousel and the Tuileries. Were the king and queen, half abandoned, going to run the risk of a siege? The Assembly was gripped with fear. What would happen if, in the fury of the assault, the king and queen were massacred? Wouldn't France, which had been moved to support the threatened king on June 20, rise up against those who killed him, as well as against those who, through their inaction, were the accomplices in the murder? Several deputies requested that the

Assembly call for the king to be brought before them. But doing this meant not only protecting the king's life; it also in a way covered his power with national protection. It perhaps also meant turning the revolutionary forces against the Assembly itself, since it would look as if it was in solidarity with the king.

The Assembly understood this and didn't capitulate. A new proposal was written, one less clear and which exposed the Assembly less seriously. It wouldn't summon the king, but it would let him know that it was assembled and that if he wished he could go to it. But this too meant tying the Assembly's responsibility to that of the king. It hesitated again, despite the visible emotion of Cambon,[4] who exclaimed that the Assembly's inaction would be at least as dangerous as action, and that it was necessary to "save the glory of the people," that is, preserve the king's life. Since the Assembly continued to hesitate and didn't make a move, remaining stagnant in the storm, the king, pressured by Roederer, the syndic of the *département*, decided to leave the Tuileries and go to the Assembly.

The royal family slowly made its way to the Assembly via the central alley of the garden, and then through the alley of the Tuileries, already scattered with dead leaves after a dry, hot summer. They passed through a half-uncertain, half-hostile crowd in order to reach the door of the Assembly. Louis XVI was never again to return to the home of kings. On this Friday, which the pious souls of the royalists would view as another Good Friday, he began his Passion. A justice of the peace appeared at the bar of the Assembly: "Gentlemen, I come to inform you that the king, the queen, and the royal family are about to present themselves before the National Assembly."

Was it a king who was coming to the Assembly, one of the powers of the Constitution come to unite with the other? Or was it an outlaw seeking asylum at the altar of the law, which he had vainly attempted to overthrow through treason? For the Assembly, he was a king, or at least the shadow of the king, and 24 deputies, those closest to the door, walked ahead of him in the growing tumult and confusion. The pomp of the Constitution was

---

4   Pierre Joseph Cambon (1756–1820)—member of the Legislative Assembly and later of the Committee of Public Safety.

thus still maintained. Vergniaud[5] was then presiding over the sitting. The Assembly had raised him before itself like a shining shield, a shield of glory, of eloquence, and wisdom. It knew that at the Commission of Twelve[6] he had been temporizing and prudent. It thus thought that in this mounting crisis he wouldn't go further than the circumstances demanded. But the people still remembered his powerful and prophetic speech of July 3, and the Assembly hoped that the afterglow of the popularity remaining to the great orator would calm the crowd. The prestige of glory momentarily supplemented the authority of the king.

When the king entered and, in accordance with protocol, took his place alongside the president, he said to the Assembly: "I have come here today to prevent a great crime, and my family and I will always feel ourselves safe among the representatives of the Nation."

As reported in the *Moniteur*, the *Logographe*, and the *Journal des Débats et Décrets*, Vergniaud responded: "The National Assembly knows its duty. It swore to maintain the rights of the people and the constituted authorities."

Royalty's ghost thus continued to live, but the Constitution permitted removal or suspension from office, and Vergniaud had not committed himself. A few minutes later, the Assembly officially recognized the constituted authorities, but it was those constituted that night by the Revolution. After the royal family had left the palace, the crowd investing the Tuileries grew. The *fédérés*, the people of the faubourgs with bayonets, pikes, and cannons arrived, swelling the crowd. Would it be possible to avoid a bloody clash? The Assembly hastily addressed a proclamation to the people, but who would see to its being carried out? The former municipal government had been dissolved and was powerless. Thuriot[7] openly proposed to the Assembly that it recognize the new municipal government, the revolutionary Commune: "I request that all the commissioners who will be going to the city be authorized to confer with those in whose hands

---

5   Pierre Vergniaud (1753–93)—Girondin leader. He was guillotined.
6   Commission established at the behest of the Gironde and established on May 21, 1793. Its ostensible purpose was to protect the National Convention against plots, but its actual goal was to contain and watch over the activities of the left. Among those it imprisoned was the voice of the sans-culottes, Jacques Hébert. Marat was vocal in calling for its suppression, and it was, indeed, suppressed, after the events of May 31 and June 2, 1793.
7   Jacques Alexis Thuriot (1753–1829)—Montagnard deputy, ally of Danton.

resides, either legally or illegally, any form of authority, and who have, at least in appearance, the confidence of the people."

The Assembly adopted Thuriot's motion, and it was the Commune that was the entering wedge of the republican revolution into the still-monarchical Constitution of 1791.

The Assault on the Tuileries

A few minutes later, the Assembly decided to allow the revolutionary Commune the provisional choice of a new commander for the National Guard. In the meanwhile, in a Tuileries devoid of the king, it appears that instructions were given to disarm. From the windows, the Swiss shouted words of friendship to the people. The door that gave onto the grand staircase opened and the people of the faubourgs and the *fédérés* joyously rushed through them. But suddenly, from every step of the staircase the trusting Revolution was greeted with a terrible fusillade. Was this an abominable trap, a trick? Or was it that in the anarchy of a small army that had suddenly been abandoned by its king and issued contradictory orders, there was an awful misunderstanding? A horrific cry of pain, death, and anger rose from the people as they were repelled. They aimed their cannons at the walls, their rifles at the windows from which the Swiss' muskets crackled. The buildings built against the palace walls were set on fire. And the sound of the cannon, deep, wrathful, and somber, could be heard; the piercing and furious sound of the fusillade, the crackling of the flames illuminated by the breaking day; a clamor, a tumult of destruction and combat filled the courtyard of the Carrousel and echoed in the Assembly. At around 9:00 a.m., a cry of panic was heard at the door of the meeting hall: "The Swiss have arrived. The chamber has been entered."

The frightened Assembly believed that the crown's mercenary soldiers were going to lay hands on them; that the treasonous king, after having vanquished the people, was going to strike the people's representatives, and that there was nothing left for it but to die and, and in dying leave to new generations the heroic memory of an immortal cry for liberty.

At the first cannon shots, all the citizens in the spectators' gallery rose: "Long Live the National Assembly! Long Live the Nation! Long Live Liberty and Equality!" The Assembly immediately decided that all the deputies would remain in their places and await their fate, to save the Fatherland or die for it.

"Here come the Swiss," the citizens in the spectators' gallery shouted again, who were both sublime in their courage and confused by the uncertain rumors: "We won't abandon you; we'll die with you!"

And they joined the Assembly in its decree: like the Assembly, they bound themselves to liberty and death. This was a heroic moment, a great moment, when, in the common passion for liberty, in the common scorn for death, all disagreements and distrust were erased; where the hearts of the men of the gallery beat with the hearts of the Girondins, of the "statesmen." The Gironde, in this maelstrom it had presided over a short while ago in the person of Vergniaud and now in the person of Guadet, again shared the people's great revolutionary passion.

The patriots' fears didn't last long. The Swiss who'd been pointed out had already been defeated. They retreated from the chateau, which had been taken by the people via the Tuileries gardens; they fell under the balls, pikes, and bayonets of the victors. What was the king's state of mind during this drama? This is an impenetrable mystery. Did he momentarily hope that the chateau would be defended and that the Revolution would be defeated? He watched the Assembly's session from the stenographer's box. The cries that announced the arrival of the Swiss doubtless echoed joyously in his heart. It's also possible that when he heard the cannons, heard the crackling of the fusillade, he regretted not having remained among his soldiers to inspire them with his presence. Choudieu, who observed him closely, affirmed that his face remained passive as long as the combat continued and that he only showed emotion when the defeat of his last defenders became known to him. Too late he ordered the Swiss to cease fire. The victorious people invaded the Tuileries, rummaged around it from the cellar to the roof, and men covered with powder and with bloodied faces entered the Assembly bearing papers, gold coins, or the queen's jewels and shouted: "Long Live the Nation!"

The Insurrectionary Commune Dictates its Duties to the Assembly

This was the victory of the Revolution and the Fatherland. It was also the victory of the revolutionary Commune. It was the latter that, by substituting itself for the legal Commune, burned the bridges behind the advancing revolution. It had to win or perish. It was the revolutionary Commune as well which, by holding Pétion and arresting Mandat, ensured the unimpeded growth of the popular forces. On the morning of August 10, the chateau having just been entered, the Commune appeared at the Assembly, not to request the legal confirmation of a power it owed the Revolution itself, but, on the contrary, to dictate laws. In its name, Huguenin, accompanied by Léonard Bourdon, Truchon, Berieux, Vigaud, and Cellier, said the following:

It is the new magistrates of the people who present themselves at your bar. The new dangers to the Fatherland provoked our election, circumstances counseled it, and our patriotism will render us worthy of it. The people, for the past four years the playthings of the perfidies and intrigues of the Court, finally had enough and felt that it was time to save the empire as it stood on the edge of the abyss. Legislators: all that remains to be done is to support the people: we come here in their name to work out with you measures for public safety. Pétion, Manuel, and Danton are still our colleagues; Santerre is at the head of the armed force.

May the traitors perish in their turn. This day is the triumph of civic virtues. Legislators, the people's blood has flowed; foreign troops, who have remained within our walls as a result of a new crime of the executive power, have fired on our citizens. Our ill-fated brothers have left behind them widows and orphans.

The people who sent us charged us with declaring to you that it again invests you with its confidence. But at the same time it has charged us with declaring to you that it only recognizes the French people, your sovereign and ours, gathered in primary assemblies, as fit to judge the extraordinary measures to which necessity and resistance to oppression have led it.

The Assembly didn't protest against the victorious Commune that claimed the right to treat it as an equal and that even renewed its mandate in the name of the people, but only so that the people would be convoked. It was this revolutionary Commune that the Assembly charged with transmitting to the people decrees calling for calm. On that same day, based on reports by Vergniaud, Guadet, and Jean Debry, it issued the momentous decrees without debate.

Its first decree invited the French people to form a National Convention, stating that the method and time of its convocation would be determined the next day. At the same time, it declared "the head of the executive power provisionally suspended from his functions until such time as the National Convention has pronounced on the measures it believes must be taken to ensure the sovereignty of the people and the rule of liberty and equality."

Its second decree declared that the ministers in place did not have its confidence and it decided that ministers would be provisionally named by the National Assembly through individual election. They could not be chosen from within that body.

Finally, its third group of decrees decided that the decrees already rendered that hadn't been sanctioned, and the decrees to be rendered which couldn't be sanctioned because of the suspension of the king, would nevertheless be considered binding and would be in force throughout the kingdom.

In reality, this signified the end of the monarchy. To be sure, it wasn't a matter of removal from office but only of suspension. The people murmured for a moment, and then protests were raised. Vergniaud harangued the petitioners. He told them that it was from respect for the people's sovereignty that the Assembly was only taking provisional measures. And the announcing of an imminent National Convention changed all worries and recriminations into enthusiasm. It appeared to the people that this new Assembly, born of their victory, was going to do away with all the ruses, falsehoods, betrayals, and half-measures which, given the danger that confronted the Fatherland, were the equivalent of treason. It was its own strength that it had a presentiment of, that it based its hopes on. The morning's combat had caused the people's anger to grow. The unexpected fusillade by the Swiss, combined with the threat of Brunswick's manifesto, gave rise to the most sinister rumors. According to Chaumette, it was being said that the cruelest of tyranny's inventions were to be employed against the patriots; that if the king had emerged victorious they would have been sacrificed in their thousands on a gallows similar to that put up by Louis XI, and that their sons, standing below them, would be covered with a blood-drenched dew. The people hunted down those it suspected of having taken part in the battle against them during the morning's ambush. And throughout that day of August 10, Louis XVI couldn't have crossed Paris without danger even under escort as a prisoner.

All day the Commune distributed cartridges, as if a terrible plot was still to be feared. But the people's anger gradually fell when they saw that they would soon exercise their sovereignty and elect the great Assembly of combat and salvation. And the dying Legislative Assembly seemed in a way to participate in the popularity of the new and unknown assembly it had just promised France.

This Convention constituted the advent of the Republic, without this having yet been openly announced. But more than anything, this was advent of democracy. No more *cens*,[8] no more privileges, no more harmful and bourgeois distinctions between active and passive citizens. Upon the report of the deputy from the Aisne, Jean Debry, given in the name of the Commission of Twelve, the Assembly voted without debate at the sitting of August 10 that all citizens aged 25 were electors:

> The National Assembly desiring, at the moment when it solemnly swears its support for liberty and equality, to this day consecrate the application of a principle sacred to the people and itself, decrees that in the future, and in particular in the formation of the upcoming National Convention, every French citizen 25 years of age, a resident for one year, and living from the fruits of his labor, shall be admitted to vote in the assembly of communes and the primary assemblies in the same way as every other active citizen, and with no other distinctions.

And so universal suffrage was established. And it wasn't only for the upcoming National Convention, but for all manifestations of national life

---

8   Property qualification.

until the end of time. And then, on August 12, the Convention again expanded the popular base, lowering the voting age from 25 to 21. It maintained 25 as the age of eligibility, but it erased, both for eligibility for office as well as the electorate, any distinction between active and passive citizens. It maintained the system of election in two steps by primary assemblies, but rather as a counsel than as an imperative, and it set the naming of electoral assemblies for August 26, and the electing of deputies for September 2.

The New Ministers

On August 10 the ministry was constituted under the name of the Provisional Executive Council. On the proposal of Isnard,[9] ever fond of theatrical display, the Assembly, renouncing individual election, named en bloc Roland, Clavière, and Servan, the three Girondin ministers the king had dismissed. But the Gironde could not be alone in benefiting from a movement it had only participated in half-heartedly and sporadically. The Assembly understood that it could only have an effect on the revolutionary people and satisfy the Paris Commune if it called a man of the Revolution to the responsibilities of power. So Danton was elected minister of justice with 222 out of 284 votes. Monge was called to the navy and Lebrun to foreign affairs.

Danton hadn't personally taken part in the assault on the Tuileries. But during the night, he was actively involved in the preparations, ready to bear the terrible responsibilities that risky day held for the leaders of the Revolution. Victorious along with the people, his thoughts were generous and clement. Beautiful were his first words at the Legislative Assembly of August 11:

> The events that just occurred in Paris prove that there is no way to compromise with the people's oppressors. The French Nation was surrounded by new conspiracies. The people deployed all their energy. The National Assembly backed them, and the tyrants disappeared. But

---

9   Maximin Isnard (1755–1825)—Girondin leader.

now it is I who, standing before you, make a commitment to perish in order to wrest from a too-long-delayed popular vengeance these same men [the Swiss] who found refuge in your Assembly. (*Loud applause.*) A few minutes ago I said this at the Paris Commune: where the acts of the agents of the Nation begin, popular vengeance must end. Gentlemen, there is no doubt but that the people feel this great truth: they must not sully their great triumph. The assembly of the Commune appeared to be filled with these sentiments, and all those who hear us share them. I promise to march at the head of those men who the people, in their indignation, felt had to be outlawed, but who they will pardon, since they have nothing more to fear from their tyrants. (*Repeated applause.*)

On August 11, Louis XVI was taken with his family to the Luxembourg palace and from there, a few days later, to the Temple. He was nothing but a prisoner.

The Consequences of August 10

But this revolution that, in Paris, had to be controlled and saved from the bloody folly of reprisals, had to be accepted by an unquestionably shocked and disconcerted France. It also had to be accepted by the army, where there was a legitimate fear that because of Lafayette and Luckner the "Constitutional" spirit prevailed.

In order to rally France to the revolution of August 10, the Assembly resorted to two methods: the papers found in the Tuileries proved the king's treason, and the corruption caused by the court. They didn't reveal all we know today, but the king's connivance with the foreigners was nonetheless clear.

The Assembly published these papers. It ordered its army commissioners to distribute them in the camps. The Jacobin societies throughout France commented on them and there rose from all of patriotic France, which unhesitatingly sent off its young people, the flower of its life, an immense cry against the treasonous royalty.

8

The September Massacres

(The allied forces of monarchy were now in open war with the Revolution. And on August 23, 1792, Merlin de Thionville proposed taking hostage the wives and children of émigrés as a result of the invasion that had resulted in cities on France's borders being attacked and on the brink of falling, with Longwy having already been taken. A levée en masse of 30,000 men from Paris and the surrounding areas was issued. Visits to homes were authorized to procure arms. Patriotic and revolutionary enthusiasm were at their height, and at the Commune its procurator "demanded that all citizens gather and camp this evening on the Champ de Mars and leave as early as possible tomorrow for the walls of Verdun and die there defending liberty or purging French soil of its enemies." The scene was set ... .)

In the summer of 1792 the forces of reaction were on the march against revolutionary France, and Verdun was invested. Nicolas-Joseph Beaurepaire, commanding the troops there, gave assurances "that he would die rather than surrender the city" [and he would later commit suicide rather than surrender]. But the Assembly was worried and asked if the inadequately fortified town, poorly defended by a population where aristocratic and royalist elements were powerful, wouldn't, like Longwy, capitulate ... . With Verdun taken before Dumouriez could send reinforcements from Sedan, the road to Paris was open. For the first time the Revolution felt the breath of the Prussian horses in their faces.

The Commune issued a declaration calling for all citizens "to immediately assemble and bivouac that very evening on the Champ de Mars, to leave tomorrow for Verdun, and to perish there defending liberty and cleansing French soil of its enemy's presence."

And it was Danton, not the Legislative Assembly, which issued the famous cry: "The tocsin that will be sounded is not an alarm; it is a call against the enemies of the Fatherland. In order to defeat them, *Messieurs*, we need boldness, more boldness, and ever more boldness, and then France will be saved … ."

Around 3:00 p.m., the cannon on the Pont-Neuf gave the alarm signal, which was echoed by all the bells of Paris. The sound of the tocsin gave rise to a patriotic frenzy in the capital. The citizens grabbed their weapons, hastily left their homes, read the Commune's posters, and in ever-growing groups headed to the Champ de Mars to enlist and receive, if it was deemed necessary, the order to immediately set out. What a magnificent movement of an entire people.

But now, while this irresistible torrent flowed towards the great plain, fearful comments began to circulate among the groups.

How can this be? We're leaving and tomorrow, after we have left Paris to go to the border, when not a single patriot is left here, the enemies of freedom will rule in the capital. Didn't you hear that a scoundrel who was executed yesterday announced that a great conspiracy was being cooked up in the prisons? Yes, in the prisons. They've become a den of aristocrats and priests. The scoundrels are announcing the imminent downfall of the Fatherland. They were seen making mysterious signs, and they've been beaming since the taking of Longwy. And to think that they were spared through favoritism; that we were promised revenge and the traitors are still alive! Even the Swiss officers who assassinated our brothers on August 10 are still breathing, and tomorrow they'll once again be able to place themselves at the head of the conspirators. When all of them, the general staff of the National Guard, the Swiss murderers, the insolent nobles, and the refractory priests, force the gates of the prisons and proclaim the counter-revolution in a city emptied of patriots, we'll be caught between the enemy without and the enemy within. What will the patriotic armies think when they learn that treason has triumphed at the very heart of the Revolution? No! No! The traitors must be executed. Since the justice of the tribunals was so dreadfully slow and timid, it's up to the people's justice to save liberty. Just a few days ago we held a memorial ceremony in honor of the victims of August 10. But what good to them are these vain demonstrations of mourning and this impious feigning of pain? They should have been avenged, but instead our cowardly indulgence towards the killers who are preparing to act again has rendered their deaths pointless. To the prisons, and may the traitors perish!

And so on the afternoon and evening of September 2, the fanaticized groups went to the Abbaye and the Conciergerie, the prisons where the counter-revolutionaries were being held. They had the prison registers brought to them and all the prisoners who had taken part in the events of August 10 or who had been involved in the court's plots were summarily judged, at which point a sinister phrase was spoken: "Set them free." Waiting for the prisoners at the gates of the prisons were avenging pikes, and the prisoners fell under the blows of the maddened people. All evening, all night the slaughter continued. And sometimes, since the rage to kill at times mixes with the rage of lust, the bodies of victims suffered obscene profanations. Ignoble passions were quenched on the corpse of Mme de Lamballe.[1] The murderers carried her head on the end of a pike and attempted to approach the Temple to show the cruel trophy to the royal family.

The massacres continued through the morning of September 3, until 2:00 p.m. But what is the point of tracing in meticulous detail this somber tableau? And what is the point of philosophizing over these sorry events? The right to revolution is not in the least diminished, for the immense social transformation that was being carried out cannot be judged based on one brief access of fury. On the other hand, I do not favor vague and cowardly apologies. There is no denying that this massacre of disarmed prisoners, even if it can be explained by sinister rumors, was the sign of an obscuring of reason and humanity.

It was absurd to suppose that after the departure of the volunteers Paris would be so stripped of patriots that a few hundred counter-revolutionaries could rule there. This was a foolish idea suggested by fear, and fear, even when it tragically blossoms into bloody brutality, is not a revolutionary force. If the men who carried out the killings at the Abbaye, la Force, and the Conciergerie had retained a modicum of lucidity and balanced reason, their consciences would have led them to ask: "Do these murders

---

1 Princess Marie Louise of Savoy (1749–92)—confidante of Marie Antoinette.

make the Revolution stronger?" And they would have foreseen humanity's long shiver of disgust. They would also have foreseen that the parties would return to and circle around the spilled blood, each side accusing the other in an unhealthy obsession. It is not a question of deciding whether individually the men who appointed themselves judges and butchers were worthy of esteem. I do not appreciate the hypocritical defense pleas of contemporaries who go into ecstasies over the people's "spirit of justice" simply because they spared and freed those imprisoned for debt. The September murderers would have had to have been drunken brutes incapable of any discernment for them to have confused the poor devils imprisoned for not having paid the wages of their child's wet-nurse with the political prisoners, who were the sole cause of their alarm. It's frivolous to think that this "act of justice" is praiseworthy.

But again, it is quite possible that many of the men who killed, uselessly and in a cowardly fashion, were honest patriots, devoted and brave. It is quite possible that they thought they were serving the Revolution and the Fatherland and were ready to brave death after having dealt it. But this is not the question. It's not their character that is in question, it's their acts, and their acts grew out of fear and the blind ferocity engendered by fear. This is why they were base, and also why they were foolish, for in the eyes of the world, in the eyes of history, they did the Revolution more harm than the prisoners they slaughtered could have done, even had they been unleashed on Paris.

The Responsibility

What was the responsibility of the parties and the authorities in this abject drama? I admit that I am unable to get to the bottom of this with any certainty, and the motives of most of the politicians remain obscure and difficult for me to decipher. It's certain that the Revolution allowed these things to happen: the authorities, all of them, intervened either late or half-heartedly. The Revolution could have stood up against the massacres at the first rumor of their occurrence. If it had really wanted to, it could have prevented them, since this was not an irresistible movement. Rather, a healthily patriotic and revolutionary passion animated the people, and their hatred was directed at the enemies on the country's borders. The murderers were few in number and it would have been easy to disperse and perhaps even convert them. Thuriot's admirable words should have been spoken to them: "We are accountable for the Revolution in the eyes of the whole world."

Let us suppose for a moment that instead of periodically sending a few hesitant and weak emissaries who, not being able to prevent the murders became their official witnesses, the entire elective assembly had gone to the prisons. Suppose that the entire Legislative Assembly and the Commune and the entire executive council had resisted this savage fury of an insignificant segment of the population. Suppose that Danton, Robespierre, and Vergniaud had taken turns recalling the Revolution to its grandeur and humanity. The murderers would have dropped their weapons. But there was no common or firm action on the part of the authorities.

It was the Commune that was notified first. It had gone back into session on September 2 at 4:00 p.m. and this is what the minutes say:

An officer of the National Guard announces (at the opening of the sitting) that several people were killed along the way and that the people are beginning to enter the prisons.

The council names MM. Dangé, Marino, James, Michonis, Lesguillon, and Moneuse as commissioners to go to the prisons to protect those imprisoned for failing to pay wet-nurses, debts, and for civil causes.

The Procurator of the Commune asks that each Section be invited to reclaim those from their arrondissement who are detained for the above-named causes, as well as soldiers detained for indiscipline.

On the proposal to release from Sainte-Pélagie those prisoners who are there purely for debt and recognized as such through verification of the records, the Council decrees that the prison of Sainte-Pélagie shall be opened. An amendment is proposed to release from prison all those held there for debt or for failing to pay wet-nurses, as well as for civil causes. So decreed.

Thus, and from all the evidence, the Commune's first impulse was to only protect prisoners held for debt. In doing so, in not concerning itself with the others, it surrendered them to the crowd. It officially established two categories of prisoners: those who weren't to have their throats slit, and the rest. This was the Commune's first thought, and though it later adopted more humane sentiments, this original impulse, which lived on despite it all, stood in the way of any decisive measures.

What was the source of the Commune's complacent abstention? Didn't it have enough grandeur of soul and thought to rise above fleeting fury and think of humanity and the future? It seems improbable to me, whatever its rage, that it thought allowing the accused to be judged by the criminal tribunal of August 17 would be a threat to the Revolution.

Did the Commune fear appearing to disavow Marat, its inspiration, its quasi-official journalist, who on August 19 had showed the people the way to the Abbaye and called for a massacre? Since August 10, the Commune had so often denounced the sluggishness of justice, the hesitations of the legal authorities, that it didn't dare intervene to put a halt to the "people's justice." And perhaps if it had stopped this popular movement it would have opened its authors to the vengeance of the law. In order for the movement to go unpunished it had to be victorious. Perhaps, too, despite the apparent reconciliation of the morning and Vergniaud's flattering effusions, the Commune, wounded in its pride as well as its authority by the Assembly's decree dissolving it, was not at all put out at showing the Legislative Assembly that, in ridding itself of the revolutionary Commune, it hadn't rid itself of the revolutionary people: "The Assembly smashed us, but now it'll see just how far the people's passion can go when they act spontaneously and no one is controlling them." Finally, from evidence that I will review later, I imagine that it saw in this popular movement, in this terrible agitation that confounded all notions of legality, an occasion to prolong its revolutionary power, to impose itself on a Legislative Assembly that was on its way out and a Convention that was on its way in. And in fact, France was in full electoral mode; the events seemed to mark even those legal powers being formed during the crisis with the seal of revolution.

But the Commune showed signs of hesitation. After having sent commissioners to protect only the prisoners for debt, according to the transcript it appears that it had had uncertain and timid second thoughts and had contemplated extending its protection to all the prisoners: "We appoint commissioners to go to the Abbaye and protect the prisoners." And a short while later: "A member recounts what is occurring at the Abbaye. The citizens who are enrolled, fearing to leave their city in the power of the wicked, refuse to leave until all the scoundrels of August 10 are exterminated."

It is evident that the Commune stood by and allowed events to unfurl. But in order to free itself of any responsibility, "the Council decrees that four commissioners shall immediately go to the National Assembly to give it an account of what is currently occurring in the prisons and the measures that can be taken to save the prisoners."

And so the Commune wanted to hand over the burden for these terrible events to the Legislative Assembly. The Assembly had gathered for a second sitting at 6:00 p.m. The delegation of the general council of the Commune appeared at the bar:

People are gathering at the gates of the prisons and they want to break them down. Most of the general councilors of Paris went to join the people wherever there was danger, but it was all in vain. Several prisoners have already been killed, and the situation is critical. The people are ready to march to the borders, but they feel a justifiable alarm concerning the intentions of a great number of persons who were arrested and accused of counter-revolutionary crimes.

Upon the proposal of Danton's friend Basire,[2] the Assembly immediately appointed twelve commissioners. But I fail to hear any cry of pity; I hear no protest from Thuriot.[3] The Assembly seems to be discharging a painful formality in silence. As the final rays of the autumn sun fell, the

---

2 Claude Basire (1764–94)—Dantonist politician, guillotined along with his fellow Dantonists.
3 Jacques Alexis Thuriot (1753–1829)—Dantonist deputy.

commissioners helplessly witnessed the slaughter. Old Dussaulx,[4] translator of Juvenal, returned to the Assembly:

> The deputies you sent to calm the people reached the gates of the Abbaye with great difficulty. There we tried to make ourselves heard. One of us climbed onto a chair, but he had hardly been able to say a few words when his voice was drowned out by loud shouts. Another orator, M. Basire, tried to make himself heard by opening his speech with well-chosen words, but when the people saw that what he was saying wasn't in agreement with their point of view he was forced to stop speaking. Each of us spoke to his neighbors to the left and the right, but the peaceful intentions of those who listened to us couldn't be communicated to the thousands of men assembled. We withdrew, but the darkness prevented us from seeing what was happening, so I can't reassure the Assembly concerning the sequel to this unfortunate event. The people are enflamed to such a point that they listen to no one. They are afraid that they are being duped.

And that is all. While the murders continued under the veil of darkness, the Assembly did nothing. It allowed the work of the night to be completed. It is all but impossible to sound the depths of people's consciousness during those fearsome and troubled hours, when all sentiments were blended together. Perhaps the Assembly felt that since the crisis of August 10 it had lost contact with the people and had no influence over them. Perhaps it thought that the Fatherland, threatened by the invader, required any and all forms of energy, even the savage, and that in repressing the peoples' excesses, there was a risk of halting its momentum. At the same time, though, I sense a pitiful calculation in their abstention. Both the Assembly and the Commune, surprised by this crisis at the height of their battle with each other, sought to shift the blame onto the other. Instead of acting vigorously, the Commune had consulted the Assembly. And there is no doubt but that some of the politicians of the Gironde thought and whispered that responsibility must be left to the Commune. If it allowed

---

4 Jean Dussaulx (1728–99)—classicist, friend of Rousseau, and moderate member of the Assembly.

the people to do whatever they wanted, the Commune covered itself with blood; if it repressed them, it entered into battle with the extremist forces it had unleashed. I see in Brissot's newspaper of September 3 a first attempt—still prudent and discrete—to hold the Commune responsible:

Sunday, September 2. The municipal government of Paris, convinced of the dangers to the Fatherland and feeling it necessary to make a grand effort to incite the people, at this morning's sitting decreed the sounding of the tocsin and the assembling of the people on the Champ de Mars to form an army of 60,000 men to go to Châlons, or wherever necessary. The intention of this proposal was praiseworthy, though events have proved that it should have been more measured ... Large groups were formed, and men spread it about that before leaving to fight the external enemies it was necessary to be freed of the enemies of the interior. They said it was necessary to attack the prisons, and principally the Abbaye, where the conspirators were held. The idea spread, and hardly had the tocsin been sounded than a certain number of men went to the Abbaye and the Carmes, where the refractory priests were held. There a large number of victims were slaughtered. We cannot go into the details of this: they must be accurately given and until now the versions differ. What appears to be certain is that much blood flowed.

This is not only a discrete reprimand. Brissot's newspaper slyly insinuates that the men scattered among the groups were carrying out instructions. And above all, it is clearly preparing to impute the "massacre" (and this is the word used) to the Commune's lack of prudence, to its need for theatrical excitement and display.

The next day, September 3, the *Patriote Français* returned to the subject of the sitting of September 2. And here we can clearly see the antagonism that paralyzed any attempt to act humanely:

A short time later the commissioners of the Assembly announced that a large number of armed and unarmed men were headed to the prisons. The Commune requested that the National Assembly come to its aid. If the Commune had exhausted all of its measures, what could the National Assembly do? And if it hadn't, what was it asking of the National Assembly? The representatives of the people didn't ask these questions; they listened only to the dying voice of the law and the cry of humanity. They immediately sent twelve commissioners to the prisoners.

It wasn't difficult to predict how successful this measure would be, dictated more by zeal than by prudence. The Commissioners returned, despairing at having made a pointless effort, and suffering from the pain of having seen those they wanted to save murdered before their eyes.

To be sure, the Assembly's démarche was not as vigorous as Brissot said it was, and if it listened to "the dying voice of the law and the cry of humanity," it did so with a heart obsessed with other thoughts. At bottom, Brissot condemns the commissioners' attempt. He sees the Commune's démarche as nothing but a trap, and he would have wanted the Assembly, by abstaining totally, to leave the Commune bearing all the responsibility for the events. And so, while death continued its labors, labors that would terribly and for so long a time be exploited to condemn the Revolution, the rivalry between parties and men paralyzed its heart. Robespierre maneuvered like the Gironde, and against them.

Robespierre Denounces the Gironde

At that same sitting of the Commune on the evening of September 2, where, like gloomy knocks at the door, word of the massacres arrived throughout the evening, Robespierre and Billaud-Varenne spoke.[5] Was it to advise clemency, to speak a humane word? No. It appears that on that bloody night the only strings that quivered in Robespierre were the strings of hatred. But he didn't condemn the people's rage that had been unleashed against the traitors and the accomplices of the crown. He denounced the Girondins. In the disorder of the dug-up soil he, the patient miner, never lost the vein of his hatred. And while the people struck enemies, he sought to strike rivals. These extraordinary lines leap out from the transcript:

---

5   Jacques Nicolas Billaud-Varenne (1756–1819)—Montagnard, supporter of the terror, and encourager of the September Massacres.

MM. Billaud-Varenne and Robespierre, as they expressed their civic feelings, described the profound pain they feel at France's current state. They denounce to the general council a plot in support of the Duke of Brunswick, whom a powerful party wants to put on the French throne.

He made this murderous accusation against the Gironde. And what is the use of quibbling, like M. Ernest Hamel,[6] over the names he mentioned?

Two names, he said, perhaps three fell from his mouth, those of Carra and Brissot. And when at the Convention's sitting of September 23 Vergniaud reproached Robespierre—about whom, he said, he had only ever spoken highly—for having implicated Brissot, Guadet, Lasource, etc. and himself in the plot denounced at the Commune on the night of September 2–3, Robespierre stood up and said with the force of truth: "That is false." To which Vergniaud responded: "I would be happy for a denial that would prove to me that Robespierre, too, was slandered." No one noted such a denial by Maximilien, and from Robespierre's response to Louvet,[7] it can be seen that in fact he only named two or three people who had already been denounced by several of his colleagues for having constantly disparaged the General Council of the Commune.

We see here the marvelous results of partisanship, and to what complaisant sophistries this honest historian allowed himself to be led. It is agreed that Robespierre gave only two or three names, but they were the names of Carra, one of the most active of the Gironde's journalists, and Brissot, who passed for the leader of the Gironde. And after having named these men— or in naming them—Robespierre accused a "powerful party:" the entire Gironde. This would have been a grave matter even if he had only accused Carra and Brissot during those tragic hours when words could kill.

Robespierre can't be defended in this matter. On November 3, he would say:

By resorting to an intolerable parallel it was insinuated that I wanted to compromise the safety of certain deputies by denouncing them at the

---

6 Louis Ernest Hamel (1826–98)—Historian of the Revolution and biographer of Robespierre.

7 Jean-Baptiste Louvet (1760–97)—Girondin legislator and enemy of Robespierre.

Commune at the time of the executions of the conspirators. I already responded to this calumny by recalling that I had ceased going to the Commune before these events and that I could not have predicted them any more than the sudden and extraordinary circumstances that brought them about could have been predicted. Do I need to tell you that a number of my colleagues had denounced before I did the persecution plotted against the Commune by the two or three people of whom we speak, as well as the plan to slander the defenders of liberty and divide the citizens at a time when they needed to unite their efforts in order to smother the conspiracy within and to repel the foreign enemies? What is this awful doctrine that denouncing a man and killing him are the same thing? What kind of republic are we living in if a magistrate who freely explains himself in a municipal assembly concerning the authors of a dangerous plot is viewed as someone who incites murder?

The sophistry is striking. It wasn't at just any time, but on the night of September 2–3 that an accusation of treason like this one was an incitement to murder. I do not know if, as he claims, Robespierre was absent from the Commune during that period. He spoke there at great length on September 1 and again the next day. And when he presided over the electoral assembly of his section on the Place Vendôme when they chose deputies to the Convention, it is inconceivable that he wasn't apprised of what was happening at the Commune. And he also knew just how much the Commune hated Brissot and the entire Gironde.

It was virtually in the name of the Gironde that the Lombards section demanded the dissolution of the Commune, giving rise to implacable rancor. And so when Robespierre, with all his authority, affirms that the Gironde is the party of Brunswick, and that it wants to raise to the throne of France the very man who signed a manifesto calling for the extermination of revolutionary France and Paris, then, whatever he might say, he has sharpened the daggers. Could the people massacre the prisoners in order not to leave a single traitor still living and then spare the traitors of all traitors, those who, under the usurped and profaned name of patriots, wanted to surrender France to the Prussian general and exacerbate their re-established slavery with the shame of defeat? Absolutely not: they, too, must be struck. Let the sinister legend to which Robespierre gave force and credit spread from the general council of the Commune to the enflamed people, and the massacres will spread even wider. The accusation made by Robespierre hypocritically tended towards Marat's policy: suppress both the Feuillant and Girondin royalists.

The proof that his denunciation was not inoffensive is the fact that the very next day the Commune ordered that Brissot's home be searched. Brissot spoke of it in the *Patriote Français*:

I thought I had provided proofs of my patriotism that were sturdy and steadfast enough to be beyond suspicion. But calumny respects no one. Yesterday, Sunday, I was denounced at the Paris Commune, along with several Girondin deputies and other men as virtuous as they. We were accused of hoping to surrender France to the Duke of Brunswick, of having received millions, and of having conspired to flee to England. I, the eternal enemy of kings and a man who didn't wait for 1789 to manifest my hatred towards them! I, the supporter of a king? I'd rather die a thousand deaths than ever recognize those despots, and even more, a foreigner!

Citizens, I was denounced at 10:00 p.m., and at that very moment murder was being committed in the prisons. Such a denunciation was likely to incite the people's fury against me, and in fact, it did incite them. Some honest souls, who think that a person should be investigated before being convicted and punished, demanded that my papers be inspected. Consequently, at 7:00 this morning, three Commissioners of the Commune came to my home. As a deputy I could have refused such a search, but when the fatherland is confronting danger every citizen, whoever he might be, must lay himself bare at the first request of the law.

For three hours the commissioners carefully examined my papers. I handed them over to them with the confidence of a man with nothing on his conscience. I had only one regret, and that was that the people, this people, to whom I am slandered and who I always defend, could not witness this examination. Here are the results: "We, after a careful search of all the papers of Sieur Brissot, and after having examined them, having found absolutely nothing that appeared contrary to the public interest, left him all his papers. Signed: Berthelon, Guermeur, deputy Commissioners, Cousteau, alias Mignon."

But what bitterness these conflicts left in people's souls!

9

The Battle of Valmy

(Foreign royalty was at war with the Revolution, and "on the borders the soldiers of the Revolution fought the battle of liberty against the first attacks of universal despotism." The army of Prussians and émigrés, under the leadership of the Duke of Brunswick, had already carried off victories at Longwy and Verdun, where the revolutionary general "Beaurepaire had committed suicide rather than surrender. But the heart of the Revolution didn't waver." Dumouriez, commanding the Revolutionary army, carries out reconnaissance and locates a spot between the Meuse and Aisne valleys and exclaims: "This shall be France's Thermopylae." He issues an appeal to the people: "Citizens, I call on you, in the name of the Fatherland and of liberty, to bring your grain and forage to our camps." He announced to the people that he will sound the tocsin to call them out to fight, asking that "all those who have firearms" should meet the army at the edge of the woods. As Jaurès wrote: "It was a strange and new tolling of the bells that would echo down the Argonne forests. The bells of the old steeples until then had rung for festivals of resignation or mystical hope ... Now they rang in the hearts of men, in the hearts of the peasants, in the hearts of the woodsmen, the great hope of liberty, the great hope of right."

But the enemy had hopes in Dumouriez. "The émigrés, who had encountered Dumouriez in the salons of the ancien régime, *thought they might be able to seduce him. But it was too soon. How could he abandon the magnificent showdown from which he could expect so much renown, and doubtless so much power?" On September 20, 1792, the battle will occur in the spot chosen by the Revolution.)*

For a brief while, the émigrés and the allies had solid reasons for hope. When the Croix-aux-Bois passage was forced they thought they would be able to surround Dumouriez.[1] But the latter, through a skillful night withdrawal on September 15, 1792, was able to break off contact. And with admirable calm, instead of rushing to Paris he held his position, with his lines anchored to the south of the Argonne forest, a bit to the west and to the rear of the route Brunswick would have to take to Châlons. His troops were posted in such a way that they could watch over the enemy and, if the latter advanced the vanguard of his troops, they could fall on his rear. And so when Brunswick and his harassed army came out onto the drenched and gloomy plains of Champagne, he was forced to finally confront Dumouriez's army, firmly positioned on the heights and reinforced by Kellermann.[2]

This was the battle of Valmy. On the morning of September 20, the Prussian army encountered Kellermann's troops to the right of the road that goes from Sainte-Menehould to Châlons-sur-Marne. Dumouriez hastened there during the course of the day to give aid and counsel. The Duke of Brunswick and the King of Prussia worriedly observed the solid army on the heights and slopes. But was it possible, now that the moment for a decisive encounter had arrived, that Frederick the Great's veteran soldiers were going to hesitate? The decision was made to attack, and when the Prussian army saw that its leaders were resolved to advance the glorious memories of the Seven Years War stirred within them. Who could defeat these veterans? Mocking the uniforms of the frail French volunteers, they said that they would "smash the blue porcelain figures" with the sweep of a hand.

The Prussian artillery, commanded by Tempelhof, opened fire with its 54 pieces. They were placed at the front of the troops, on a plateau facing the mill of Valmy, surrounding it in the form of an arc. The French artillery responded with a power and a precision that surprised the enemy, but didn't yet cause them any worry.

---

1   Charles-François Dumouriez (1739–1823)—a professional solider before the Revolution, as a friend of Danton's he obtained important military posts after the Revolution. He commanded the armies of the north and the Ardennes. Though initially responsible for important victories of the Revolution's armies, after a series of defeats he was accused of treason and did, indeed, become a traitor to the Revolution, going over to the Austrians.

2   François Christophe Kellermann (1735–1820)—a career military officer, he commanded the Army of the Moselle at the time of the battle of Valmy.

The Prussian infantry slowly advanced, in perfect order but with no élan. With an ordered and firm step, it approached the slopes where our army was positioned. A slight hesitation could be seen in the latter, as if past defeats, those of Rosbach and others, weighed on them.

But the shadow of the past played no role here. New forces were coming to life; a new world was rising. Let the Prussian army dig among its memories of glory like a miner extracting whatever bit of gold is left from a long-exploited mine: the revolutionary souls bore a virgin treasure of enthusiasm and strength.

Kellermann knew this, and at the decisive moment he evoked the grand sentiments that had been stirred to life. Upright and motionless under the bullets raining around him, he raised his hat on the tip of his sword and cried out: "Long Live the Nation!" The entire army, from the mill heights to the base of the slopes, cried out: "Long Live the Nation!" All of the radiant energy accumulated in these words over the past three years was communicated to every heart.

The nightmare of the past melted away. And just as the cloudy sky of Valmy was cleared by the thundering of the cannonade, in the same way the shadows of doubt and fear instantly vanished.

And now it was the Prussian army that was surprised. The French cry resounded like the cry of an entire people. Are we fighting an entire nation? The French artillerymen, despite the losses it suffered from the Prussian artillery, didn't fire back on it, concentrating its fire instead on the decimated infantry.

The Duke of Brunswick took fright. Wouldn't he lose the best of his army in an attack with no artillery cover?

He ordered his men to halt. And then, after a few minutes of dazed hesitation, he pronounced the decisive phrase: "We won't fight here." *Hier schlagen wir nicht.* And the retreat began. The Prussian army withdrew to the plateau.

According to the ordinary rules of war, this could hardly be considered a defeat. When you set out to attack an enemy position and realize that it is stronger and better defended than you had thought, you renounce the attack so as not to waste your forces. This is an incident of no great importance and an easily repaired mistake.

And yet, from that moment the Prussian army's momentum was decisively broken. Like a man who still looks vigorous but whose physical and moral force is worn out by a long train of sorrows, fatigues, and trials, and who succumbs to a new disappointment, the Prussian army and its leader, bent under the weight of the melancholy impressions of the preceding month, became aware of its total exhaustion at Valmy.

The invader felt that he not only had against him the immense and diffuse force of the revolutionary Nation; he saw, he became aware that in just a few days that Nation had been able to form an organized, mobile, and resistant force, capable of both firmness and enthusiasm.

When it encountered this new and fervent power, the invading army, exhausted, ill, and supported by no ideal, felt all the more profoundly its own misery. And it allowed itself to slide down the walls of an abyss where there were no outcroppings to stop its fall and gather itself. It was discouragement and impotence that led to its defeat.

Since the defeat was far more in the hearts of the invader than in their bodies, Kellermann and Dumouriez failed at first to grasp the full meaning of that great day. But Goethe, the great and clear-sighted poet who had accompanied the Prussian army, immediately saw the grandeur of the event: "In this place and on this day, a new epoch in the history of the world is beginning." It was September 20. The same day the National Convention held its first session at the Tuileries.

10

The Trial of the King

(Already, before the events of August 10, 1792, "addresses demanding Louis XVI's removal from the throne began to arrive." On July 23, a petition from Angers had said, "Legislators, Louis XVI betrayed the Nation, the law and his oaths. The people are his sovereign. Pronounce his removal from the throne and France is saved." But the Gironde hesitated, and one of their leaders, Guadet, issued an appeal to the king: "The Nation alone will certainly know how to defend and preserve its liberty; but it asks you, Sire, one last time, to unite with it to save the Constitution and the throne." But on August 1 of that year, a declaration issued by the Duke of Brunswick, leading the foreign counter-revolutionaries, "in the name of the King of France declared the men of the Revolution and the revolutionaries to be outside the law." As Jaurès says, "This definitively ruined the king."

With the king dethroned on August 10, 1792, the major military victories of the Revolutionary armies, particularly Valmy, having ensured its survival, and the Republic having been declared in 1792, the fate of the monarch had still not been decided, despite the passing of time. It would be decided by the National Convention, where diverse opinions existed. He would ultimately be guillotined, and Jaurès analyzed the positions of those in the Convention who would make that decision.)

On August 10, 1792, Louis XVI was suspended from his functions as king and imprisoned in the Temple. On January 21, 1793, he climbed the scaffold. Why did the Revolution take five-and-a-half months to judge and execute him when it was in its interest to move quickly? If the king had been judged and executed in October, as soon as the Convention had met, the country would still have been under the impressions of August 10 and, still angered, would more easily have accepted the bold stroke. Since the

Revolution wanted to discourage the royalists and shock Europe with an irreversible act, the trial should have been the first thing the Convention dealt with. In doing so, it would have marked its labors with an inviolable seal. What is more, in late September and October, Europe was stunned by the Revolution's unexpected victories. The king's death would have turned this shock into total confusion, and it's possible that the European coalition would have disintegrated.

In any case, in September and October, the English did not appear determined to go to war, and the rapid and ferocious sentencing of the king would not have sufficed to push them towards it. The world would have been surprised by the rapidity of the event and immobilized by the thunderbolts.

Why did the Convention delay? It was because of the original mandate it had received. The Legislative Assembly had stepped aside so that the Nation itself could decide on the fate of the monarchy and the king. The monarchy was abolished on September 21. The king's fate had to be settled urgently and immediately. Despite its boldness, did the Convention feel an unspoken disquiet? Was it held back by the remnants of superstitious respect and the first stirrings of a feeling of pity for this man, whom misfortune had made almost human without completely depriving him of age-old prestige? It tied itself up in formal difficulties and judicial scruples:

Can Louis XVI be judged for the crimes he is accused of committing while on the Constitutional throne? Who should he be judged by? Will he be brought before regular tribunals, like any other citizen accused of a state crime? Will you delegate the right to judge him to a tribunal formed by the electoral assemblies of the 83 *départements*? Is it not more natural that the National Convention judge him itself? Is it necessary or appropriate to submit the judgment to the ratification of all the members of the Republic gathered in communal or primary assemblies?

These were the questions posed by Mailhe in the first words of his preliminary report of November 7 and which the legislation committee "profoundly and at great length discussed."

The Thesis of Inviolability

In truth, this long debate was futile. How was it possible to retain the thesis of royal inviolability? It is true that the Constitution declared the king's person inviolable and held only ministers responsible, though it stated that for certain acts the king "was considered to have abdicated" and decreed his removal. But this constitutional procedure supposes that the Constitution had not been attacked at its roots. If the king's offenses, his treason don't place the Nation and liberty in mortal peril; if the monarchy can survive the king, then yes, the king should be judged in accordance with the Constitution, since the Constitution remains in place. But if the king has been involved in long-standing conspiracies, undermining the Constitution itself; if by his connivance with foreigners armed to destroy the Constitution he has all but killed it; if the just anger incited by his crimes has forced a frustrated and defiant people to a new revolution, then how can a Constitution of which nothing is left because of his offenses, be applied to him?

In fact, since August 10, France was not a constitutional, but rather a revolutionary state. The suspension of the king and his internment at the Temple were revolutionary acts. The Convention itself was a revolutionary assembly, since it had not been convoked by virtue of the Constitution of 1791 and, like the Revolution, it had received its unlimited powers from the people. It was thus manifestly as a revolutionary assembly that it had to judge, and it was quite strange that there was any discussion of this matter.

It was clearly the sole revolutionary tribunal competent to judge. Handing the judgment over to a jury formed of two jurors per *département* chosen by the electoral bodies would have been an act of dangerous folly. It would have been a parody of the regular forms of justice, for in a question in which the life of the Nation was at stake this jury would not have been able to escape the passions of popular opinion and the hints, the pressing suggestions, of the Convention itself. This judgment was, par excellence, an act of sovereignty, since it involved the fate of liberty and the Fatherland. It was thus sovereignty—that is, the Nation itself—represented at the Convention, that had to judge. There was no longer a

Constitution, since that of 1791 had been abolished and the new one had not yet been formulated.

In this interval between Constitutions, there was only one power left: the Nation. Or rather, all powers flowed back to it as if to their source. It was precisely because the Convention did not have a purely judicial mandate but rather a political mandate, a total mandate, that it should judge, for it was impossible to separate the judging of Louis XVI from the overall judging of the political and social state of France. It would have meant dismembering sovereignty and mortally dividing it against itself to detach from the total political power exercised by the Convention the judging of the king, which involved the entire political life of the Nation. And let it not be objected that the Nation was both judge and plaintiff and that this is contrary to the rules of justices. When a king has betrayed a nation, where in that nation can one find a citizen who is not both judge and plaintiff?

As a member of the Convention wrote: must we seek judges on another planet?

It would be strange for the Nation to be deprived of its right to judge because of the very immensity of a crime which, by offending every conscience and every being, deprived a people and all the individuals of this people of the vulgar impartiality of a judge. In this sense it is not only to the Convention, but to the entire Nation that De Sèze could have said: "I seek judges among you, and all I find are accusers." But these words were only dangerous for Louis XVI who, in betraying an entire people, forced an entire people to be both judge and accuser.

The Montagnard Thesis: Saint-Just

But this being so, would it not have been more honest to strike rather than judge him? This is what, in an odd meeting of the minds, Kant and Robespierre both concluded. Kant thought that on August 10 the Revolution would have had the right to strike the king in the same way one strikes an enemy in combat, but that claiming to judge him by substituting

a new law for an older one was a mockery. "And I say," exclaimed Saint-Just
in his November 13 speech,

> ... that the king must be judged as an enemy; that we have less to judge
> him than to combat him. I would even say that a Constitution accepted
> by a king does not bind the citizens: even before his crime they had the
> right to outlaw him and expel him. It would astound posterity that a
> king should be judged like a citizen. To judge means to apply the law.
> A law is a legal relationship, but what legal relationship is there between
> humanity and a king? A king should be tried not for the crimes of his
> administration, but for the crime of having been king, for nothing in the
> world can legitimize this usurpation, and whatever illusion, whatever
> conventions royalty wraps itself in, it is an eternal crime against which
> every man has the right to rise up and arm himself. It is one of those
> criminal acts which even the blindness of an entire people cannot justify.
> It is impossible to reign innocently: the folly of this is too obvious. Every
> king is a rebel and a usurper.

This is nothing but sophistry. For unless Saint-Just ignores history, he must
recognize that the institution of monarchy is not the work of a handful
of bold men: it corresponded to historical necessities, and all that could
be said in 1792 was that these necessities no longer held true and that
nations were now able to govern themselves. The question is then posed:
by what right can we make the individual who was king pay for a fate he
is no more responsible for than any other man? Or if Saint-Just ignores
history, if he extends the present hour into the past, if he believes and says
that at any moment in the past centuries men could have shaken off the
royal yoke the way it was now being shaken off, then it is all of humanity
that is criminal, and the people should punish themselves for their lengthy
and cowardly slavery, as they should punish kings for their lengthy and
arrogant domination.

Saint-Just alleges in vain that the blindness of the people doesn't excuse
the usurpations of kings, nor does it excuse the abject servility of the people.
And here again, why concentrate on Louis XVI's head alone a punishment
that should strike the humiliated faces of peoples as it does the haughty

ones of kings? And to say that Louis XVI should be struck a blow, not because of the crimes he committed in the exercise of his functions as king, but solely because he was king, means being too severe towards one man and too indulgent towards complicit humanity.

Nor is it true that no legal relationship existed that allowed for Louis' judgment by the French people. Since the Revolution of 1789, an agreement had intervened between historic tradition and the new law, between the royal institution and popular sovereignty. This agreement would have lasted if the royals had been honest and faithful to their word. It was the Constitution itself that was the "legal relationship" between the king and the Nation that was denied by Saint-Just. And even when the Constitution fell, the Nation maintained the right to demand accounts of Louis XVI for the betrayals that had nullified the pact between the crown and the people. The king wasn't freed of his felony by the fall of the Constitution against which he had committed his felony, and it was this felony that the Nation had the right to judge.

Robespierre's Opinion

In his speech of December 3, Robespierre reached the same conclusion as Saint-Just, but for different reasons. Like him, Robespierre wanted there to be no judgment: he wanted the king to be executed as an enemy without benefit of trial.

But it wasn't his status as king he invoked; it was the crimes he committed against the Nation: "People don't judge in the same way as judicial courts. They don't issue sentences; they cast lightning bolts. They don't condemn kings; they cast them back into the void."

The fight had begun between Louis XVI and the Revolution. August 10 was the first blow; death would be the second. On August 10, the people made no claim to passing judgment: in order to defend themselves they struck out. They were now going to strike the decisive blow and forever rid themselves of the tyrant: "The tyrant must die so the Fatherland can live." Judging Louis XVI implied that he could be innocent, and if Louis XVI was innocent then it was France that was a rebel, it was the Revolution that was a crime. And so, no trial, no indictment, no lawyers, no judgment, no new delays, but rather a measure of public safety.

What is worthy of note in Robespierre's thesis is that it is not a trial when the sentence is imposed on the judge in advance, whatever the defense of the accused. After August 10, it was not possible for the Convention to proclaim Louis XVI's innocence without unleashing the counter-revolution. It was bold, and in a sense noble, to proclaim this vital need of the Revolution and not tie up in legal formalities the act that would save liberty and the Fatherland.

But this idea was too forceful for France's hesitant and troubled conscience. It lacked the boldness to strike without trial. It didn't want to deprive itself of the benefits of publicizing Louis XVI's crimes and, in keeping with the essential forms of justice, it wanted these crimes made known to the Nation and the world through a public debate where the accused could make his voice heard. Perhaps Saint-Just's and Robespierre's haughty and summary proceedings would have been possible in the immediate aftermath of August 10. The death sentence for Louis XVI would then have appeared to be the consequence of a battle. In December, it was too late. Robespierre himself noted the change in mood: "Last August, when the partisans of the crown were in hiding, anyone who would have offered apologies for Louis XVI would have been punished as a traitor. Today they raise their heads with impunity." And Robespierre concluded: "Don't delay. Waste no more time with hypocritical and timid formalities."

Marat's Opinion

But there is no doubt that it was no longer possible to pronounce oneself so summarily without going against public sentiment. M. Ernest Hamel in his *Histoire de Robespierre* wrote in this regard:

Is it true that at that moment Marat, leaning over to Dubois-Crancé, said to him, "with these doctrines we'll do the Republic more harm than all the tyrants combined." This, at least, is what an extremely conscientious historian [Vuillaumé] claimed, though we don't believe this for three reasons. First, because such scruples seem to us to be totally contrary to Marat's genius and habits. Secondly, because Dubois-Crancé, an extremely shady character, deserves no credence. And finally, because he has completely omitted providing us with the least proof of the authenticity of such an allegation.

It is clear that M. Hamel is scandalized at the thought that Marat could find Robespierre extreme and impolitic. But he has a false idea of Marat. The latter was at times quite thoughtful and prudent, careful not to enflame the forces of counter-revolution. It was precisely in that month of December that he accused Cambon, because of his motion on the religious budget, of having upset the constitutional priests, and made known a letter from several of them.

There is no doubt that he condemned Saint-Just's and Robespierre's line of reasoning. We know that he held Robespierre in high esteem: he was the only man he never attacked. He had also been impressed by Saint-Just's first speeches and he characterized his manner with great subtlety. He wrote on December 1: "The sole orator who gave me any pleasure at the tribune was Saint-Just. His speech regarding staple goods demonstrated a feeling for style, a dialectic, and a vision. Once he has matured through reflection and has renounced showiness, he will be a man: he is a thinker."

But on this point he stood apart from Saint-Just and Robespierre. I would like to point out that he didn't praise Saint-Just's speech regarding Louis XVI. In fact, Marat's opinion was that Louis XVI should have been judged in accordance with legal forms. He feared that if the country was not reminded of the king's most flagrant crimes through a solemn trial the death sentence would meet resistance. He expressed his opinion:

Your legislation committee, with a series of reasons drawn from natural right, the rights of people, and from civil law, has made it clear that Louis Capet must be brought to justice. This was necessary for the education of the people, for it is important to lead all the members of the Republic to this conviction by the different paths appropriate to the quality of their intelligence.

It is clear that Robespierre's summary proceedings did not appear to him to be capable of convincing. And since Marat deposed his written opinion at the Convention on December 3, the very day Robespierre spoke, it is quite likely that he showed some irritation with the latter's views. Robespierre's intransigent and clear-cut opinion made Marat look like a moderate. If M. Hamel hadn't been absorbed and fascinated by the contemplation of Robespierre, if he had referred to Marat's writings, he would have found the words attributed to him by Dubois-Crancé quite plausible. Marat insisted on his idea: Louis XVI must be judged with ceremony and severity. And in his December 13 issue of *L'Ami du Peuple*, Marat, who was usually in such a hurry to bring things to a conclusion, complained of the unthinking impatience that risked depriving the Convention's decision of some of its authority:

> It is with pain that I saw the patriotic members of this Assembly fall into the trap that was laid for them. How could they not see that the other side sought to have them carry out misguided measures by pushing them to hastily judge Louis Capet! I call for them to reflect. They should pronounce on the fate of the former monarch with the greatest calm and wisdom, less for their own honor than to deprive his henchmen of a pretext to slander them by accusing them of having killed him with the sword of the law.

Marat is obviously thinking here of the sitting of December 12, where several members of the extreme left proposed that only four days be granted Louis XVI to examine the evidence and present his defense or have it presented for him. Marat was so concerned with satisfying public opinion that he was even accused of being lukewarm, and had to defend himself in his newspaper:

> In putting Louis Capet back on the throne after his flight to the enemy, the representatives of the Nation granted him remission of his previous crimes. If it is appropriate to place him on trial in accordance with the Constitution, at the very least in order to silence his henchmen, I think we must limit ourselves to the acts committed after that date. Because

of this simple observation friends have concluded that I am playing tyranny's game, and enemies have concluded that I was commiserating with them in their plight. The latter found this mysterious, the former an abominable bit of foolishness.

Whatever the case, even if the Convention sees that the defenders of Louis Capet abuse legal forms, not to save the tyrant but to make his crimes known and to prove to the universe that in condemning him it isn't condemning an innocent man to death, it still has it in its power to reject this vicious practice and punish a conspiratorial monarch and to treat him as a public enemy taken weapon in hand.

And so Marat would only rally to Robespierre's and Saint-Just's point of view if the other proceeding, that is, judgment in accordance with legal forms, raised difficulties and failed to resolve the crisis. But in essence his viewpoint is directly contrary to theirs. Far from viewing the king only as king; far from treating him as if the entire nation saw in him anything but an enemy, he wanted to judge him for his crimes and in accordance with the Constitution. He granted remission for the crimes committed prior to Varennes because public opinion saw his being returned to the throne as an amnesty. Yet again, it is surprising that M. Hamel erred so seriously concerning Marat's tactics.

But what I want to point out is that Saint Just's and Robespierre's position was an isolated one and that it appeared to almost the entire Convention to be a paradox and it presented no difficulties capable of halting or slowing down the trial. If, from the first days, the Convention had clearly confronted the problem, then between late September and early October it would certainly have decided that there was cause to judge Louis, that he should be judged by the Convention, and that all legal forms would be complied with.

(The king was executed on January 21, 1793. As Jaurès wrote:

> *The sentence was just, not only from the revolutionary point of view, but from the point of view of Louis XVI who, in accepting the Constitution, in which popular sovereignty was inscribed, had recognized the new law ... The blow*

that was delivered by the Revolution against monarchy, a profound and decisive blow, remained, and the feelings of pity, the fleeting reappearances of counter-revolution, would not prevail against the force of that sovereign act. Kings might briefly return, but they would henceforth be nothing but ghosts. France, their France, is eternally regicide.

The king's head fell "because the opposition is irreducible between the former monarchical law and the new law of popular sovereignty. It was thus the Nation itself which struck with the force of its new principle, and the blow it delivered was prolonged into the infinite, like the principle in the name of which it struck.")

11

The *Enragés* against the High Cost of Living

(In 1792–93, peasant revolts broke out throughout France, and the working class of the cities reacted with increasing strength to the high cost of living, particularly of the staple of the working family's diet, bread. The Jacobins were reluctant to take measures to control prices, for "in the first months of 1793 [such measures] frightened them. Wouldn't they risk alienating the commercial bourgeoisie?" Into the breach stepped the key figures of the left of the Revolution, Jacques Hébert, both as deputy procurator of the Commune and in his avatar as Père Duchesne, the voice of the sans-culottes, Jean-François Varlet and the priest Jacques Roux. Around these men "a kind of social party formed that wanted to place economic problems in the forefront. It wanted to denounce and combat hoarding in all its forms."

Varlet, aged only 21 and so not eligible for elective position, "sought to act outside and on the elected assemblies." Roux attended meetings at the Cordeliers and the sections of the Observatoire and, most importantly, that of his Gravilliers neighborhood:

> On the streets crowded with people, in the modest shops where the artisans waited for customers, he spoke to everyone, with the women as well as the men, knowing from his experience in the church that the woman could play a decisive role. And he passed from attacking the king to hoarders: "What good was it to cut off the head of the tyrant if every day you are slowly devoured by speculators and monopolists."

The great social movement of the sans-culottes, the Enragés, *who took their program from a manifesto written by Roux, took form.*

In February 1793, the movement took matters into their own hands. On February 22, the Jacobin Club is visited by women asking for a place to discuss the issues confronting them. When the club refused them, the leadership was hissed and booed, and from the stands people shouted that "among them were merchants and hoarders who grew wealthy on public misfortune." Two days later, washerwomen visited the Convention to make their case for their need for basic goods. And on February 25, 1793, perhaps the result of an inflammatory article by Marat that appeared that same day, but probably not, since the article appeared at virtually the same hour the riots occurred, shops were pillaged by a working-class crowd, their immediate needs resolved by direct action.)

The Revolutionary Forces in Paris

The death of Louis XVI had enflamed revolutionary passion and enabled the Revolution to taste the bitter savor of death. The pressure of the joint threats of external war and internal dissension led some to say that the guillotine was a solution and that the death of the king hadn't exhausted its pacifying virtues. Without uttering a protest, in February [1793], the Jacobins heard these sinister words: "The national razor must be taken around France." And yet, the guillotine was not yet on the agenda, though the still inchoate idea of liquidating the Girondins was beginning to make itself felt. The king's trial had provided a terrible argument against the Girondins: "They had wanted to save the king."

The revolutionary groups that had been so active from late July to late September 1792 and throughout the period surrounding the events of August 10 and which had then been restrained by the sovereign authority of the Convention, assembled anew and entered into action. They planned to pressure the Convention and obtain more energetic measures in the economic, social, and political spheres.

Before August 10, the revolutionary force had been made up of the delegates of the sections and the *fédérés* called to Paris. This revolutionary force, mainly directed against the crown and the Tuileries Palace, had had a complex and sly attitude towards the Commune of Paris: it had both dominated and used it. It had made use of Pétions's remaining popularity without binding itself to his weakness. There was a kind of extra-legal Commune that functioned alongside the legal Commune, one that made use of it before replacing it. For a moment, the revolutionary Commune of August 10 had been the master of Paris, and one of the main forces of the Revolution.

In December 1792 and January 1793, the provisional Commune, heir of the revolutionary Commune of August 10, still carried out large-scale actions. Through its procurator Chaumette and his deputy Hébert, it was in communication with the popular elements, but it wasn't vigorous or bold enough to stand up against the Convention and impose a more daring policy on it, and to a certain extent it was held back by the mayor, Chambon, who leaned toward the Girondins. Even more, like all lasting forms of authority, it had gradually taken a turn towards legality: it had been caught up in the formidable gears of the Convention. Often called to the bar to give an accounting of the state of Paris, troubled by the memory of the September Massacres, which had been disavowed by all, it was no longer capable of a great, spontaneous revolutionary undertaking. Though Hébert and Chaumette could very well involve themselves in a popular movement, they weren't determined enough to incite such actions or persistent enough to organize them. And although the most ardent and impatient section of the people of Paris wanted to eliminate the Girondins, tax foodstuffs, and declare war on the rich; although it wanted to push the Convention in this direction, or even to force it to act, it couldn't count on the open and direct action of the Paris Commune.

The motive force was elsewhere, in the sections and among the *fédérés*. The latter, when they came to Paris in late July 1792, had but one goal: to save liberty by combating the king. They hadn't taken sides in the quarrel between Robespierre and Brissot and didn't distinguish between Girondins and Montagnards. What is more, their sympathies would more likely have gone to the Gironde than the Mountain, since at that time it was in the front ranks of the Revolution and because the *fédérés* from Marseilles were fond of Barbaroux.[1] But they had no problem taking lodging near

---

1   Charles Jean Marie Barbaroux (1767–94)—the voice of the Marseilles representatives at the Convention, he was an opponent of the Jacobins and the left in general. Guillotined.

the Cordeliers and allying themselves with Danton, and the spirit of Paris, which was increasingly hostile to the Gironde, soon entered them. Barbaroux himself, in a letter addressed January 30 to his friends from Marseilles, sorrowfully noted the change in the *fédérés'* disposition [...]

If it looked like there had been a rapprochement between the *fédérés* from Marseilles and the Girondins when the former requested they be allowed to return to Marseilles, this only appeared to be the case. Naturally, the *fédérés* wanted to return to their homes, and Barbaroux, their deputy, supported their request at the Convention. In doing so, he hoped to regain his popularity among them. In any case, the Gironde no longer had any interest in keeping in Paris men who, under the influence of the city, were distancing themselves from them. It's true, though, that the Montagnards didn't appear to show any especial concern for the Marseillais battalion that they'd worked so hard to win over, since they prohibited its return to Marseilles and placed it at the disposal of the minister of war who, if he so desired, could send them to the border. The Mountain was afraid that new appeals would be made by the Gironde and by binding them to military service it discouraged in advance any *fédérés* who might consider coming to Paris to support the Girondins. But in fact, many *fédérés* had allowed themselves to be won over by the extremist parties, and they could become precious allies for the revolutionary groups of the Paris sections.

Through these men, Paris grew and became all of France. Thus, when the delegates of the sections spoke at the Convention it was no longer in the name of Paris, it was in the name of the entire revolutionary people of France, represented by the most devoted of patriots. United with the *fédérés*, they constituted the entire revolutionary Nation, and it would be extraordinary to crush the Gironde with the *fédérés* that they had called to their defense. The tactic of the most active sections was thus to unite with the delegates, to gradually bring along and compromise the Commune, and in so doing break the resistance of the Convention.

Revolutionary anger had been rising in the sections since December. What? On August 10, the people were murdered by the king and yet five months later the Convention has not yet tried the assassin? It hesitated, it argued. What? Incited by tyrants, the entire world is arming itself to avenge the death of the tyrant? We have to abandon shops and workplaces and march to the borders again while the very men who encouraged these despots by their reluctance to strike the king continue to govern, to dominate the Convention! What? The people give their blood, and while they exhaust themselves saving the Fatherland, they are ruined and starved by the constant rise in the price of food! And the law doesn't strike the speculators who cause the value of paper money to depreciate, the hoarders who drive up the cost of living! The people must organize, act, and assist the democrats of the Convention who are too fearful, too chained to scrupulous legality to strike the speculators! The people must either assist them or compel them!

From December 30, the first outlines of an organization, the first attempts at revolutionary pressure, become visible when the delegates of the 18 sections, along with the wounded of August 10, went to the Convention to demand they hasten the death of the king.

This organization defined and asserted itself on January 17 at a demonstration with the Paris Commune. I read in the account given in *Le Moniteur*:

January 17—Yesterday a deputation of *fédérés* presented itself at the Council to invite it to participate today at a fraternal ceremony that was to be celebrated on the Place du Carrousel, where their brothers perished on August 10. It was decreed that the members of the Council would participate as a body in this ceremony and would take the solemn oath along with the *fédérés* of the 84 *départements*, the Marseillais, and the 48 Sections of Paris.

This morning the General Council adopted the terms of the oath in this form: "We all swear to be faithful to the French Nation; to maintain the unity and the indivisibility of the Republic; to defend unto death humanity's sacred rights, liberty, and equality. Finally, we mutually swear to indissoluble unity and fraternity. In the same way, we swear eternal war on all tyrants under whatever name they might present themselves."

The Council left at 12:30 p.m. to go to the Carrousel, where the *fédérés* of Marseilles and the other *départements* could be found, as well as the citizens of the sections. They gave each other the civic accolade and took the oath together. On the way back, the members of the Commune mingled with the *fédérés* and entered the Council hall, which had never been so packed.

The Commune's procurator [Chaumette] ordered that the account of this day be engraved on stones from the Bastille, one of which will be sent to each of the 84 *départements*, and finally that a tree with the name Tree of Fraternity be planted on the Place du Carrousel.

Several *fédérés* took turns speaking and, in the name of the 84 *départements*, swore unity and fraternity with their brothers, the Parisians.

Fraternal kisses were exchanged. Finally, all the citizens withdrew and, to the sound of the drums, they danced the Carmagnole on the Place de la Maison Commune.

And so the *fédérés* , who had themselves been won over by the extremist parties of the Revolution, began to annex the Commune. They were a force for action, and they would gradually push the Commune to act.

The Petition of February 3, 1793

On February 3 the new organization made its official appearance at the Convention itself. "Federalist petitioners," calling themselves, according to the minutes, "defenders of the Republic one and indivisible" took the floor to defend Pache. Most importantly, "a deputation of the 48 sections of Paris, of the General Council, and of the united defenders of the 84 *départements*" demanded laws against speculation in paper money. Following the example set in early August, when the revolutionary sections placed Pétion, the mayor of Paris, at their head in order to provide themselves with as much legal cover as possible and in this way impose themselves on the Legislative Assembly, it was now the weak mayor of Paris, Chambon, who presented the deputation and spoke in its name. It was under cover of the law that the new organization made its entry into the Convention.

What is immediately striking in the declarations and manifestos of these revolutionary groups is their predominant concern for economic questions, the accent placed on social demands. Even when they appear to be proposing an exclusively political object, even when they demand that the Convention hasten the death of the tyrant, it is not mainly for political reasons, it is not to strengthen liberty, to punish the traitors, or to frighten despots, or at least it is not mainly for this that they do so. It might be said that for them Louis was a symbol of a long reign of iniquity and poverty whose very memory they wanted to erase, and there is a note of social anger in their words that is more profound than the conflicts between the monarchy and the republic, between liberty and tyranny. Pity for the king seemed to them an insult to more heartrending sufferings, because the latter are undeserved and an offense to humanity itself, which finally expected that amends would be made. [To quote from one of the declarations:]

That woman who cries today over the fate of Louis Capet also went to the crossroads to see the execution of a father who, revolted by the despicableness of a hoarder, attempted to lighten the weight of the cost of his basic needs.

We, more just, will not plead the cause of the tyrant, but rather the cause of all of humanity against that of the tyrant. We demand the punishment of Louis in the name of those lives stifled before they could grow by forced labor and poverty under an oppressive regime. We demand it in the name of all those who, since Louis' elevation to the throne, were sacrificed to the luxury and prodigality of his court; in the name of the patriots sacrificed in the colonies under the iron of counter-revolutionaries paid for by Louis; in the name of the victims swallowed up until 1789 in the state prisons; in the name of the innocents who died in the torments of the Question until public indignation forced him to banish that odious regime from France; in the name of the unfortunates who perished on the gallows by order of ignorant and iniquitous judges to whom he had sold the right to implement justice; in the name of all those who died in poorhouses and hospitals through the negligence of the officials who had been placed in their posts because of the abuses of his reign; in the name of those unfortunate soldiers he entrenched in his palace on August 9 and who, stupefied by an intoxicating liquor, he exposed to the peoples' fury; in the name of the brothers of our *départements* who died in the war against liberty, undertaken in concert with him by the tyrants of Europe in order to re-establish his absolute power; and in the name of the widows and orphans who his betrayals deprived of their support.

Yes, when these groups evoke the grievances of the revolutionary period they seem to view them as superficial and accidental. Their argument against the king is based on the permanent poverty of the people. What they don't forgive the monarchy for is having created suffering and degradation, not by accident, but as part of the normal course of events. Even when they allude to the unmistakable crimes of the king, to those that resound down history, to bloody events like those of August 10, they present them in a new and unexpected way. They seem to be saddened less by the death of patriots fallen while fighting for liberty than by the degradation of the mercenaries of the tyranny. The Swiss soldiers of August 10, whom the people hunted down for several days are, par excellence, the victims of oppressive royalty: it was royalty that debased them, that dehumanized them, and through them the delegates sympathized with the entire people, whose ignorance and poverty made them receptive to the stigmatizing temptations of despots. By a kind of evocation and all-embracing insurrection, which would mobilize even the past victims of tyranny, they brought back to life all those who died in poverty or despair or foolish resignation; all the victims who suffered in the penal colonies and lay on the pallets of poverty and ignominy. This was monarchy judged from the poorhouse, where the impoverished shivered with fever; from hovels where the people in rags, worn out by forced labor and hunger, gave birth to new generations capable only of continuing the age-old sufferings.

These revolutionaries had a feel for the social depths, for the hidden dramas of popular life. And far from being enthralled by the spectacle of superficial conflicts, they delved deep into the subterranean layers, and there they saw a kind of never-ending murder, the silent and continuous smothering of countless seeds. Yes, countless seeds of life, of joy, of strength were crushed by overwork or were aborted under a thick layer of poverty. This is truly a new note, and suddenly the circle of judges gathered around Louis XVI expanded and deepened. It was royalty viewed from the asylums of poverty, of illness, of forced labor, of hunger.

Royalty, but also society. This indictment, this threat extended beyond the king. And tomorrow, with the king gone, all poverty, all injustice, all degradation must disappear, and the new rulers, the new privileged ones will be asked to account for the poverty that still exists, for the iniquity that continues, for the crushing labor that goes on, for the human degradation that hasn't ended. And I know of nothing as tragic as this indictment which, attacking an already condemned monarchy, strikes a blow against an entire society and even threatens the new one. As far as I'm concerned, Marat, too involved in the political struggle, in the battles of the Convention, in the conflicts and maneuvers of parties, too exclusively concerned with bringing down the Gironde, his immediate enemies who he slanders daily, no longer strikes so profound a note. And perhaps he never did. And so we can see that from its very beginnings, it was a feeling for social demands that animated the revolutionary organization of the *fédérés* and the sections.

In truth, despite all the energy drawn off by the external war, every great revolutionary event made the people more receptive to the social question. I have already said how a whole movement of ideas tending towards social equality grew from the troubles of August 10, from the victory of the people and democracy. A movement so strong that the Revolution thought that property was threatened and briefly organized for resistance.

But it was precisely to the extent that political equality became a more solidly established fact that social inequality offended the people. The Revolution, through the death of the king, through universal war, assumed growing responsibilities before humanity. How could it bear them if it didn't demonstrate that it truly wanted the good of all men and that, without leveling conditions, it wanted at least to ensure the independence and well-being of the entire people? The more it was forced to fight and kill, the more it should have shown that it possessed profound ideas of kindness and peace.

Père Duchesne

The people hadn't forgotten that the Law of the Silver Marc[2] and the privilege of active citizenship had deprived them of the right to vote,[3] and

---

2   Proposed law that would have required any candidate for the Assembly to possess the value of 50 days of work.

3   "Active citizens" were defined as those who paid three livres in taxes, far beyond the means of the popular classes.

if they were humiliated by this they were also proud to be able to say to the bourgeoisie that they interpreted the Rights of Man better than they; the letter of the Constitution was on the bourgeoisie's side, but the Rights of Man were on theirs.

The people were no longer demanding the Republic and the removal of the king as they had in July; they at times seemed to be making amends for their boldness in this matter. But they still had before their eyes the shining light of the Republic, and a deeply seated instinct told them that this was a logical extension of all that had occurred, that it followed naturally along the path of events. The people were angered by the sudden fortunes of bourgeois speculators, the boldness of hoarders, the ferocious selfishness of the colonials.

To the egoism of the bourgeoisie, they proudly opposed the Rights of Man, which the selfishness of the bourgeoisie evaded, attacked, and deformed, and they knew that their upright conscience was in accord with the purity of their ideals. Given the universal overturning of conditions and fortunes and the enormous rearrangement of interests, the people no longer felt that poverty and servitude unavoidably weighed on them like a rock. Even in their suffering, they could sense so ardent a stirring, so rapid a transformation in the age-old relationships of men and things that they conceived the remote possibility of forms of liberty where they would finally find happiness.

However willfully crude Hébert's newspaper was, I often feel in it the great heartbeat of popular sentiment. Is there nothing but theatrics in the affected cynicism of *Père Duchesne*? I wouldn't say so, although I detest its foul-mouthed style that was gobbled up by the proletarians. But it was sincere in that it instinctively understood popular sentiment and effortlessly reflected it. Marat was a loner who constructed an entire revolutionary system in his head and who furiously attempted to impose it on events and men. In every crisis of the Revolution, and whatever the people's sentiments, Marat proposed a dictator or a military tribune to execute the traitors. To be sure, even in the depths of his underground dwelling he heard the sounds of the crowd, the cries of suffering, even the whisperings of treason, and he responded to them with piercing appeals and fearsome words. Sometimes, with his angry and sublime cry of pity, he touched the soul of the people and left an enduring emotion there. At other times, he astounded with the strange lucidity of his vision, by the amazing encounter of his improbable prophecies with improbable events. But this unremitting anger and endless suspicion wore out the people: they occasionally needed to catch their breath and weren't always in a feverish state. They abandoned themselves to the simple joys of life, breathed in the air, the sun, and confidence, giving men credit when it was due. Marat, who didn't leave them a single person to admire (except Robespierre) and nothing to hope for, exasperated them and kept their nerves in such a state of tension that they snapped. Unlike the underground man, Père Duchesne is the man of the streets and the crowd; of the arbors where good wine is drunk while cursing the hoarders who drive up its price. He kept an eye on, denounced, and scolded the tribunes of the people. But he at times demonstrated a rugged tenderness for them that responded to the people's need to love. Closer to popular ideas, in periods of crisis, Père Duchesne didn't dream of a cheerless dictatorship. He demanded a republic after Varennes; a broad, popular government that wouldn't mistreat the king's son but which would have no need of him.

Repulsed by the votes of the Assembly and the repression on the Champ de Mars, he didn't persist in his furious imprecations. He momentarily seemed to renounce his beautiful dream of a republic, but deep down in his soul he maintained the euphoria of liberty, a joyous hope for the republic that would burst forth on August 10. Père Duchesne doesn't bang his feverish head against walls of his cellar: he knows that in the popular soul the forces of life, sometimes silent and unperceived like deep waters, accumulate and suddenly reveal themselves in astounding geysers.

In addition, while Marat, worn out and despairing, thought there was nothing left to do since everyone was preaching the literal respect for the Constitution, Hébert accommodated himself to this passing phase and blissfully continued along his way. Between December 15, 1791 and April 12, 1972 Marat, whose newspaper was selling poorly, put down his pen while Père Duchesne, with increasing success cried his great anger, his great suffering, and his great joys: "I am the real Père Duchesne, and I don't give a fuck!"

For more than a year, with an extraordinary range of tone, he scolded, grew angry, and took joy, passing from sentimental abandon to sudden distrust. Listen to how he originally admired Mirabeau in his issue number 10: "It doesn't surprise me if the eloquent Mirabeau takes so much pleasure in crushing them [Abbé Maury[4] and his friends] … Keep on talking about the Fatherland, dear man; our heart plays the violin whenever you open your mouth to perorate in our august assembly."

What we hear here is the echo of the women of the markets, calling him "our little father Mirabeau" at Versailles. But suddenly, Mirabeau's complicated political schemes begin to worry him (issue no. 12): "We see that your damn face gave us a mortal fright. It's not enough to have a nice mug, you've got to have a beautiful soul, do you hear me, my good friend?"

This is a true reflection of the peoples' mixed worries about and affection for Mirabeau. Marat is lacking in such rich tones.

And then the speculation in the *assignat* made itself felt in the summer of 1791, and Hébert launched a vigorous campaign against the monopolists (no. 14) and gives us a piquant portrait of the revolutionary capitalists:

Much as I've cried out against the fucking money merchants, against those triple Jews who seize our *écus*; much as I've hunted them down, chased after them with my whip, the asses dare to show their faces again and sell all the little *assignats* that we so impatiently waited for. Who would be cowardly enough not to reject such incompetents, not to descend on them, give them a serious beating, and then send them back all bruised to the thugs in whose name they act?

I don't know what damn policy has prevented us from getting to the source of these maneuvers that have so often caused despair among the people and the army. There's a mob of jackasses who lead public opinion, who pretend to serve the interests of the people, who caress them with one hand and smack them with the other. Thunder of the gods! Won't I ever get my hands on one of them and treat him the way he deserves? Do these damn speculators think they'll be the only ones to escape punishment? What? We'll have crushed the nobility, the parliamentar-

---

4   Jean-Sifrein Maury (1746–1817)—reactionary priest who fought against the emancipation of the Jews and joined the émigrés in 1792.

ians, the clergy, and these Arabs will be spared? Let them tremble, these monsters! The day will come when the people's fury, having reached its height, will make them feel the effects of a terrible but just punishment. [...]

And then he attacked the clergy, but in keeping with the popular sentiment of the period, he was careful to distinguish between priests and religion. He speaks ironically of the

> ... gratitude owed the Jews who, because they engaged in usury with our former prelates, introduced into the sanctuary all the vices that have made us open our eyes ... Upon seeing how the priestly buggers mixed religion with their passions I think that God wouldn't recognize himself in it. But fuck, he'll now see our hearts laid bare and will see that we are all brothers, that we love our good king, and even more, the Nation.

Frightened by the fanatical movements that were beginning to take shape, Hébert wrote: "We have to stop our women from getting mixed up with the affairs of the priests, for if their damn tongues decided to start wagging on questions they know nothing about we'll never see the end of it" (no. 16). His anger is colorful in the face of the persistent emigration of hard currency: "Can it be that those asses [the émigrés] before leaving sent a magnetic stone to all foreign countries in order to attract all our specie? Oh, fuck! There's some magic involved here. [...]"

The end of the Constituent Assembly approaches:

> The National Assembly is limping along. It's an old hooker, once an honest woman but who, because she spent too much time in the capital, has gone wrong and prostituted herself for money to the executive power and the aristocrats. But fortunately, goddamit, she's reaching her end, and we see the day of her burial coming with as much pleasure as a child does in seeing that of a grumpy old tutor who was the bane of his existence.

If the Constituent Assembly displeased the popular party by revising the Constitution so that it favored the executive power by making the conditions for voting and electability harsher and by limiting the freedom of the press and the right to petition, Père Duchesne was also worried about what its offspring, the new Legislative Assembly, raised under the law of the Silver Marc, would do: "The famous law of the Silver Marc," he exclaims in issue 58,

> ... will forever prevent us from having deputies as skillful and honest as [Robespierre and Pétion]. If it had been in place before the Estates General you can bet that three-quarters of the brave buggers who shut up the nobility and the clergy wouldn't have been elected and we'd more than ever be in the claws of despotism.
>
> If we can, we have to prevent this law from remaining in place much longer. I don't mean by this that we should revolt against the decrees of the National Assembly, for even when there are unjust ones it's better to submit to them than to cause all kinds of disorder and civil war. But fuck, we have to shout so loudly that our cries will resound in the depths of the Manège [where the Assembly met]. I fully expect it to cause most of the aristocracy and the false patriots—who are veritable horses, or rather mules from the Auvergne—to buck when we speak of the People and of Liberty. But fuck, all ears aren't stuffed, and among those scoundrels there are still good men who will take our side. Didn't we recommend to you that you tear down the ancient idols and raise onto your shoulders the poor people who for so many centuries were down in the mud? You destroyed the aristocracy of Nobles and the Clergy and you are establishing one that is a thousand times more odious, that of Wealth.

The news of the king's flight[5] spread like wildfire. Hébert, who kept daily track of popular feelings but who lacked Marat's sharp foresight, hadn't seen it coming. The widespread popular sentiment immediately made itself felt in *Le Père Duchesne.* He felt the stirring of the people, their fearful and joyful excitement in the face of the unknown, and, in several tableaux of a vulgar and idyllic realism, if I can use those terms, he

---

5   To Varennes on June 21, 1791.

skillfully brought to light the contrasting emotions of the conservative and moderate bourgeoisie, which retreated, and the people, who marched into the future. Almost all of issue 59 is powerfully written, and since Hébert is above all a reflector, it is the people themselves that we see on the stage:

> "What are we going to do with that fat pig?" ask all the curious bystanders, referring to Gilles Capet.
>
> "But," the president of a Section says, "he's still our king; he's inviolable and we mustn't stop respecting him, obeying him." "Bravo," says a battalion commander. "It's only the hotheads who speak differently." What the fuck do you mean, hotheads? Is it being a hothead to prevent someone from setting the house on fire?
>
> I sent all the active citizens to go fuck themselves somewhere else and consoled myself wetting my whistle at a little café near the docks. Goddam if I wasn't rewarded for the troubles all those damn buggers caused me! I had no sooner sat on a stool than I heard someone singing as loud as can be: "*Ça ira! Ça ira!*[6] Long Live the Nation!" I stuck my nose outside and what do I see? A bunch of brave buggers armed with pikes walking arm-in-arm with the drinkers of the night before. Where are you coming from, I ask 'em? Are there still Bastilles that need to be taken? "Oh Père Duchesne, where were you? We just took the oath to die for the Fatherland and this vow won't be the vow of a son of a bitch, like that of the fucking pig who falsely swore and who ruined the Fatherland."
>
> "Well, Père Duchesne," Mother Caquet the fish-scaler says to me, "what do you think of our fucking king of diamonds? What I think, goddamit, is that we need to throw him in the nut house, in the insanity ward, since there are no longer any cloisters to hide him away in like our ancestors did to lazy and imbecilic kings." As the clock tower tolled, Cateau the oyster shucker shouted: "Let them all be fucked. No more Capet, no more court, no more Austrian woman. No need for an aristocrat to govern us and some good fellow who's like us could fill the

---

6   "*Ça ira!*" ("Things will be fine"): refrain of a particularly virulent popular revolutionary song.

position just as well as that fucking piglet who only knows how to drink himself silly."

It's said that the people are sovereign. We should try out our rights by giving ourselves someone we think appropriate. We won't put a crown on him, since that snuffs out common sense and virtue. But goddammit, we want him to always be direct, like Père Duchesne.

"Like Père Duchesne! Like Père Duchesne," they all shouted together.

"I support the motion," said Old Man Bondo, the strongest of the strongmen of the port and the marketplace. "And I request that Père Duchesne be named regent of the kingdom during the imbecility of Gilles Capet, former king of France. Long Live Père Duchesne! Long Live Père Duchesne!'"

So no sooner am I proclaimed regent than they promise to protect me with three hundred thousand pikes. You bet that *ça ira!*

"What will you do Père Duchesne, when you assume the Regency?" I'll begin by kicking the ass of all the false patriots who slithered like snakes into the National Assembly, the city government, and the departmental government. I'll assemble a new legislature composed not only of Active Citizens but of all the good people, poor and rich, who will deserve that honor through their patriotism and their talents.

When the legislative body is well organized in this way I won't be so fucking insolent as to admit that no one is my equal, to pretend to unite within myself half the strength of the Nation, to devour all by myself enough wealth to allow half the citizens of a *département* to live.

I'll content myself with doing nothing but watching over the machine and warning the workers when it's not working right. I'll protect the arts, I'll support commerce, I'll slice the necks of all the speculators. In the meanwhile, Gilles Capet will have ended his shameful life in his lunatic asylum and his abominable wife will have croaked in La Salpetrière.[7] Their son will have grown up, having been raised in labor and poverty, and will have forgotten his original attire. He will have learned to be a man and a citizen. People can, if they want to at that time—if they need to—make him, I won't say king, since you can't have one if you want to

---

7 Originally a powderworks, at the time of the Revolution it was a hospital and prison, largely for prostitutes.

be free, but if a first functionary is needed people can cast their gaze in his direction and he can succeed Père Duchesne.

What a strange subjugation of the intelligence which, even in its powerful, foul-mouthed revolt against royalty, isn't yet able to completely free itself of the royal hypothesis.

But this was the people's first, confused glimpse of the Republic. Hébert's article laid out what was probably the boldest limit of popular thought at that time. It's almost a Republic and it is a democracy without any distinction between active and passive citizens; socially, it means laws against speculators, but with no new arrangement of property.

This quasi-republican exaltation declined after the king's return, and a calmer Père Duchesne would pay a fictional visit to Louis XVI at his Tuileries Palace to congratulate him for having accepted the Constitution and to warn him, in a half-confiding, half-scolding tone, to remain faithful this time. Hébert even allowed himself to be enthusiastic the day the Constitution was proclaimed in Paris. "The sound of the cannons resounded in my heart."

But despite it all, the people of 1792 continued to feel the strange sentiments of deliverance, of joy, and of worry that had gripped popular consciousness at the news of the king's flight. For a few days the people had scorned and insulted the disloyal, fleeing king. For a few days, the people had felt superior to the royalty they condemned, to the revolutionary bourgeoisie that hadn't taken a clear position against the king. All of this ennobled the proletarians; all of this prepared them to judge from above not only royalty, but also the bourgeois oligarchies that sought to exploit the Revolution. *Le Père Duchesne* was rough on the bourgeois hoarders in those first months of 1792 (no. 68):

I saw all our merchants, all our retailers, the grocers, the liquor sellers, the wine-makers, in a word, all the buggers who make it their jobs to steal from us and poison us, I saw all of them profit from the money shortage enriching themselves after having snatched all our *écus* and sold them to the émigrés. Afterwards they made all the coins disappear and now all that's left is paper money and *sols* are more rare than *double louis* once were. [...]

After dealing with the hoarders of *écus*, he went after the hoarders of foodstuffs (no. 83):

"Fuck! I'd hoped that after the abolition of the duties on goods brought into Paris I would be able to get a few extra bottles every day, but fuck no. Instead of being cheaper and better the wine is as expensive as in the past and poisons us the way it always did. I'd also thought that the prices of other things would go down, but grocer André and his confreres are as determined as ever to make us pay the same price for pepper as before. [...]

Fuck! So we've gained nothing with the doing away of the customs barriers? We're charged new taxes and we still pay the same duties on basic goods! Good God this can't be! Wherever there's an illness there's a remedy. New legislators, it's up to you to find it. It's your duty to do away with the new abuses. Hang every financier and all the damn merchants who speculate on the citizens' substance and grow fat on the blood of the unfortunate. Call the Lombards Section; they'll show you the secret.

You'll soon understand, goddamit, that there is an infamous conspiracy to reduce us to the last extremity this winter. [...]

And so the tone of popular protest rose. In these words, we already see prefigured the regime that the Terror applied to the economy. The Revolution didn't consider touching private property, of substituting communism for exchange and competition. It thus had no other resource for containing the bourgeoisie's speculation than striking the merchants with fear. *Le Père Duchesne* threatens them with hanging; the scaffold will soon follow.

It was in this way that the economic reasons for the Terror made their appearance.

Le Père Duchesne wasn't yet calling the people to insurrection or for a new revolution. He deplored the fact that the Constitution was a failure, that it wasn't inspired by a great democratic and popular spirit. And he provisionally resigned himself (no. 84):

> If the voice of the people of Paris hadn't been stifled we wouldn't have had a hastily cooked up Constitution, a veritable harlequin's costume where there are magnificent pieces stitched to rags. If the Constitution had simply been drawn from the Rights of Man it would one day have been the law of the universe. But what's done is done, and just because the horse has only one eye that's no reason to kill it.

As we can see, *Le Père Duchesne* accommodated itself to the sometimes precipitous, sometimes slow and uncertain movement of popular ideas. But soon the people, momentarily worn out by Marat's continuous state of exaltation, would again feel the need to hear that strident and passionate voice. On its own, *Le Père Duchesne* seemed insufficient and vulgar.

On April 4, 1792, the Cordelier Club addressed a petition to Marat asking him to return to the scene. The letter was signed by Hébert as president. *L'Ami du Peuple* reappeared on April 12 and now people made themselves heard with two voices, one cheeky, good-humored and often foul-mouthed; the other bitter, heartrending, vibrant with passion and thought, with delirious excesses, and prophetic tones.

The Position of the Jacobins

Robespierre didn't dare go so far as to completely deny the popular character of the movement, but after having briefly recognized it, he harped at length on the theme of a counter-revolutionary plot. Indeed, the Revolution was lost if, under the pretext of repressing hoarding, it allowed the people to take the road of pillage, or if it allowed the property system to be shaken before either society or people's minds had prepared a new one. "As I have always loved humanity," Robespierre said,

> ... and since I have never sought to flatter anyone, I am going to speak the truth. This is a plot hatched against the patriots. It is the intriguers

who want to destroy the patriots. There is a just feeling of indignation in the peoples' hearts. I maintained, surrounded by persecutors and without any support, that the people are never wrong. I dared proclaim this truth at a time when it was not yet recognized. The course of the Revolution demonstrated it.

The people have so often heard the law invoked by those who wanted to place them in the yoke that they mistrust such language.

The people are suffering. They have not yet harvested the fruits of their labors. They are still persecuted by the rich, and the rich are still what they always were, that is, harsh and pitiless (*Applause.*)

The people see the insolence of those who betrayed them; they see the fortunes accumulated in their hands; they feel their own poverty, but they do not feel the need to take the measures needed to arrive at their goal, and when we speak to them the language of reason they listen only to their indignation towards the rich, and they allow themselves to be led into false measures by those who usurp their confidence in order to mislead them.

There are two causes. The first is the people's natural disposition to seek the means of easing their poverty, a disposition natural and legitimate in itself. The people believe that lacking a protective law they have the right to protect their own needs.

There is another cause. That cause is the perfidious designs of the enemies of liberty, of the enemies of the people, thoroughly convinced that the only way to hand us over to foreign powers is to alarm the people about their staple goods and to make them the victims of the excesses that result from this. I have personally witnessed these acts. Alongside honest citizens we saw foreigners and the opulent garbed in the respectable attire of the sans-culottes. We have heard said: "We were promised abundance after the death of the king and we are unhappier since the poor king is no more." We have heard people declaim, not against the intriguers and counter-revolutionaries in the Convention who sit where the aristocrats of the Constituent Assembly sat, but against the Mountain, against the Paris deputation, and against the Jacobins, whom they described as hoarders.

I am not saying that the people are guilty. I am not saying that these actions are a crime. But when the people rise up, shouldn't they have a goal worthy of them? Is it puny merchandise that should concern them? They didn't even profit from this, for the sugar loaves were carried off by the valets of the aristocracy. But even if we suppose that they profited from an uprising, in exchange for this small advantage what are the drawbacks that might result from it? Our enemies want to frighten anyone who has any property. They want to convince them that our system of liberty and equality is subversive of any form of order, of all security. The people must rise up not to grab sugar, but to bring down the brigands.

The difficulty Robespierre found himself in was obvious: he didn't want to lose contact with the revolutionary energy of the people, even if it had gone off the rails; but he also didn't want to alarm the wealthy. He shied away from the question of staple goods.

The Jacobins so feared the results of the events of February 25,[8] the advantage the Feuillants and the Girondins could draw from them against the democrats throughout France, that they sent an address to the affiliated societies. There too, more clearly than Robespierre had done, they denounced the riot as a maneuver by the enemies of the Revolution. The question of staple goods had only been a pretext: "In order to cause an explosion a more-than-suspect orator delivered a petition at the bar of the National Convention whose style and inspiration revealed the true instigators of these proceedings." It was émigrés who had secretly returned, disguised royalists, and aristocrats who had incited and led the movement: "Our alarm was redoubled when, for the first time, we heard from our public galleries spectators who were either misled or planted respond to our pacific counsels by calling us speculators and hoarders." In the groups people shouted "Long Live Louis XVI," and the Jacobins went as far as to say that "the warehouses of the hoarders were respected; that the shops of patriots received preferential treatment." This isn't true. The report in the *Révolutions de Paris* affirms the contrary: "What is extraordinary,"

---

8   Date in 1793 when the people invaded the stores of Paris to take the goods they needed to survive (see below).

this newspaper wrote, "is that the smallest retail shop was treated like the biggest warehouse: no one, or almost no one, was spared." We can see from this that the warehouses weren't spared. But a note on the bottom of the page adds: "A few Jacobin grocers were respected." This is totally contrary to what was affirmed in the address. I don't believe that there was a decision to respect the Jacobin merchants, any more than there was a decision to attack them in particular. Depending on which events chance placed before him in a movement that was widespread and confused, every observer believed he'd gotten to the bottom of things. The truth is that the marching orders were "Against everyone, be they Jacobins or Feuillants: they're all merchants." This indifference to political differences among the mercantile class is precisely what characterizes the ideas of Jacques Roux.

The Jacobins were more accurate when they pointed out that the oldest quarters remained inactive. And this is a decisive confirmation of what I said above concerning the petit-bourgeois character of the February movement and the new party. The address says:

A remarkable circumstance is that those neighborhoods where the *civisme* is most ardent and the people less well-off and more numerous did not feel any effects. In the faubourg Saint-Marceau not a single merchant was troubled. Protestors leading women from the distant neighborhoods went to the faubourg Saint-Antoine in vain. They weren't able to lead along the good and vigorous citizens who live there. These are the people of Paris.

But the Jacobins drew the conclusion that elsewhere, in Gravilliers and the quarters of the center of the city, the movement was stirred up against the Revolution.

Hébert allied himself with the Jacobins in this campaign. His crude verve and impudent imagination served their tactics. He pushed the Jacobin explanation to the point of caricature. If we are to believe him, the events of February 25 were nothing but an aristocratic masquerade, a masked riot where the émigrés were disguised as sans-culottes. And it was, of course, the "Brissotins" who organized the whole spectacle. First, they "caused the bread to be stolen from the bakeries" in order to create panic and provide a pretext for crowds to gather:

That band of swindlers didn't grow discouraged and, reinforced by English guineas, it cooked up a new plot. Former marquises dressed as coalmen and wigmakers, countesses got up as poor wretches, the same ones who asked for grace the day Capet lost the taste for wine, scattered around the faubourgs and the markets squares to incite the people to revolt and brigandage. "Grab the shop owners," they said. "Force the grocers to give us sugar and soap at the price we want to pay. We've been suffering too long, we pay for everything in its weight in gold. It's time for this to end." [...]

I don't speak from love of the shopkeepers. I think that most of them are bad citizens and that they deserve what's happening to them. But it's for you, my sans-culotte friends, who are being led astray that I speak. Fuck! They want to divide you at a moment when you all should be brothers. They want you to devour each other when you should be marching on the enemy. Scare the hell out of the crowned brigands and their slaves. Once this task is done, go back home to destroy the traitors and soon you'll see abundance reborn. What would you say about an *Enragé* who would see his house in flames and who, instead of putting the fire out, would amuse himself by brawling with the first person he saw? Parisians, know your true enemies! The ones who do you the most harm are the Brissotins and the Rolandins.[9] Make them dance and, fuck! I'm sure that *ça ira* in the end.

This is a grotesque and degraded parody of the sublime tocsin sounded by Danton in moments of peril. It was also an attempt to remake the bloc of left revolutionaries in order to direct the impatience of a portion of the people against the Gironde and to push the economic question to the background of the Revolution. Believing Jacques Roux[10] had been brought

---

9   Supporters of Jean-Marie Roland (1734–93), leader of the moderate Gironde, a firm enemy of the Jacobins. Guillotined along with his wife, Manon.

10   Jacques Roux (1752–94)—along with Jacques Hébert the most important figure on the left of the Revolution. He was most notably the author of the central text of the sans-culotte movement, the *Manifesto of the Enragés*.

down, and also needing to attack him in order to justify the conduct of the Council of the Commune which hadn't assisted the movement, Hébert insisted in issue 220 [of *Le Père Duchesne*], "These are the same jerk-offs who, in order to prevent us from thinking about them, have retailers pillaged in their stores so as to cause famine and civil war."

And at greater length in issue 221:

While our armies in foreign lands were preparing to be attacked; while, fuck, all our generals had abandoned them and were strutting backstage at the Opera; while the Austrian columns were about to attack our soldiers, the rogues paid off by England pillaged the stores of Paris in order to incite disorder at a moment when we were busy recruiting for the army. Brave sans-culottes, do you have any doubts now that this was a plot to destroy you? Repent having fallen for this charade and swear to exterminate in the future all the jerk-offs who'll be foolish enough to lay such traps.

One might think that Jacques Roux, combated by all, disavowed by all, was done for, buried. Even the sections were abandoning him. At that moment, the provisional Commune, which had succeeded the revolutionary Commune of August 10, proceeded to its definitive establishment in accordance with the terms of municipal law. The delegates who had been designated by each section to be part of the General Council of the Commune and the municipal body were to be subject to a vote by all of the sections, which would admit or reject the proposed representatives. It appears that the nomination of the new Mayor Pache, proclaimed on February 14, decided the authorities to speed up this operation, which was dragging on. [...]

It is only on March 2 that the minutes of the Commune mention the results of the vote of the sections:

We have received the tallies from 45 sections for the admission or rejection of citizens who will form the General Council of the Commune. The Mont-Blanc and the Panthéon-Français Sections refused to submit their vote. Forty-six citizens, among them the priest Roux, were rejected.

The transcript names him alone, and the Commune wanted his rejection to be trumpeted. It should be observed that the majority of sections refused to sanction Gravilliers Section's choice Jacques Roux. The section didn't abandon him, or rather didn't have to pronounce against him, for municipal law quite naturally dictated "that the [first] three candidates chosen by an individual section will not be subject to the test [of an eliminatory vote]." But this raises a question: was Jacques Roux's elimination pronounced by the majority of sections before February 25 or after? Was it a general rejection of his policies or, more precisely, a rejection of the events of February 25 and the role he had played in them? A strict reading of the Directorate's decree makes it appear that the vote should have been completed the evening of the 23rd in all the sections, since the results were to have been brought to the *Hôtel de Ville* the next day, Sunday, February 24. But there were often delays in these operations. A vote that had to deal with 140 names, even without debate, even with people voting simply by sitting or standing, is quite a long one. And it is quite possible that the sections weren't able to finish on Saturday, February 23' and that they assembled again on the following days. If Jacques Roux had been eliminated the evening of the 23rd that would underline the importance of his role. It would, in fact, be demonstrated that even before the outburst of February 25, his propaganda against the merchant class worried the citizens of the sections throughout Paris. But it seems to me infinitely more probable that his exclusion was a result of the sugar and soap riot. I don't think that his semi-secret propaganda could, before the 25th, have spread far enough to compromise him throughout Paris. Moreover, the fact that it was only at the sitting of March 2 that the vote of the sections was discussed indicates that these sections continued to vote to confirm or remove from office until that date. Finally, the Pikes Section wouldn't have felt the need to communicate its anti-Jacques Roux views to the Council of the Commune on February 27 if he had been eliminated by the majority of the sections on February 23. On the contrary, it is quite probable that the wishes of the Pikes Section, known and expressed on February 27, succeeded in precipitating the rout of Jacques Roux in the sections.

Roux, hunted down everywhere, had to struggle to maintain a base of support at least in the Gravilliers quarter that had originally delegated him.

The course of a revolution is the result of these countless obscure struggles, barely suspected by the history books.

We find in the transcript of the Commune's sitting of March 19 in *Le Moniteur* of the March 24 that […] "The Temple and Gravilliers Sections have not yet sent their minutes, though they've been invited to do so three times."

These are the two sections over which Jacques Roux had the greatest influence. That of the Temple, neighboring Gravilliers, was in solidarity with it, and there is little doubt that the delegates from the Temple, who, like Jacques Roux, were expelled by the Gravilliers Section, must have been his partisans. Did the Gravilliers Section show signs of hesitation, some fear at compromising itself with Jacques Roux by not purely and simply re-electing him as several sections had done with their delegates? This re-election was obviously illegal since the vote in all the sections would have been a travesty if each section could delegate to the Council of the Commune those rejected in the general vote. But the Gravilliers Section probably wasn't held back by any concern for legality. I believe that the attitude of these two sections, Temple and Gravilliers, responded to the priest's prudent and wise policy: what's the use of wearing yourself out in a conflict against the Commune, one that is undignified and a dead end? On March 19, the Commune decided that "The municipal body considers that the re-election of members rejected by the majority of sections was an offense against the rights of these same sections." It was much better for the Temple and Gravilliers Sections to demonstrate through an extended abstention that, wounded by the vote that excluded Jacques Roux, they had no interest in the life of the Commune and formed an independent force capable of retreating into itself. This is precisely what these sections initially did. And then, working together in a way that demonstrates the inspiration of a single will, they named new commissioners.

The storms of revolution and civil war rumbled ever louder in March and April. What difference did it make to Jacques Roux that he was no longer officially a delegate to the Commune? He wasn't lacking in means of action. What was essential to him was maintaining the sympathy and confidence of the Gravilliers Section, and it seems that this never wavered. When Jacques Roux would speak at the Convention and put forth his program it would be as "orator of the Gravilliers deputation" as well as that of Bonne-Nouvelle. These central sections thus remained the unshakeable fortress of Jacques Roux and the new party that Hébert and Marat already called the *Enragés*.

Jacques Roux was far from being defeated on February 25 for, despite the deafening anathema of most of the advanced revolutionary forces, his ideas had suddenly made great progress: they were now on the Revolution's agenda. The ideas of legally regulating exchange and countering the economic power of wealth in and by the Revolution were now asserted everywhere.

In the face of the all-enveloping agitation only Condorcet's newspaper, the *Chronique de Paris*, continued to support absolute commercial freedom. According to him there is no artificial method for preventing the rise in prices [...]; the remedy is a corresponding and proportionate rise in all prices, the price of labor as well as that of material. [...]

This is all fine when all is going well. But the economist forgets one important thing: that this operation supposes both space and time. Space is needed so that, if necessary, the nation can issue a call for foodstuffs, material, and products, for if there is a category of products whose supply is too limited those who monopolize it can raise their prices to such a degree that society cannot raise all prices to a corresponding level. And time is needed as well, for it is not with the snap of a finger, it is not by a kind of instantaneous reflex, that the worker's salary can be accommodated to abrupt variations in prices.

But the Revolution had at its disposal neither space nor time. Through nearly universal war, and especially because of the enormous discredit of the *assignats* outside of France, it became increasingly impossible for it to purchase on the foreign market: economically, France was on the point of being a nation besieged. Materials and foodstuffs, limited to what the country itself produced, could thus easily be hoarded. This was made even easier because once the amount of purchasable materials became limited, the means of purchase which the upper classes disposed of increased and even became super-abundant. The enormous quantity of *assignats*, issued for reimbursement of the debt and for offices of all kinds, when added to the cash already on hand, placed an immediate, insatiable, and avaricious purchasing power in the hands of the capitalist bourgeoisie. In this sense, the legal and democratic arrangement that allowed those who acquired national lands to pay them off in twelve annuities left the capitalists with an enormous amount of money, both metallic and paper. Saint-Just pushed things a little far when he later wrote (April 1794) in a retrospective review of the Revolution:

The many annuities allowed the purchasers the time to speculate on public staple goods using the value of their property. And this policy of annuities which, at first glance, seemed to facilitate sales, was relatively mortal to the French economy and to prosperity. In fact, the owner of a large amount of paper money settled a first annuity and paid 5 percent for the others, and these funds, used to monopolize foodstuffs, produced for him a profit of 100 percent. The state thus earned 5 percent on the annuities and the people lost 100 percent through the villainy of the factions. This option of twelve annuities was not for the poor citizens, who didn't purchase property. It was for the rich, in whose hands the funds were left that fed speculation.

Yet again Saint-Just exaggerates. He distorts the intentions of those who adopted this system, and he underestimates the immense service it rendered to the many small-scale purchasers. But it is true that the means of purchase, accumulated and immobilized in the hands of the rich, were used for purchasing all the available food and material in a fashion that could be called frantic. From this flowed an impressive increase in activity, but one that was disordered and harsh. With this enormous power of acquisition operating in a closed market that could not renew itself by the influx of foreign materials, France was like a basin into which no water is poured but whose contents are sucked out by suction pumps of prodigious power.

In the long run, an equilibrium would no doubt have been established between the higher price of food and material, and the price of labor. In the long run, too, the producers would have adapted to the new state of affairs and have taken on only those enterprises for which they could supply themselves with primary material, thus allowing the big merchant monopolists to become big industrial monopolists. But the Revolution was a crisis hemmed in in both time and space. It was necessary that in two or three years it either emerge victorious or disappear. And yet, during these two or three decisive, tragic years, which bore the destiny of the world on their narrow base, equilibrium could not be found.

12

The Revolution of May 31 and June 2, 1793

(After a series of military defeats in Belgium and the treason of the defeated general, Dumouriez, who had been defended by the Girondins and who called the Convention "a bunch of imbeciles led by wretches [and] declared that it is time to be done with anarchy and re-establish the former constitution, that of 1791, that is, a tempered monarchy," as well as the Gironde's bringing of Marat up on charges of provoking the violation of the national representation for his attacks on the Girondins, "the revolutionary investing of the Gironde had begun. In this struggle it was the Mountain that had to win, for it had on its side not only the active forces of Paris, but because it alone acted vigorously in line with the Revolution and the Fatherland."

The events that will occur between May 31 and June 2, 1793, the open and physical attack on the Gironde, can only be understood if we see that the Mountain "had reached the disastrous conclusion that their enemies were traitors, either for the benefit of the royalists or the Duc d'Orléans. In any case, they were no longer in agreement as to how to defend the threatened Revolution, as a result of which there no longer existed between them the necessary bond without which legality is nothing but an empty word."

Not only the Mountain and Marat, but the revolutionary sections also attacked the Girondin leaders and had an address read at the Convention on April 15, 1793 that accused 21 Girondin leaders of "violating the people's faith." In doing this, the General Assembly of the sections "took a singularly bold initiative, which obliged it to carry things to the bitter end."

The Girondins attempted a riposte in the sections, at the end of April calling moderates to their support, but this would be in vain, for "it was Hébert, it was Père Duchesne who, in these days of direct combat ... was the interpreter of the people's passion." The revolutionary forces were united and determined, having "long since taken control of the mechanism of the sections; they'd occupied all the influential posts," while "the forces of modérantisme *lacked unity and were incapable of acting as a unit." Nevertheless, aware of the dangers confronting them in May 1793, the Gironde counter-attacked, condemning the sans-culottes and the sections and arresting Hébert and Varlet, their leaders. As Jaurès said, "One could say that the Gironde wanted a fight, and that it had to be to the bitter end." It all but provoked the left by forming the Commission of Twelve "charged with examining the political situation and seeking out all the plots that threatened liberty and the law," a Commission made up largely of Girondins, and entirely of enemies of the Mountain.*

On May 26, the meeting at the Jacobin Club was a stormy one, where the "unmasking" of the Girondins and the shutting-down of the Commission of Twelve was called for. On May 28, Hébert, released from prison, spoke at a meeting of the Paris Commune, where he received a crown of laurels, which he then placed on the head of a bust of Rousseau. "A female citizen in the audience brought out another crown and placed it on Brutus' [bust's] head.")

While the Commune crowned Jean-Jacques Rousseau and Brutus, the most active revolutionaries of the sections understood that the hour of the final conflict had arrived. Already, on May 28, the battalions of the moderate sections had mobilized and promised their assistance to the Convention, that is, the Gironde.

Could this aggressive return of *moderantisme* be smashed with words or even by vigorous Montagnard resistance within the Convention? Would the Commission of Twelve be given the time to recover from the alert of May 27 and prepare its revenge? The Cité Section, which had resisted the Convention's order to hand over its minutes, and whose president, Dobsen, had been arrested, issued a summons to all the sections for the next day, May 29, in order to organize the insurrection.

The Role of the Committee of Public Safety

In the meanwhile, at the Convention, on that same May 29, the Committee of Public Safety, inspired by Barère[1] and Danton, made a final attempt at delay and reconciliation.

---

1 Bertrand Barère (1755–1841)—deputy of the Plain and member of the Committee of Public Safety.

On the previous day, as if it wanted to attenuate the harmful rifts that were about to open throughout France, the Convention had sent through Robert Lindet a pacifying and sagacious circular to the representatives on mission: "We must not resemble the generals and ministers of the monarchy who, in hard times, imputed to each other both the errors of individuals and the common misfortunes. Citizens, it is in difficult circumstances that we must stand together. May events never alter out unity."

Barère, who thought he had calmed and forestalled any difficulties by proposing the Commission of Twelve, an idea which had turned out badly, read a long, well-balanced and totally useless report in which he spoke of every faction, weighing the services and faults of them all, inviting them to mutual tolerance and concord. What was the use, though, when war thundered on all sides?

Danton, on the previous day, had unleashed his fury against the aggressive revival of the Gironde, which had re-established the Commission of Twelve, exclaiming: "If the Committee preserves the tyrannical power it exercised and which I know it wanted to extend over the members of this assembly, then, after having proved that we surpass our enemies in prudence and wisdom, we will surpass them in boldness and revolutionary vigor"; he tarried over this desperate attempt at rapprochement.

M. Bornarel has noted (and this remark constitutes a discovery) that Danton, who almost never wrote, had in this instance collaborated in Barère's report and had inserted into it the most pressing and eloquent appeals for unity and peace. The testimony of the *Républicain, journal des hommes libres de tous les pays*, in its May 30, 1793 issue, is decisive in this matter:

Barère then presented the report of the Committee of Public Safety on our internal and external situation. It is too extensive for a rapid analysis to be able to satisfy our readers. We want them to dispose of it in full. But we will nevertheless say today that we owe the so-often slandered Danton, who is frequently depicted in the most horrific colors, the paragraph where the Commission makes known the need for a republican Constitution; the establishing of primary schools; the strengthening of property; the return to order; the rule of law and morality; and above all the stifling of those passions that divide the representatives of one people and which do nothing but turn the palace of unity into the palace of discord.

Cambon's[2] testimony [...] confirms that of the *Républicain*. It is Ducos who, in the *Chronique de Paris* of May 31 points this out in these terms: "Applause greeted a passage read by Barère: 'What you just heard,' exclaimed Cambon, 'was nevertheless written by a man who has been slandered, by Danton.'"

Barère, who attacks Danton in his *Memoires*, appears to have forgotten this collaboration, but it is none the less certain that it occurred. Danton, with the showiness that was at times joined to the vigor of his eloquence, declaimed:

Upon entering this building where the assembly sits, both the foreigner and the citizen are struck by the sublime inscription which is in itself a constitution; it contains all of our duties, revives the hope that animates us, exalts the courage that you must bring to your labors, and makes the tyrants of Europe grow pale with fear. The word "Unity" that is inscribed over the gate of the national palace should be seen by all the *départements* and engraved in the hearts of their deputies.

The unity of 25 million men, the unity of so many wills renders you invincible. [...]

There is a sadness about all this rhetoric about unity. The time for it had passed and demoralization had already set in. No words could now heal sickened hearts. Danton felt defeat approaching; he had been vanquished because he had been unable to maintain unity. His broad revolutionary ideas had been smashed and mutilated by the brutality of passions and events. Yet he nevertheless maintained contact with the revolutionary forces while continuing to pursue this chimerical attempt at reconciliation, going so far as to join with the Plain[3] and collaborate with its leader.

---

2   Pierre-Joseph Cambon (1756–1820)—member of the Convention and president of the Finance Committee, he played a key role in the confiscation of Church property and spread of the *assignats*. He was an important actor in the downfall of Robespierre.

3   The moderates of the Revolution, who sat between the Gironde on the right and the Mountain on the left of the Convention.

It is difficult to know precisely what transpired in the discussions held at Charenton, where Robespierre, Danton, and Marat exchanged views.

The Girondin Dulaure, in his *Historical Sketches of the Events of the French Revolution* provides an unlikely account of them. [...] According to Dulaure it was at these meetings that the entire plan that would unfurl in May was decided upon, notably the gathering of the delegates of the Sections at the Bishop's Palace on May 15. But how can the least credit be granted a historian who reports that Pache, Robespierre, Danton, and Marat deliberated over the restoration of the Bourbons?

Garat also speaks, though more vaguely, of these meetings in Charenton:

On that same day [that is, May 30], or one of the previous or following days (I'm not certain of the date), the leader of the first division of the interior, Champagneux, brought me a large number of copies of a placard in which Robespierre, Marat, Danton, Chaumette and Pache, who was called the "Political Escobar," were accused of holding nocturnal meetings in Charenton where, protected by an imposing armed force, they deliberated over the means of organizing new September massacres. [...]

What is certain is that if Pache, Robespierre, and Danton deliberated it was, on the contrary, in order to find a way to resolve the crisis without bloodshed or doing harm to the Convention. Even on May 29, Danton had not yet totally renounced that hope, and Robespierre only renounced it on May 29, when the Convention committed the error of re-establishing the Commission of Twelve and when the Cité Section began to set the revolutionary forces in motion.

Robespierre's Call to Insurrection

At the Jacobin Club on the evening of May 29, Robespierre publicly admitted the impotence of the legal methods he had stuck to until then. He invited the Paris Commune, which was again fearful about the aggressive revival of the Gironde and the Twelve, to resistance:

If the Paris Commune, to which the defense of the interests of this great city is confided, does not raise a cry to the whole universe against the persecution directed against liberty by the most vile conspirators; if the Paris Commune does not unite with the people, does not form a close alliance with them, then it is violating its primary duty and it no longer deserves the reputation for siding with the people which it has maintained until today. In these latest moments of crisis the municipality must resist oppression by demanding the rights of justice against the persecution of patriots.

When it is obvious that the Fatherland is threatened with the most pressing danger, the duty of the people's representatives is to die for liberty and to see that it triumphs.

Robespierre was expressing support, in advance, of the revolutionary action of the Commune, and he all but called on it to take over the leadership of the movement. Perhaps he wasn't frightened of the anarchic deluge that might result from the unorganized initiative of the sections and the *Enragés*. And he then added, with a melancholy laced with threats:

I am unable to prescribe to the people the means for saving themselves. This is not something given to one man. It wasn't given to me, who am exhausted by four years of revolution and by the heart-rending spectacle of the triumph of tyranny and all that is basest and most corrupt. It's not up to me to point out these measures, I who am consumed by a slow fever and above all by the fever of patriotism. I have spoken, and I have no other duties to fulfill at this time.

To those who with nearly superstitious confidence expected him to cut the Gordian knot, Robespierre responded: I can no longer solve the problem; this is beyond the strength of one man. Only the collective action of the people can put an end to this crisis.

Coming from a Jacobin Club that had long been bound by legality, this was finally an open call, or at least the official consent to, insurrection. Robespierre's words were fully understood, for the emotion at the Jacobins was great and a tumult arose, the passionate prelude to action on the streets.

Billaud-Varenne, as if to clarify Robespierre's ideas and to take them to their logical conclusion, recalled the daily worsening misfortunes that were befalling the Fatherland and freedom, in particular Custine's[4] defeats and the progress of the rebellion in the Vendée, and he concluded by denouncing the futile policy of the Committee of Public Safety: "Unity was mentioned in Barère's report, as if it were possible for virtue to join forces with crime. There were thirty ringleaders who had devised the plan of the conspiracy." And he proposed measures of public safety.

Even before Robespierre spoke and with his usual formal prudence committed himself completely, the Maratist current showed itself to be stronger than the Dantonist one at the Jacobins. Legendre, Danton's friend, having proposed the dispatching of a quite benign circular to the French people, was called a "beguiler." Bentabole had replied to him by bitterly attacking Barère's report, which the Jacobins knew full well Danton had collaborated on. "It's not very likely," Bentabole said, "that the Jacobins will go along with Barère's report. He said good things and this deputy has rendered many good services, but at heart he's a moderate."

Bentabole had been applauded, and Robespierre, with his acute understanding of the moral crises that were overwhelming the people, understood that the legalistic Jacobin Club was going to take the revolutionary path without him. He went along with this new policy in order not to break with the central force of the Revolution, in order to both strengthen and organize the movement.

But it was the delegates of the revolutionary sections who would take the measures of public safety proposed by Billaud-Varenne. The Cité Section had originally summoned the delegates for 4:00 p.m. on May 29 at Notre Dame. But it thought that it would be better to meet in a more private place in order to deliberate in complete confidentiality, so the delegates gathered at the Bishop's Palace, where the secret revolutionary committee called the Commission of Six had been meeting since May 28. There were two sittings on May 29, one at four o'clock and the other in the evening, and the insurrectionary delegates deliberated at the same moment that at the Jacobin Club Robespierre agreed to the insurrection.

---

4   Adam Philippe de Custine (1742–93)—revolutionary general; after a series of defeats, he was considered suspect and guillotined.

In these insurrectionary sittings at the Bishop's Palace on May 29 there were, so to speak, two levels of deliberations. On the first level, there was a relatively public meeting, where the delegates of the sections and the electors of August 10 discussed the events of the day and the decisions to be taken, in quite a moderate tone. But on the second level, and in a darkness propitious for the preparation of a *coup de main*, a small number of Commissioners from the sections who were tacitly invested with an executive mandate decided on the means of action. It appears that the Commission of Twelve, at least if we are to judge by the notes left by one of its members, the Girondin Bergoeing, was notified by its police only of the less critical of the deliberations. It seems not to have known of the constituting of an executive committee. The note given to the Commission of Twelve concerning the afternoon's sitting hardly makes clear a plan of action. [...] However, there was another sitting in the evening, and at that one the action plan was clearly laid out. [...]

The object addressed by most of the orators was a swift general uprising and extensive measures in Paris.

One of the methods proposed by a member, who said he was from the Théatre-Français Section, was to disarm all the rich, the aristocrats, the Feuillants, and the moderates, which he said had been accomplished with great ease in that section and one other. "We assembled," he said,

> ... a few canoneers and we told them that the Convention had promised to arm them. That that body had done nothing about this, and that they had only to pay a fraternal visit to the homes of those mentioned above to take their rifles from them until the time comes when we can take their *assignats* and *écus* from them.

(This individual remark, which has an air of authenticity, certainly didn't express the general spirit of the delegates.)

Another general measure proposed by Dufourny,[5] still in the name of the Commission of Six, was to commit all the sections to deliver an address

---

5   Louis-Pierre Dufourny (1739–96)—in the lead up to the Revolution, Dufourny had published a *Cahiers* in defense of day laborers and the poor. A member of the Jacobins, he was considered a Dantonist, but escaped their fate.

at the Convention asking it to punish Isnard's crime against Paris,[6] so that having once set all Parisians in motion they could be led to the same goal.

What is more, people have spoken of delivering harsh blows, and we have always counted the right side of the Convention and the Commission of Twelve among the most dangerous enemies of the Fatherland. In any case, it all comes down to this: organizing an insurrection similar to those of July 14 and August 10 and the immediate execution of this measure. In order to do this, the assembly was adjourned until tomorrow at 9:00 a.m., from which time it shall be permanently in session.

What can be seen in this key communication made to the Commission of Twelve is that everything was in place for the insurrection by May 29. The plan for it had been devised, since Dufourny silenced those imprudent individuals who might have divulged it. It had its executive organ, for the Commission of Six spoke to the delegates as a sovereign and Dufourny warned them that if they deliberated too long they would miss the party. We can thus see that the Executive Commission was assured of being followed by the sections as the instant it gave the signal to begin, and that it was resolved not to hesitate before any obstacles or objections that even the delegations of the sections, preoccupied perhaps with their responsibilities, might oppose to them. At the same time that the Commission of Six determined to set things in motion through the energetic initiative of a tiny minority, it busied itself with widening the spontaneously created movement, with bringing along and compromising all of Paris. To that effect, Isnard's speech, which had wounded and alarmed all Parisians, the wealthy as well as the sans-culottes, was invaluable. Contra Isnard, it would have been simple to raise up all of Paris, and once risen up Paris could be led to march against the Gironde. When Blanqui, who so passionately studied all the revolutionary forces of 1793 said, "A movement isn't created, it's diverted," he formulated the tactic of leadership and revolutionary substitution that Dufourny recommended at the meeting at the Bishop's Palace.

---

6   Isnard, as president of the Convention, had responded on May 25, 1793 to a deputation denouncing Hébert's arrest by saying that if uprisings continued "Paris will be obliterated."

But in order to lead along all of Paris, to combine in one movement the proletarians and the bourgeois, the sans-culottes and the merchants, Paris had to be reassured about property, and this is why I noted a short time ago that the sharp remark made at the Bishop's Palace about the rich, from whom first their arms would be taken and then their *"écus* and their *assignats"* was nothing but a quip. From May 29 on, reassuring property-owners was one of the most important and pressing concerns of the revolutionaries of the Bishop's Palace, which is proved by what Hassenfratz would say the next day at the Jacobins:

> The Cité Section invited the 47 other Sections to send its commissioners to meet with it in order to deliberate concerning the means of ensuring public safety. The meeting took place yesterday. The first deliberation had as its object calming the fears of property-owners. To that effect, the section decreed that all property is under the safeguard of the sans-culottes, who promise to hand over to the sword of justice whoever makes the least attack on property, and all the members of the Section have sworn to die ensuring the observation of this law.

Obviously, the idea of the Cité Section, the most ardent of all of them, the one that had taken the initiative of the convocation, was shared by all the sections.

The May 31 Sitting of the National Convention

At the Convention as well, the Mountain, particularly the Robespierrist Mountain, was determined to succeed. Its salvation, as much as the salvation of the Revolution, made this imperative. It had to either vanquish or perish. If the Gironde emerged victorious after these days of crisis, it would certainly carry out harsh reprisals. Levasseur states quite clearly in his memoirs that the Montagnards were forced to strike if they weren't themselves to succumb [...]

The Montagnards, at the sitting of May 31, were in a difficult situation. The insurrectionary plan that was aimed to rid them of their adversaries was sufficiently advanced to compromise the Mountain, but it wasn't yet vigorous enough to destroy the Gironde.

The forces from the sections that began to gather at the Carrousel were divided and hesitant. Only those in the galleries were passionately devoted to the Mountain, and what could they have done against a resolutely violent attitude on the part of the Convention? The latter was hardly moved when Pache[7] calmly announced to it the dismissal of the municipality and its revolutionary re-establishment. He didn't disavow the Bishop's Palace, saying, "We have gratefully assented." In so doing, he legalized the revolution: he communicated with the National Convention, not by virtue of the powers he held by law, but by virtue of the mandate he held through the insurrectionary sovereignty of the people, expressed by the delegates of the sections. He was admitted to the honors of the sitting. The Gironde doubtlessly saw an ultimate safeguard in the man it had so often slandered and who seemed to be called upon to play a calming role.

The news that Hanriot wanted to fire the alarm cannon caused a storm. The commandant of the armed force of the Pont-Neuf Section notified the Convention

…that Hanriot, provisional commandant of the Paris National Guard, having given the order to fire the alarm cannon, and the guard at the Pont-Neuf post having refused to do so, he had referred the matter to the departmental government, which passed to the order of the day, motivated by the law that prohibits firing the alarm cannon without a decree from the Convention.

He awaited the orders of the Convention and asked to be permitted to speak.

The Girondins were indignant. What does this Hanriot want? What is this impertinent man, this seditionist preparing? Let him be summoned to explain himself. Mathieu and Valazé flew into a violent rage. They were supported by the petitioners of the Pont-Neuf, who repeated that the departmental government reminded everyone that the law prohibits the

---

7 Jean-Nicolas Pache (1746–1823)—Girondin politician; minister of war in the first Girondin government, formed by Roland.

firing of the alarm cannon. Vergniaud seemed primarily concerned with preventing the conflict from worsening. "If there is combat," he exclaimed, "whatever its success, it will mean the destruction of the Republic." But he, too, wanted to know who sounded the tocsin, who ordered the firing of the alarm cannon. And in fact, it had just sounded, and the Mountain worriedly wondered how it would maneuver. If it disavowed Hanriot, if it summoned him, if it turned him over, it would disorganize the popular movement, which it needed; it would cause confusion and doubt in the ranks of the patriots; and it would give the Gironde an advantage that would easily grow in a confused and bewildered Paris. If, on the contrary, it backed Hanriot, if it took the side of the man who fired the alarm cannon despite the contrary order given that morning by the Commune, despite the unfavorable opinion of the *département*, it risked being dragged into positions more extreme than those of Pache, Hébert, Chaumette, and Lullier: it would merge with the *Enragés*, and fall into the hands of Varlet[8] and the violent militants. In order not to undermine the Revolution through weakness, it exposed itself to undermining it through overreach and foolhardiness; it risked unleashing panic and raising up the *départements* against it.

Only one man could pull the Mountain out of its difficulties. One man could, by his thundering speech, echo the alarm cannon, and advocate for the insurrection and the Revolution before the Convention, while at the same time turning the emerging movement from the ultra-revolutionary direction that the Bishop's Palace wanted it to take: Danton. He who for several weeks had hesitated and lost his intensity, in the heat of this crisis found again his impetuous and subtle boldness. And by appeasing it, he amplified the revolutionary voice of the alarm cannon resounding over a Convention either comforted or invigorated. First, we must be rid of the Commission of Twelve: "Paris must do away with the Commission. It doesn't exist in the same way as the Convention. The Commission you created is inopportune." […]

He concluded by demanding that the suppression of the Commission of Twelve be put to a voice vote. This was a brilliant stroke of authority and political wisdom. Interpreting the alarm cannon in this way deprived the

---

8   Jean-François Varlet (1764–1837)—*Enragé* leader and publicist.

Gironde of a pretext for summoning Hanriot and entering into conflict with the revolutionary Commune. It was as if the tranquil and legal force of the people had borrowed a thunderous voice in order to be heard by the legislators. The *Patriote Français* said (and it should be said in passing, these few words again confirm Danton's collaboration with Barére), "The so-often slandered Danton, who had written so touching a paragraph on unity in Barère's report, Danton spoke with the fury of a man tugging the cord of the tocsin."

No, it wasn't fury. It was the noble rage of a man who had tried everything to avoid a terrible crisis; who had run up against the blind selfishness of the factions and who ran up against it yet again when he tried to moderate events that he couldn't prevent. How could a man of as generous and proud a character as the young Girey-Dupré, editor of the *Patriote*, so badly underestimate the great revolutionary? Girey-Dupré, writing about the sitting, said with calm dignity and a serene courage:

Immortal glory to the representatives of the people who didn't despair of the Republic and who, ready to die, went to their posts to the funereal sound of the tocsin, to the gloomy rumbling of the alarm drum. I want to imitate their courage; I want to share their fate in everything. And may I also share their glory. I owe it to the French people; I owe it to my conscience and my character, my character whose independence the tocsin, the general alert, and the cannon cannot change; I owe it to posterity, whose more august tribunal, more fearsome than all the revolutionary tribunals, will judge both me and my enemies; I owe it to the free men of the entire earth to bluntly and dispassionately speak the truth. In times of great danger the republican soul rises above petty hatreds and vulgar fears.

Alas, by what misunderstanding did this republican soul, upright and young, enthusiastic and good, which soared above petty hatreds, by what blindness did he not recognize in Danton's great soul the same native generosity and the same detachment from narrow passions? Danton did not sound a murderous tocsin against the threatened Girondins. As far as was in his power, he limited the effects of the people's anger. First, it must be noted that it was not the 22 men denounced by the sections that he wanted to have judged, it was only the members of the Commission of Twelve. In doing so (and this hasn't been sufficiently noted) he placed the leaders of the Gironde, its most illustrious chiefs, Brissot, Vergniaud, and Guadet, outside the debate. Even more, he could hope that after the political suppression of the Twelve, the people, disarmed of their hatred, would no longer surrender themselves to individual revenge. Finally, it wasn't the trial of a party, the trial of a tendency that was initiated against the Gironde. It was because of specific acts imputable to the Twelve that the members of the latter would be interrogated, judged and, if necessary, sentenced. Yet it was only the eminent men of the Commission of Twelve, Douze, Boyer-Fonfrède and Rabaut-Saint-Étienne who, won over by Garat's influence, had taken sides against the violent measures, against Hébert's arrest. Would it then be the turn of unknown associates to be attacked?

But this was a chimera. How could it be hoped that the people would exclude the best-known and responsible chiefs, those they had learned to detest the most, those who had played the weightiest role in events? What would become of the Revolution if the Girondin faction, surviving the Commission of Twelve, continued its labor of denigration and paralysis? Danton's repugnance at striking the Gironde was almost invincible, and there was a barely perceptible trembling in the hand that "tugged the cord of the tocsin." How many precautions he takes against the possible violence of the *Enragés*! And he announces that as soon as the Commission of Twelve is dissolved the Bishop's Palace must "cease to exist." [...]

The Disappointment of the *Enragés*; Their Actions at the Commune

A mixture of disappointment and fervor was felt by the most vehement revolutionaries of the Bishop's Palace and the Commune. No, the decisive blow hasn't been dealt, but we will begin anew, and this time we won't listen to the advice of the timid. At the sitting of the Commune, even before the Convention broke up and it began to look as if the movement had only partially succeeded, recriminations flew. Why was the municipality so hesitant and weak?

A citizen mounts the tribune and proposes taking the swiftest and surest measures, saying that time, which should only be used for action, shouldn't be consumed by long speeches [this was said for Chaumette's benefit]. The procurator of the Commune, while applauding the zeal and patriotism of the orator, observed that prudence must be joined to the grandeur of measures; that the aristocrats could ask for nothing better than to see the citizens of Paris led in the opposite direction, acting riotously without knowing where they're going or which way they're inclined.

The speaker insists on the measures he proposed and accuses the procurator of the Commune of weakness and offers to preside over the Council and lead the revolutionary operation.

Whatever the boldness, boldness in action or boldness in vanity, of the unknown orator, for such a proposal to have been made the revolutionary credibility of the official leaders of the Commune had to have been badly harmed by the more or less unmistakable failure of the day:

The deputy procurator of the Commune [probably Hébert] takes the floor and, speaking in the same sense as Chaumette, he invited the citizens to return to their sections and to frankly lay out the reasons behind the failure of that great *journée*. He condemned the impetuosity of the people who devised the plan; he thinks it will be time to carry out tomorrow what was proposed to be executed today.

The Commune, harshly attacked, denied any responsibility. It accused the Bishop's Palace of having acted too hastily, that is, of having sounded the tocsin and the alarm cannon before being certain that the vast echo of the sections would respond. Hébert committed himself and the Commune for the next day. "No, right away," shouted the impatient ones who didn't see that it was every bit as impossible to restore that declining day to the highest revolutionary height as it is to return the setting sun to its zenith:

"A citizen, to whom these measures appeared pusillanimous, offers to place himself at the head of the Parisian battalions and to go to the Convention." The Commune rebelled at the brutality of the plan:

> The General Council expresses its indignation and horror at such a proposal. The citizen who is its author is invited to go to the office and to declare his name, his position, and his profession. He responds to the various interpellations and requests that he be heard until he has completed his motion. He insists that he had no other intention than that of arresting the suspect members of the Convention in order to hand them over to their *département* so justice can be done. The Council, attributing the speech to the ignorance and lack of experience of the speaker believes there is no need to follow up on this affair.

But what could the follow-up have been? And how could it have punished a man who did nothing but make the insurrection's true goal clear?

> The mayor takes the floor. He makes it known that the people of Paris are capable of distinguishing between its true friends and the fanatics and imbeciles who seek to lead them astray and involve them in wrong-headed actions. He proves that the measures that the previous speaker just proposed would forever split Paris from the *départements* and would lead to civil war.

What game was the Commune playing? And where did this sudden severity towards a plan that the mayor had already submitted to the Convention in April in the name of the sections come from? Did it think that the game was lost and that the prudent thing to do was to remain silent? Or was it that, if the people went to the Convention and imposed the arrest of the already-denounced Girondins, it wanted the movement to be spontaneous and to emanate directly from the people? But experience had just demonstrated that without a vigorous push and a sure and centralized leadership the people would not march, and the Revolution, like a squeaky and discordant chariot, would get stuck in a rut.

But the more the Council of the Commune hesitated, the more the men of action pressured it. It tried to appease them by publishing vague and dilatory revolutionary measures that didn't respond to the immediate needs of the crisis. What difference did it make that it decreed that tomorrow, "during the day, all suspect citizens shall be disarmed and their weapons turned over to those patriots who have none," if these patriots aren't invited to use them, if they can't wrest from the Convention even through threats, the bringing to justice of the traitors? What difference did it make that the Council decided "… that the forced loan shall be applied in conformity with the method previously indicated by the Commune; that the products of this loan shall be employed to assist the widows, fathers, mothers, wives, and children of those citizen soldiers who serve the fatherland in our armies, as well as for the manufacture of arms and the wages of the citizens who will form the salaried revolutionary guard of Paris"?

Yes, what difference did all this make? The proposals were the lies of a dilatory philanthropy evading its present duties, evading its revolutionary duties. The Commune, flapping around in the void, fooled no one and discredited itself. It was at precisely that moment that Jacques Roux chose to make his reappearance with the draft of a new address to the Convention, one that was without any shadow of a doubt of a socio-political nature, one where the question of the right to live would again be posed.

The stubborn priest unquestionably savored the humiliation and embarrassment of the impotent Commune. He felt a prideful and bitter joy at repeating his formulas in front of his weakened and debased enemy of yesterday, intoning them in much the same way he'd have recited bitter litanies tasting of death at the bedside of a dying man. And the attack on the official Commune was redoubled:

A young citizen climbs to the tribune and proposes the most violent measures. The Council invites the imprudent young man to withdraw. He continues speaking. But finally, ceding to the remarks of the former president Dobsen, and repelled by the indignation manifested against him by the Council, he withdraws from the tribune.

In the meanwhile, the delegates of the neighboring Communes of Bercy, Sèvres, Drancy, and Bourget vowed to ally themselves with the Parisian movement. But which movement, if Paris remained dormant? And so the decisive motions were repeated. "A member requests that the members of the Convention denounced to public opinion be arrested." If this wasn't the program of the "day" then what did it mean? And how could the Council of the Commune disavow what, just a short while before, Lullier and Robespierre had requested in the name of the established authorities of Paris and the *département*? But Chaumette had lost control: "The procurator of the Commune rises up with indignation against this proposal presented for the third time. He says that if anyone tries to repeat it again he will denounce him to these very people who applaud without realizing they are applauding their own ruin."

Is the Commune going to throw itself between the Revolution and the Gironde? Will it cover for the latter? For a moment this seemed to be the case, so thoroughly did it seem to be bending under the weight of this *journée*, whose futility was overwhelming: "A member proposes to post at the door of the hall the formal disapprobation of any option tending to violate the national representation." Thus the 22 Girondins were placed under the protection of the Commune, which was frightened by the direction it was heading and evaded the decisive motion: "It is observed that this disapprobation is in people's hearts; that the citizens and the established authorities of Paris are too aware of their obligations to need to be told what they were."

This was not one of the Commune's shining moments, but rather one where it demonstrated nothing but weakness, false agitation, systematic impotence, and hypocrisy. But it's impossible not to feel that it was going to be overwhelmed, swept away.

Vergniaud's maneuver congratulating the sections had initially caused surprise. When the commissioners of the Commune charged with corresponding with the National Convention wrote to the Council that afternoon, they said: "We are doing this on Vergniaud's proposal, which will perhaps surprise you." And perhaps this contributed to the General Council of the Commune's yielding the way it did. But upon reflection, the revolutionaries of action understood the advantage they could gain from this. The glorifying of the sections and the applauding of popular force constituted, in suspect form, the capitulation of the Gironde. The enemy was frightened and had to be pushed as hard as possible. Levasseur, whose impressions were so acute, assures us that this was a triumph for the Mountain:

The Plain abandoned the Gironde, or rather the Girondins abandoned themselves. For in the presence of the battalions armed against them, at the sound of the tocsin, the alarm cannon, and the Assembly, Vergniaud proposed declaring that the Paris sections had deserved well of the Fatherland. It can be imagined that his inexplicable motion was greeted on our side with joy. The Commune itself rejoiced. This fact alone proved to it that its enemies had neither the will nor the courage to fight.[9]

The Meeting at the Jacobin Club

That evening at the Jacobin Club, the events of the day were judged more clearly and firmly than they were at the Commune. The deputies who joined them after leaving the Convention had watched the battle from its very heart. They viewed the horizon from a greater altitude than did the Commune, which had spent the day in a dip in the terrain, waiting for news and remaining inactive. And yet the Jacobins also didn't reach any conclusions. They clearly saw what was dangerous and deceptive in Vergniaud's maneuver: it was the appeal to the vast and diffuse people, still weighted down by instinctual servitude and conservative prejudices against the revolutionary committees, against the active and resolute groups. Hadn't Guadet already expressed his confidence in the presidents of the sections? Boissel pointed out the threat:

The sections must be established as popular societies. They mustn't be involved in public affairs otherwise they'll render completely useless all the revolutionary measures that the representatives will decree. These measures mustn't be impeded by enemies of the state. In a word, the

---

9   Spoken at the May 31 session of the Jacobin Club.

sections must do nothing but keep an eye on and disarm suspect individuals.

What does this mean? The answer is that the most ardent men of the Mountain feared the counter-revolutionary intervention of a still poorly educated people. If the sections remained or became sovereign, they might wreck or weaken the movement. Doesn't the correspondence from Marseilles (*Journal de la Montagne* of June 1) say that in that city "advantage was taken of the absence of our brave sans-culottes—who went to risk their lives against the enemies of the Republic—to establish in Marseilles a system that oppresses them," and that "all the rich, all the big capitalists, too cowardly to take up arms and even to speak expressly of the sans-culottes, seized control of the sections and insolently dominate them." Is it not known that "in these spurious sections, where the people's voice is stifled, horrors are spit out against the Jacobins of Paris, against all the societies who profess the principles of pure republicanism."

The "spurious sections" of Paris, bought off by the aristocrats, might also become dangerous: unless they were closely watched they would respond to the insidious appeal of the Gironde. Boissel's implicitly revolutionary conclusion was that it was necessary to count less on the diffuse and uncertain force of the people than on the vigorous and coordinated action committees. In reality, he proclaimed the bankruptcy of the confident tactics of May 31 that had been abandoned and proposed a more concentrated and effective one for a day in the not too distant future. Another citizen continued along the same lines: "Citizen Mittié told you that fear led Vergniaud to perform a good deed. For my part I look upon it as an act of gratitude to the aristocrats for having prevented the patriots from giving their insurrection the character it should have had."

Unless they were organized and led, nothing definite and vigorous could be expected from a people still enslaved to all the traditions of the past. A soldier was enraged by the attitude of Paris on the Fête-Dieu. The day before, on May 30, in his police bulletin, Dutard had written to Garat:

> [...] I saw acts of repentance there. I saw there the comparison everyone made between the current situation and that of the past. I saw the deprivation the people felt at the abolition of a ceremony that was once

the Church's most beautiful one. I saw the regret the people felt for the loss of profits earned by thousands of workers from this festival as well as others. People of all ranks, of all ages, stood there shamefaced, silent, saddened … Some people had tears in their eyes. The priests and the cortege looked to me to be quite happy with the reception they received.

It was precisely this reception that worried and angered an outspoken militant at the Jacobins: "I was supposed to leave 36 hours ago and I delayed my trip because the alarm cannon was supposed to be fired a week ago. Yesterday I saw with indignation the National Guard still escorting the Holy Sacrament."

Here we see the revolutionary seed of Hébertism. Did this sentimental reaction that weakened the people's strength have to be combated? Here, too, is the signal for the united and dictatorial action that would take the place of the feeble undertaking of May 31. For the Jacobins were determined to carry things to the bitter end. The Commission of Twelve was deposed:

Was it necessary to wait until today to destroy the most flagrant monument of despotism? It was only this evening that you were able to obtain this salutary decree. We must not rest. Renounce all hope, cowardly enemies: it is chimerical, and liberty stands so steadfast that it will triumph over all your efforts.

Hébert told you that the members of the dictatorial commission were outlaws and were subject to arrest. I say that all citizens must pursue these dictators and the 22 deputies unworthy of the people's confidence, and I think that the people must remain on the alert as long as the 22 haven't paid the penalty for their crimes.[10]

The Investing of the Convention

(The massive presence of the people at these events was considered so vital that the revolutionary committee in charge of the events "requested that a list of

---

10   Words spoken by an unidentified citizen, quoted in A. Aulard's *La Société des Jacobins*, vol. 5, p. 216.

sans-culotte workers be drawn up in each section and that each of them receive six livres … the salary for three days. May 31 and June 2, that made two days. The third day would be the decisive one, and they had to be paid in advance." The crowds attacking the Girondins and investing the Convention was enormous.)

The investing of the Convention caused it to become more cramped with every passing moment. Women blocked the corridors and soldiers posted by Hanriot guarded the exits.

Barère, whose courage grew beyond its normal height when the majesty and integrity of the Convention were being brutally threatened, was enraged by these degrading measures:

It's not up to slaves to make the law. France will disavow those that emanate from an enslaved assembly. How can these laws be respected when you only made them when surrounded by bayonets? We are in danger, for the new tyrants are keeping a close watch on us; their instructions imprison us, and that tyranny is in the Revolutionary Committee of the Commune. If the General Council doesn't take prompt measures to avoid violence it deserves condemnation. There are members of it whose morality I wouldn't want to vouch for.

The movement that threatens us is a tool of London, of Madrid, of Berlin; one of the members of the Revolutionary Committee, named Gusman, is known to me to be Spanish. People, you are being betrayed.

But what was the use of all this? What did this semi-resistance mean? And why did Barère, who agreed to demand the Girondins' resignation under popular pressure suddenly feign independence? What armed force could he have counted on? And how could he hope to pit the Revolutionary Committee of the Bishop's Palace and the General Council of the Commune against each other, both under revolutionary influence?

The left of the Convention was in a terrible fix. It wanted to strike the Gironde, but if it was already dangerous to go against the body that represented the nation, how much more dangerous would it be to do so under the threat of the insurgent streets? What would be left tomorrow of the Convention's privileges, that is, the moral authority of the Revolution itself? Levasseur accurately noted this immobilizing distress in his *Memoirs*:

A kind of stupor reigned in the Assembly. Even we members of the Mountain, who wanted to put an end to the domination of a handful of colleagues incapable of fulfilling their functions, couldn't look without pain at this attempt at popular insurrection against the only official body capable of saving the fatherland. No one asked for the floor; there were no discussions ... Aside from five or six men of action, among whom not a single friend of Danton could be found, the Mountain shared the right's consternation. President Mallarmé had left his chair in disgust, and Hérault de Séchelles silently presided over a mute Assembly.

However, Danton, wanting to avoid any excesses by the popular forces and to safeguard the dignity of the Convention, and, willing to go as far as necessary in order to do so, demanded that the Committee of Public Safety find the source of the order by which the soldiers were blocking the doors of the hall. He said, "You can count on the zeal of the Committee of Public Safety to vigorously defend the majesty of the Nation, which is being insulted at this moment."

Lesain, a captain in the armed force of the Bon-Conseil Section, who had given the instructions, was summoned to the bar, and Barère abruptly told the Convention to leave the hall and to deliberate amidst the armed force, as if to feel its own freedom and affirm it to the world.

This showy display of pride was the most frivolous and vain act that they could have committed. The armed revolutionary force that surrounded the Convention wanted the Girondins to be struck down. In order to prove it was free, though surrounded by bayonets, the Convention should have protected the Gironde. Either what Barère proposed was simply for show or it meant violent, open conflict between the Convention and the armed revolutionary sections.

What sweet revenge for Vergniaud who, on May 31, had unsuccessfully attempted to organize a mass sortie from the Convention. Reading Barère's *Memoirs* it is difficult to see what plan he'd formulated, or even if he had one at all. [...]

It appears from a few lines in one of Marat's writings that Barère would have liked to lead the Convention a great distance away, as far as the Champ de Mars, and it would have been dispersed there after having vowed not to allow the insurrectionary force to do violence to its decisions. But in that case, the Convention, without intending to, would have become a center of counter-revolutionary *moderantisme*. Marat showed a good deal of political sense in not wanting to be associated with this sortie that was either useless or disastrous, and by bringing the Convention back. He wrote:

The general is requested at the bar; he can't be found. Several officers appear and declare that they weren't the ones who gave the orders. The tumult grows; there's much to-ing and fro-ing on all sides and it is said that all is lost, that a foreign guard is holding the Convention captive until the time comes to slaughter it. How small the so-called wise men are! They were frightened by a handful of sentinels armed with pikes who guarded the doors, allowing no one to enter or leave, a measure of caution taken by the best citizens in order to prevent a few deputies of the faction from being mistreated by a handful of rogues planted in the crowd. Amidst all this disorder it was proposed that the president leave at the head of the Convention. He descends from his seat, almost all of the members follow him, and he presents himself at the bronze door. The guard clears the way. Instead of going back and noting the falseness of the clamor, he leads the Convention on a stroll in the courtyards and the garden. I had remained at my post with thirty Montagnards. The people in the galleries, impatient at not seeing the assembly return, grumbled loudly. I calm them down. I fly after the Convention and find them at the bascule bridge from which it is said Barère proposed to lead it to the Champ de Mars. I urge them to return to their post. They return and again take up their functions.

The Plain had been able to see that the sections were determined to be done with all this. At the passing of the Convention the people had shouted: "Vive la République! Save us! Down with the 22!"

The Arrest of the Girondin Leaders

It wasn't only Hanriot's cannons it would have had to fight, but also the Revolution itself that the Gironde would have had to combat if it wanted to continue the fight to save itself. Couthon demanded that the deputies who had been denounced be placed under arrest, along with the ministers Clavière and Lebrun. He was applauded and the decrees, immediately rendered, struck Vergniaud, Brissot, Guadet, Pétion, Salle, Chambon, Barbaroux, Buzot, Birotteau, Rabaut-Saint-Étienne, Lasource, Lanjuinais, Grangeneuve, Lesage (of the Eure-et-Loire), Louvet (of the Loiret), Valazé, Doulcet, Lidon, Lehardi (of the Morbihan), and all the members of the Commission of Twelve, except Boyer-Fonfrède and Saint-Martin) and the ministers Clavière and Lebrun.

After having thanked the Assembly, the *département* of Paris offered hostages taken from among them equal to the number of arrested deputies in order to assure the *départements* of their safety.

No, it wasn't the lives of the Gironde that the revolutionaries were after. Vergniaud, on one of those tragic days had exclaimed: "Give Couthon a glass of blood to drink, he's thirsty." Vergniaud was wrong; Couthon wasn't thirsty for blood. But the Gironde had become a mortal danger to revolutionary France. It had to cease to exist. On June 2, its political power collapsed.

("What undid [the Girondins,] what turned them into a critical, paralyzing force, mortal to national and revolutionary action, was simply their party spirit reduced to a spirit of faction and coterie ... There's no question that class conflict would soon mix with the political conflict of parties, but at that time this wasn't the heart of the matter ... It was party egoism that the Revolution had to eliminate at risk of death. It eliminated it.")

13

Marat's Assassination

(In the summer of 1793, as the influence of the Enragés *and the Hébertists was about to reach its apogee, Marat was campaigning to purge the leadership of the armies fighting the reactionaries in the Vendée and the north. "He didn't unmask treason, but rather weakness, the lack of vision and energy" of the Representatives on Mission and the Committee of Public Safety. For Jaurès, "Marat, with his admirable disinterest and horror of intrigue would have fought Hébert and his friends the day he'd have seen they wanted to dominate the Convention." But he wouldn't have the time.)*

As the Girondin party in Normandy stumbled and disintegrated, a young girl from Caen, Charlotte Corday, headed to Paris, either to save or avenge those she considered martyrs of the Republic. She whipped up her enthusiasm by admiring the heroines in the plays of Corneille.

Believing that Marat was the guiding hand behind despotism, anarchy, and murder, she had resolved to kill him. The evening of Sunday, July 13, 1793, she insisted on being received by him. He was in the bathtub where he stayed much of the time, since the day an inflammatory illness began devouring him. A plank placed across it held up the inkwell and the sheets of paper he still blackened with his ideas and his fevers. She spoke a few words to him and stuck a knife in his heart. He gave out a cry, called for his companion Simone Evrard, and died.

Charlotte Corday, having sacrificed her own life in order to kill a man she considered villainous, made no effort to flee. Before the revolutionary tribunal she explained her act in a few clear words, words of a heroic and fatal simplicity that attested to what petty proportions she had reduced the problem of the Revolution. Beautiful, young, modest, and proud, wrapped for her trip to the gallows in the red shirt of parricides, she left in the people a strange image of nobility, heroism, and blood, which disquieted many. She had killed Marat, but above all she had killed the Gironde. Who would take seriously the Girondins' rants against the Maratists and those they called assassins? First Lepeletier[1] had been assassinated and now Marat. The men who had been denounced as murderers were themselves murdered. Even among those who were prejudiced against Marat, anger and hatred were succeeded by shock and even pity. One of the motive forces of Girondin propaganda was smashed.

The Convention and the people gave Marat a triumphant funeral. The sorrow of the poor and the workers was great. They had lost a friend, an advisor who didn't flatter them; one who, when the need arose, knew how to warn them and speak to them harshly. Marat's death was a great misfortune for the Revolution. Perhaps if he'd been able to live one more year he would have been able to prevent the fatal events that would later occur. His sister said, "If my brother had lived, Danton would not be dead." What did she mean? Probably that he would have prevented the Hébertists' violent campaign against Danton and reconciled Danton and Robespierre. But why grant him this sovereign influence and nearly august prestige that in truth death alone gave him? He would in all likelihood have been overwhelmed by events. In June and July, he was close to Hébert and his friends, though he would probably not have followed them to the bitter end. Had he become an obstacle to their restless ambition, he too would have been slandered and in all likelihood left behind. Or perhaps, with the worsening of the revolt in Lyon and the treason in Toulon, in order to remain in the vanguard of the movement he would have been driven to murderous follies and adopted Hébertist policies. It's impossible to say with certainty whether he would have guillotined the Hébertists or been guillotined along with them.

Almost immediately after Marat's death, the Hébertists and the *Enragés* fought each other to assume his popularity and name. Jacques Roux claimed he was continuing his newspaper and brought out *The People's Friend by the Shade of Marat*. It's clear that he didn't lack boldness. After Marat's terrible article of July 4,[2] Jacques Roux had gone to Marat's house, as we learn from a police report from Greive to the Committee of General Security:

---

1   Martyred Jacobin, assassinated for his vote for the execution of the king.
2   Marat had written a ferocious attack on Roux in that issue of *L'Ami du Peuple*.

The Citizens Crosnier, Allain, and Greive, being at the home of Citizen Marat on the morning of Tuesday the ninth of this month, Jacques Roux arrived to demand from Marat the retraction of what he wrote concerning him in his newspaper, saying that he had left at his home his baptismal certificate that proved that his name wasn't Renaudi, as Marat had said. Marat responded with his characteristic firmness ... Roux answered him in the most mealy-mouthed of tones, in the falsest language, in a way that rendered him in our eyes as base as he was dangerous. As soon as Marat dismissed him, and before going down the stairs at the end of a long landing, he stopped for a moment and cast a prolonged vengeful gaze at Marat that is difficult to describe, one that left with us the most profound impression. And so the moment we learned of Marat's dreadful death our suspicions, especially those of Greive, immediately fell on the vindictive priest.

It was precisely when he was suspected of being Charlotte Corday's accomplice that Roux assumed Marat's name and attempted to regain his standing at the Commune. On July 19, he explained the famous address saying that a few expressions that shocked listeners were the effect of a "petulant imagination." In doing this, he sought to have consecrated the bold act by which he seized Marat's political and popular heritage.

But at the same moment Hébert was exclaiming at the Jacobin Club:

If a successor is needed for Marat, if a second victim is needed, one man is ready and resigned to this fate: myself! I will be only too happy to die as long as I carry to my grave the certainty of having saved my fatherland! But no more nobles! No more nobles! It is the nobles who are assassinating us!

Marat's embalmed heart hung like a relic in the vault of the Cordelier Club, now become the sanctuary of the Revolution. Robespierre, irritated by this maneuver, protested against the excesses of the funereal honors. "Jealousy," Bentabole shouted at him. But Robespierre knew that the Hébertists were going to make Marat's canonized heart speak in their support, and he wanted to break the spell.

14

Dechristianization

(In its early days the Revolution had attacked Church property and made the clergy take an oath of loyalty to the Republic, but the abolition of religion was not part of its program. The Jacobins—and Robespierre in particular—were deists, and considered atheism an enemy of the revolutionary project, though as we will see the installation of the Cult of the Supreme Being in 1794 would contribute to Robespierre's undoing. The sans-culottes, however, saw things differently, and in the second half of 1793 unleashed a militant campaign of dechristianization.)

On the religious question Hébertism was nothing but vain and superficial violence, incoherence and contradiction. From August to December 1793, an intense dechristianization movement made its appearance. A portion of the revolutionary people rose up not only against non-juring priests and the Church, but against Christianity itself, and they attempted to tear the Christian idea from people's minds by destroying the symbols and emblems that allowed it to enter through their eyes. What we had here was a war on a religion as a means of war on belief. It was priests who had fanaticized the Vendée and who were accomplices of the wealthy egoists of Lyon. The Revolution would only be safe, human liberty would only be firmly established, when the power that controlled souls and forced them to submit to all the tyrannies of the earth and heavens disappeared. And there was no need to distinguish between juring and non-juring priests, between constitutional priests and refractory ones. What had the constitutional priests done? What did they do in the Vendée, in Lyon, in Toulon, in Marseille, in Lozère? Either their inertia and timidity made them secret accomplices of the enemy, or they were powerless. Their semi-fanaticism had less of a hold on the ignorant than the wholehearted fanaticism of the non-juring priests. If the constitutional priests didn't serve as a hoped-for diversion, if they didn't serve as a caution useful to the Revolution among the believers and the simple, then what was their role? And why should the Revolution continue to lend itself to a compromise that was nothing but a fraud? For in order to protect the constitutional priests, in order not to offend "their faith," the Revolution was forced to be gentle with the refractory priests as well. Acting in this way, it wasn't possible to get to the heart of things and lay bare the roots of the falsehood that supports the entire Church, be it constitutional or refractory. Let us thus have done with it, and since fanaticism forms a thick layer over the intelligence, one impervious to reason. Since it is pointless to talk to men who believe mechanically, that mechanical habit must be destroyed. It must be proved to these fools that the God they adore is nothing but powerlessness and the void, and to do this the instruments of His religion must be taken from Him. The sacred vases must be seized and profaned in the sight of the heavens in order to prove to the simplest of fanatics the nullity of a God who isn't even able to defend himself. It took philosophy centuries to liberate minds through ideas; the chains that were forged by the slavery, that is, ignorance, must be smashed by force. And so we see chalices and the monstrances attached to an ass wearing a stole, wearing a mitre on his head, and beating his flanks with a host tied to his tail, demonstrating the ridiculousness of the old religion and forever disgusting the believers in a faith that lends itself to such degrading parodies.

The revolutionary people, the people of the sections, had grown familiar with the Church, for patriotic meetings took place in churches. The representatives on mission preached war for liberty from the pulpit, so how could they allow the enslavement of minds, that is, war against liberty, to be organized within these same walls? All the vases, all the torches on the altar were the arms of counter-revolution: let them be smashed and melted and made into weapons for the Revolution or to give a Revolution drowning in paper money the gold coin it needed. The bells had already been taken down from the belfries, melted and made into cannons, and the rope of the bell pulls had been made into the cordage of the ships outfitted by Jean Bon Saint-André against the English.

But it wasn't enough to manhandle religion: priests must be made to confess that they had lied, that they misled the people. Taking their ornaments from them was a good thing, but having them reject their stoles and then trample on them was even better. And the ultimate triumph of reason would be for the priests to de-priest themselves, to reject the God they had so long spoken of and reveal to fanatics the emptiness of the tabernacle where human illusion had resided for centuries. A great triumph! On November 7, Cloots,[1] Léonard Bourdon[2] and a handful of others convinced Gobel, the Bishop of Paris, to go to the Convention and abjure his functions. Other abjurations followed. Large numbers of priests resigned, either out of revolutionary enthusiasm, or because the Gospels, from which they had removed its supernatural coloring, had become mixed in an ambiguous grisaille with the Declaration of the Rights of Man, or to rid themselves of a function that every day became more difficult and false, or perhaps from cowardice.

Chaumette rejoiced and the Commune, not wanting to leave the people's imagination idle, instituted a great civic festival to replace the religious ones. It proclaimed the Cult of Reason, and on November 10, before the statue of Liberty "raised in the place of the former Holy Virgin," voices were raised to celebrate the freeing of man. The Convention, invited in the evening for a repeat performance of the festival, went as a body to Notre Dame. Reason (in the person of Citizeness Momoro) came down from her throne and embraced Laloy, the president of the Convention. Hébertism seemed to be master of Paris and the Revolution.

To be sure, there might have been a certain grandeur in this radical and brutal attempt at dechristianization, and we can see the theoretical justification that could have been advanced. The human spirit bears a heavy burden of superstitions and habits, and if a violent shakeup could make this age-old burden fall from its shoulders overnight what a deliverance that would be! How free humanity would be, and how much more boldly intelligence would enter into the mysteries of the world when the outdated,

---

1 Anacharsis Cloots (1755–94)—Prussian noble who moved to France. Self-proclaimed "Orator of the Human Race," he was guillotined along with the Hébertists.
2 Léonard Bourdon (1754–1807)—member of the Jacobins, the Paris Commune, and the National Convention. He was close to the Hébertists.

traditional forms of belief have disappeared. It would even be possible to again put forth the great religious interpretations of the universe once there was no longer any risk of their being confused through superficial analogies with the superstitions of the past, or of their being exploited by the cunning of the Church to ensure its domination. After all, force is able to smash beliefs that were formed unthinkingly. Blind habit is also a form of force, the brief violence of the hour of liberation does nothing but abolish the effects of the slow and hidden violence of the centuries.

This is true, but the Hébertist operation could only succeed—or even be attempted—on one condition. Hébertism had to take clear sides on the one decisive question: did it simply want to mock and insult religion, or did it want to uproot it? If all it wanted to do was insult it, then the movement was as sterile as it was base; and if it wanted to uproot it, it had to openly proclaim that the freedom of religion inscribed in the Constitution was an illusion and a danger. It had to think and it had to say that Christian belief—the principle of servitude—had no right to assert itself. It is only in the name of right that such profound revolutions can be carried out. If the Revolution didn't have the courage to say "I don't recognize Christianity's right to exist and I will crush all of its manifestations, either collective or individual," then the war on religion was nothing but an ignominious display and the most vulgar form of tyranny. But Hébertism didn't even pose the problem, and it wavered pitifully between demagogic violence ennobled by no principles and retreats dictated by foolishness and fear.

Fouché[3] announced, in the memorable decree of October 9:

Article 1—The ceremonies of the various religions can only be held in their respective temples.

Article 2—The Republic, not recognizing any dominant or privileged religion, every religious emblem found on the roads, on squares, and generally in public places, will be destroyed.

---

3   Joseph Fouché (1759–1820)—one of the most notorious figures of the period. After being a representative on a mission responsible for the gunning-down of counter-revolutionaries in Lyon in 1793–94, being accused of fraud during his activities, he survived the revolution to be Napoleon's minister of police.

Article 3—Under penalty of imprisonment, it is forbidden to ministers and priests to appear in their costumes anywhere but in their temples.

Article 4—In every municipality all dead citizens, of whatever religion, shall be taken to a place designated as the common grave covered by a funeral veil on which shall be painted Sleep, accompanied by a public officer, surrounded by their friends in mourning attire and a detachment of their brothers-in-arms.

Article 5—The common place where their ashes shall repose shall be isolated from any habitation and planted with trees under whose shade a statue of Sleep shall be raised. All other signs shall be destroyed.

Article 6—On the gate to this field, consecrated by a religious respect for the ashes of the dead, shall be written "Death is an eternal sleep."

At bottom this was a moderate decree. It respected the freedom of belief and even that of religion. I know full well that the inscription "Death is an eternal sleep" has materialist pretensions, and it could be said that it expressed official materialism, mandatory for the dead if not for the living. In truth, the inscription is more infantile than aggressive and is even more anti-scientific than it is anti-Christian. Sleep is a function of life; death is its dissolution. To speak of sleep meant flattering the need to survive; it meant prolonging the form of life, wrapped in silence and repose. Death is more dramatic and poignant: it is the dissolution of form, the dissolution of consciousness. Man wonders if this dissolution is apparent or real, provisional or definitive. This is the problem of death and it is too facile to elude it through a myth as childish as the ideas of savages. What is more, Fouché's decree respected the official and constitutional organization of religion, which it couldn't touch. It limited itself to restricting cults to the interior of their temples. It was a law for the regulation of religion and was neither decisive nor profound.

(Jaurès summed up the dechristianization campaign: "Christianity would not have lasted eighteen centuries if all that was needed was Hébertism in order to overthrow it. And neither Hébert nor Chaumette had paid attention to this: that in order to proceed effectively at wresting the people from Christianity, in order to annihilate belief by destroying its emblems and prohibiting its ceremonies,

it had to be applied simultaneously all over France ... But Hébertism knew that if it were to throw itself into this policy it couldn't apply it everywhere with sufficient rapidity and simultaneity ... Hébertism did nothing but change superstition's décor ... No, it isn't possible to do without the spirit in order to liberate the spirit.")

15
The Dictatorship of Public Safety and the Fight against the Factions

(In September 1793, "the crisis of staple goods reached its paroxysm." Radical measures, measures long called for by the Enragés but resisted by the Jacobins, were necessary. Laws against hoarding and a forced loan of a billion francs, had already been put in place, but had failed to appreciably change things for the working class. On September 4, "the Commune was invaded by a large mass. They were the poor, the artisans, proletarians who had come to shout that they had had enough of starvation prices, of increasing shortages, of the daily rise in the cost of living." On September 29, the general maximum was finally passed: prices were raised a maximum of one-third their 1790 level, while wages were increased by 50 percent.

These radical measures required a strong body to see to their execution, and "it was the Committee of Public Safety that increasingly became the force behind action and regulation." Danton, named to it, preferred not to serve, while Robespierre "didn't take long in realizing that his place was now on the Committee."

But the Committee would be known not just for its role in enforcing economic measures: "Under its impetus revolutionary terror asserted itself within France ... The law of September 17 ordered the drawing up of lists of suspects." The Terror was launched. On October 16, Marie-Antoinette was condemned (Jacques Roux would be at her side on the way to and at her execution). On October 31, 21 Girondin deputies were executed.

New military victories followed, with the English driven from Toulon, which they had briefly conquered, and "the Committee reestablished unity of operations, concentrated armies and responsibilities, and invested its confidence in young, heroic, and wise officers." In early October 1793, the new Revolutionary calendar was adopted, with Year One being the proclamation of the Republic.)

What can the Nation's reawakening be attributed to? To the energetic and vigilant actions of the revolutionary power. How could victory be sustained until total liberation? By the unity and action of the revolutionary forces organized into a government.

This is what Robespierre understood, and it is the idea he expressed in a note to himself laying out his plan of action upon entering the Committee of Public Safety. It was found among his papers and probably dates from September 1793:

What is the goal? The implementation of the Constitution for the good of the people.

Who will our enemies be? The depraved and the wealthy.

What methods will they employ? Slander and hypocrisy.

What causes might allow the use of these methods? The ignorance of the sans-culottes.

The people must be enlightened. But what are the obstacles to the education of the people? The mercenary writers who lead them astray with their daily and impudent impostures.

What should we conclude from this?

First: That these writers must be proscribed as the most dangerous enemies of the fatherland.

Second: That virtuous writings must be widely distributed.

What are the obstacles to the establishment of liberty? Foreign and civil war.

What are the means of ending the foreign war?

—Placing republican generals at the head of our armies and punishing those who betrayed us.

What are the means of ending the civil war?

—Punishing the traitors and conspirators, especially the guilty deputies and administrators; sending patriotic troops under patriotic leaders to reduce the aristocrats of Lyon, Marseilles, Toulon, the Vendée, the Jura, and all the other places where the standard of rebellion and royalism has been raised; and to make a terrifying example of all the scoundrels who insulted Liberty and spilled the blood of patriots.

1—The proscription of perfidious and counter-revolutionary writers; distribution of virtuous writings; 2—Punishment of traitors and conspirators, especially guilty deputies and administrators; 3—Appointment of patriotic generals; removal and punishment of the others; 4—Subsistence and popular laws.

This is the governmental program that Robespierre laid out and which we have seen partially implemented. This is in no way a program of permanent dictatorship. What he proposes is the application of the Constitution, that is, the return to a normal regime where democracy shall govern and where power will not be concentrated in a committee. But in order for the spirit of the Constitution to be applied, that is, "for the good of the people," the people, freed from foreign and civil war, must be able to see to it that the Constitution functions.

Is a nation abandoned to the free play of parties in a condition to save itself? No, for the wealthy class is too selfish and the poor class, the class of sans-culottes, is still too ignorant. What does this mean? It means that in a time of crisis it is necessary that a strong government, bearing within itself all the energy and all the power of the Revolution, rise above the two classes, mastering the selfishness of the one and enlightening the ignorance of the other, thus preparing the advent of legal democracy.

Robespierre expressed his idea more pointedly in phrases that may well have caused him to alarm himself, for he crossed out these striking words:

The people ... What other obstacle is there to the education of the people? Poverty.
When, then, will the people be enlightened?
When they have bread and when the rich and the government cease to bribe perfidious pens and tongues to mislead them.
When their interests are merged with those of the people.
When will their interests merge with those of the people?—Never.

This implacable and pessimistic "never" appeared to trap the Revolution in a perpetual vicious circle. And the logical conclusion would have been a kind of eternal dictatorship fighting against, in the interests of the people, their incurable ignorance. Robespierre's real idea was that the Revolution could only be saved through the power of a revolutionary government supported by the Convention, but achieving the concentration of all fighting forces. Dissolving or weakening the Convention, dissolving or weakening the Committee of Public Safety was thus an inexpiable crime against the Revolution: it meant surrendering it to anarchy, that is, the enemy.

The Committee of Public Safety

While the Committee of Public Safety was being organized, was working, fighting, and smashing federalism and the coalition of armies leagued against it, it was constantly spied on by intriguers and threatened by the factions. And it sometimes wondered if, after having escaped Girondin anarchy, the Revolution wasn't going to succumb to demagogic anarchy.

This was the stirring drama that overwhelmed revolutionary consciousness between September 1793 and May 1794, and which tortured Robespierre to the point that he was ill and exhausted.

The Hébertists initially insidiously sought to discredit the Committee of Public Safety and then to violently overthrow it. They were a group of men apparently led by Hébert but which recruited its members primarily among the revolutionary agents of the ministry of war. The war offices, most of the Cordelier Club, and a portion of the Commune: these were the forces that Hébert had at his disposal to attack and destroy the Committee of Public Safety.

What did these men have against it? What did Hébert, Ronsin, and Vincent have against the Committee of Public Safety? And what was the plan of national and revolutionary action they opposed to the Committee's?

Could they accuse it of negligence, weakness, or cowardice in the administration of a France in peril? Through force of energy the Committee of Public Safety was able to meet a crushing task. All day long, each member of the Committee of Public Safety worked with his staff, and in the evening, gathered in a small chamber, they deliberated over the workings of the government, sometimes until 2:00 a.m. The members were each assigned specific functions.

Robespierre, Saint-Just, and Couthon were what the people called "the men with supreme control," that is, those who watched over the general policies of the Revolution. Barère, Billaud-Varenne, and Collot d'Herbois were primarily charged with the correspondence with the representatives on mission, with the elected authorities of the Revolution, and with reports to the National Convention. Finally, there was the group of "examiners." These were the specialists: Carnot and Prieur, who had oversight over the army, Jean Bon Saint-André the navy, and Robert Lindet, who had the immense task of seeing to the provisioning of France, Paris, and the armies. There were countless details to be attended to on a daily basis. These were overwhelming responsibilities which all of the members of the Committee shared, for the measures taken by any one of them was signed by all of them.

It is a mistake to believe that Robespierre was a speechifier in love with general ideas and adept only at phrase-mongering and theories. The form of his speeches, in which he often proceeds through allusions, where he usually wraps substantive reports and extremely detailed accusations in general formulas, has contributed to this misunderstanding. In fact, he kept himself up to date on the details of all revolutionary activity throughout the country and in the armies. And with an incredibly sustained mental effort, with a meticulous concern for the real, he attempted to evaluate the true value of the men the Revolution employed.

At the Jacobin Club, he had access to the most detailed information and was ready to rectify the vague allegations and accusations of quarrelsome demagogy. These men didn't limit themselves to governing from their offices: they were in constant contact with the violence of events and passions.

Jean Bon Saint-André toured the ports, quelled the sailors' riots, eliminated the counter-revolutionary general staff, and aroused the enthusiasm of the crews by the power of justice and his obvious concern for the welfare of all and the grandeur of the free Fatherland.

Carnot traveled to the battlefields to ensure the execution of his plans, and he set an example of combative vigor and courage in the attack.

Saint-Just overcame the weakness of his overworked nervous system to confront the dangers and din of war in the front ranks.

And what a battlefield the Jacobin Club was for Robespierre! How bitter and harsh a life it was to go there every evening, to a popular assembly that was often raucous and defiant, and give an account of the day's labors, dispel hatreds, and disarm slander. What a fearsome task it was to govern and speak, to rule over the forum, and to get the people to accept governmental discipline. But by doing this the Committee of Public Safety avoided turning itself into a narrow coterie; it was by doing this that it was in contact with revolutionary life.

Could the Hébertists reproach the Committee of Public Safety for its poor choice of generals, for too much complacency towards the officers of the *ancien régime*? This was Hébert's refrain in June, July, and August: "Drive all the nobles from the army!" In saying this, he replaced with the glib intransigence of a general slogan the difficult labor of purification and renewal that presupposes individual judgment. He seemed to forget that it wasn't enough to drive out the nobles; time was needed to test the new men who replaced them.

The Committee of Public Safety was extremely vigilant. Robespierre's first words in his June note were that Custine must be closely watched. And it wasn't only Custine, it was also victorious Houchard[1] who climbed the gallows.

It is difficult to attribute specific responsibility for the August and September disasters in the war in the Vendée. They were owed as much to a general anarchy that the Committee of Public Safety wasn't able to immediately bring under control as to the incompetence and vices of men. And I am reluctant to accept Philippeaux's[2] vehement accusations against

---

1 Jean-Nicolas Houchard (1739–93)—Commander of the Revolutionary Army of the Moselle; he was guillotined after failing to pursue the victory he won at the battle of Hondschoote on September 8, 1793.
2 Pierre Philippeaux (1756–93)—as representative on mission in the Vendée, he had attacked the generals fighting there as well as the government emissaries. He was guillotined along with the Dantonists.

Rossignol[3] and even Ronsin,[4] for the former's partisanship revolted Robespierre. But if we simply look at the facts and results, neither Ronsin nor Rossignol nor Léchelle[5] demonstrated remarkable military ability. Rossignol, the best of them, the most honest, the most sincere, and the most upright, modestly recognized his own insufficiencies. The hazards of war only turned for the Revolution when the Committee of Public Safety intervened vigorously in October and put an end to the disorder that neither the ministry of war, where Hébertist influence dominated, nor the Hébertist leaders sent to the scene were able to prevent or suppress.

If the Committee of Public Safety erred in October in naming the incompetent Léchelle to command one of the large armies of the west, it was done on the recommendation of the Hébertists and in order to avoid a break with them, to prove that it was not from a spirit of coterie and jealous exclusion, but in the interest of the Revolution that the Committee of Public Safety was reorganizing the armies of the west and changing commanders. Léchelle, in any case, quickly stepped aside, making way for Kléber.[6] It was during this period that the Committee of Public Safety picked out, encouraged, and raised to the highest ranks the army's young, intelligent, and heroic leaders, men like Marceau, Kléber, Jourdan and Hoche, who would cause European counter-revolution to beat a retreat. Shouldn't Hébert—who denounced men wildly, and who was flagrantly guilty of slander in regard to the representative and envoy to the armies Duquesnoy and his brother, General Duquesnoy—have been able to recognize in the new generation of revolutionary fighters men of firm intelligence and noble hearts? Instead, he smothered every heroic bud by damning every officer with the same suspicions and the same loquacity, until he was finally able to distribute all the gold braids and plumes to a few incompetents of the war bureaus and the sections. Did the idea for

---

3   Jean-Antoine Rossignol (1759–1802)—revolutionary general fighting against the counter-revolutionaries in the Vendée.
4   Charles-Philippe Ronsin (1751–94)—ally of Hébert, he was executed along with him after serving as general of Paris.
5   Jean Léchelle (1760–93)—general in the Vendée. He died under suspicious circumstances after a crushing defeat at the Battle of Étrammes.
6   Jean-Baptiste Kléber (1753–1800)—successful general of the armies of the Revolution; he later served Napoleon, dying during the Egyptian campaign.

an offensive utilizing large masses of men that saved the Revolution come from Vincent or Ronsin, or even from the minister Bouchotte? No, it was from Hoche[7] and Carnot.[8] And I've already noted that Marat who, in June and July reflected the opinions of the war bureaus in military matters, opted for a dispersed defensive war, that is to say, certain defeat and the rapid demoralization of the armies of revolutionary France.

The royalist Mallet du Pan, a well-informed observer who hated democracy, the Convention, and the Committee of Public Safety, saw clearly the decisive and colossal labor of the latter, its enormous impact on the armies. He remarks on "the art of enflaming hearts and minds which the Convention made impressive and frequent use of." And he added [...]

You[9] have to fight against something that didn't exist during the first campaign and to only a slight degree at the beginning of the second: impassioned armies battling against the armies of sovereigns; a fanaticized military mass to which is opposed mercenaries indifferent to the object of the dispute and whose discipline has not spared them from defeat.

How could the armies have had this confidence and magnificent élan if the Committee of Public Safety hadn't taken a broad view; if instead of recognizing merits and services, it had sacrificed everything to a narrow Parisian coterie eager to occupy all posts; and if it hadn't ended the divisions and quarrels that might have paralyzed the soldiers' élan by establishing firm unity in government and administration?

The armies' power resided in the revolutionary unity organized and symbolized by the Committee of Public Safety.

Did it strike the internal enemies of the Revolutionary with enough force? Was it too stingy with the royalist blood of the Girondins? This is what Hébert and his people constantly insinuated. They constantly called for an escalation in the use of the guillotine. Really, what a small number

---

7   Lazare Hoche (1768–97)—after enlisting in the National Guard, Hoche rose through the grades in the regular army, where he was a successful general, particularly in the Alsace.
8   Lazare Carnot (1752–1823)—member of the Committee of Public safety, he was accused of participating in massacres in the Vendée.
9   This passage was addressed by Mallet du Pan to Lord Elgin in a memo dated February 1, 1794 [note by Jaurès].

of heads! Let's make the baskets bigger! But at this game it would have been all too easy to go further than the Hébertists. The only method of Terror that a wise politician could accept, unless he was drunk on blood, was that of Robespierre: "Set terrifying examples." Examples, and not executions. In order to show peoples and kings that not even feelings of pity could weaken the Revolution in the face of royal crime, it was enough to strike Marie Antoinette after striking Louis; the former queen after the former king. To demand the head of the king's sister, Madame Élisabeth, as Hébert did day after day, was nothing but a cruel tactical maneuver aimed at embarrassing the government, at setting it at odds with humanity if it surrendered to this call, and with the extremists if it resisted. In order to set an example, guillotining Marie Antoinette was enough. It was certainly pointless to crassly insult her and, by slandering her, allow her a kind of vengeance in the court of history.

Chaumette and Hébert showed themselves to be poor revolutionaries when the former before the Council of the Commune and the latter before the tribunal that judged Marie Antoinette, accused her of having depraved her son in order to better rule over him in the event of a regency. Hébert served the Revolution poorly when he added that Marie Antoinette and Élisabeth, the mother and the aunt, took the child between them and prematurely brought on his puberty in order to later subject him to their whims when he would be king. Marie Antoinette issued a sublime cry of revolt: "I appeal to all mothers!" And this appeal, which the ignoble *Père Duchesne* caused to burst forth from a tortured heart, has been a recruiting tool for reaction for more than a century. And perhaps Chaumette was ill-inspired when he complained at the Council of the Commune that the condemned were allowed a mouthful of eau-de-vie before they left prison for the gallows. It seems this gave them the courage to defy the Revolution through their attitude. Did the Revolution need its enemies to be cowards in order for it to be strong? In a few months from this time one will be tempted to say: "If need be, give Hébert an entire gourd of alcohol so he'll die in a less cowardly fashion." But no, there will be enough sinister mockers around his tumbril, we can keep our contempt to ourselves. It was also enough of an example to cut off the heads of the 21 Girondins whom it was possible to lay hold of. Yes, you're seeing right: that's Brissot's fertile head and Vergniaud's inspired head in the basket. I imagine that the lesson was as striking as their minds were. What need was there to call for the scaffold, as Hébert did, for the 73 Girondins who signed in June a protest against the events of May 31? Denounced by Amar's report on October 3, 1793, they would have been sent before the Revolutionary Tribunal had Robespierre not intervened. He demanded an adjournment to wait for the report of the Committee of General Security, and the men were imprisoned instead of decapitated. Yet another grievance of Hébert's against Robespierre! But why did Hébert stop there? There weren't only the 73. Those who called for the appeal to the people before executing the king also needed to be struck. And aside from the Convention, there were the 20,000 citizens who signed the petitions against June 20, against the [National Guard] encampment in Paris.[10] There would have been an enormous stampede on the road to the guillotine and the exemplary force of the sentence would have been lost in a haze of throat-slitting.

But if Hébertism was lacking in revolutionary clear-sightedness in its use of death, if it was lacking in higher principles of government and military tactics, did it at least have a social plan to oppose to the internal policies of the Committee of Public Safety? Did it have a theory and a method for relieving the people's sufferings, for educating the proletarians and freeing them of the oligarchic yoke of property? I seek and I find nothing but incoherence and the void.

The End of Jacques Roux

For his part Jacques Roux had the first elements of a system, yet Hébert relentlessly continued the fight against him that he had begun in February and March 1793 and taken up again in June. After the hammer blow of late June and early July, driven from the Convention, driven from the Cordeliers, condemned by the Jacobins, Jacques Roux would have been reduced to nothing if he hadn't been supported by the faithful sympathy of the poor in his Gravilliers quarter. He was a strange priest who, when questioned at the Cordeliers as to his profession, answered "confessor of

---

10   Demonstration on June 20, 1792, calling for the recall of the Girondin ministers.

the sick," and who, sympathetic to the distress and doleful piety of poor women, bore consolation and exaltation from pallet to pallet, his speech a mixture of Christian resignation and popular revolt. This man, who urged the dying to have faith in an unknown world and who solicited from them a final anathema against the present world where iniquity and wealth triumph; this angry priest, who descended from the garrets of the poor ashen with pity and anger, and who on the streets and in the shops fanned the flames of the revolt of the infirm who had no bread, of the worn-out workers who were left without heat by the high price of coal and froze in anticipation of death; this ferocious mystic, atheist against the Church and Christian against the bourgeois, a revolutionary ever ready to curse the Revolution if it didn't justify its existence by continuing to advance; this enigmatic man had touched more than one heart. Unremarked, he had got himself back on his feet after the terrible blows that had nearly finished him off when his enemies, doubtless to court the Convention, made a new and withering accusation against him: he had dared lay a hand on the name of Marat, whose ownership Hébert aspired to. He had to be eliminated. "Marat's widow" Simone Évrard, the woman who had been his companion, was used against him, lamenting the fact that Roux was making "Marat's shade" speak, since Marat's family was Hébertist.

But more than anything else, they attempted to dishonor him by denouncing him as a thief. Accused in his section of having, while president of the Cordeliers, embezzled its funds and in particular of having failed to pay into the cashbox an *assignat* of 200 livres he received on behalf of the club, he defended himself mightily. He affirmed that several of the sums written in the register of the club had, in fact, not been paid out and that upon leaving the presidency he had had to make good the deficit from his own funds (which is extremely likely). As witnesses to his beneficence towards and solicitude for the poor, he called several of the women he had assisted, women for whom he had taken up collections, to testify in his behalf. They spoke of him with extreme gratitude. But this attempt to crush him disgusted him, and one evening he attempted to take his revenge at an assembly of the section. He made a serious accusation against one of his main adversaries, Chemin. He regained his authority over the section, had the bureau on which his enemies sat dissolved, and was appointed to the presidency. Roux had made his triumphant return to the Gravilliers Section. Around him his friends, the carpenter Natey and others, spoke out angrily against all those who had defamed Jacques Roux. Would Hébert and the Commune allow the party of the Gravilliers, the party of Jacques Roux to be reconstituted?

Roux carried out his *coup de force* at the section on August 18. On August 21, Hébert denounced him at the Jacobins:

This infamous priest, who has great influence at the Gravilliers Section, had decreed that an address would be presented at the Convention to obtain the removal of the established authorities and to accuse the mayor himself of hoarding.

Fortunately, he added, that section recognized its error, repealed its decree, and it will doubtless be the first to denounce the villain who willfully led it astray.

This appeal was heard, and on August 22, the civil and watch committees of the Gravilliers, which were trying to counter Jacques Roux's influence over the section, carried out a demarche at the Commune. Truchon said in their name:

Citizen magistrates, you must have been told that last Sunday, around midnight, Jacques Roux entered the assembly of the Gravilliers Section. There he removed the president and the secretary, and also had removed, in favor of a party he formed, the civil and watch committees, as well as the police superintendent, placing several individuals under arrest. The section is in a state of complete disorganization. We ask that the council appoint commissioners to go to our assembly and rehabilitate the public functionaries who were illegally removed.

Chaumette, hardly surprised by this action, immediately rose to issue a demand:

I find in all this two serious crimes, one more serious than the other. The crime committed by Jacques Roux in arbitrarily removing the public functionaries and casting the lightning bolt of arrest at several citizens is, without any contradiction, very serious. But the one he committed in pronouncing the dissolution of an assembly of the sovereign people, in bringing to it the spirit of discord and division, is much more reprehensible. Jacques Roux has attacked the sovereignty of the people. Whoever renders himself guilty of this crime is a counter-revolutionary, and every counter-revolutionary must be punished with death.

Chaumette proposed that the Council decree "that all the charges and evidence against Jacques Roux be sent to the police, and that the Council name six commissioners to immediately reorganize the Gravilliers Section and restore order there."

How many times had revolutions of this kind been carried out in the sections during the period when the Commune was disputing them with the moderates and the bourgeois? But when it came to Jacques Roux, everything was a crime. Hébert attacked mercilessly, accusing him of inciting pillage, of provoking insurrection, of feigning poverty while at the same time distributing considerable sums in the section: in sum, of being a hypocrite: "This man once said at the electoral assembly that he could not care less about religion. The next day he said mass and normally says it every day."

Finally, the police administrator, Froidure, announced that "an arrest warrant had been issued for Jacques Roux and several members of his party and he must question him as soon as possible."

This was the inevitable conclusion. How could Jacques Roux fight back, having Robespierre and Hébert against him? Both of them called him "the infamous priest."

However, Roux's friends didn't abandon him. A delegation from the Gravilliers Section was chosen (notes communicated from the Section's registers by Bernard Lazare[11]) to find out the reason for Roux's arrest. He was released on bail on August 27, but the investigation continued. Once again the accusation of theft was thrown in. Roux was accused of having kept for himself a portion of the collection he made for the poor. All the

---

11   Information noted by Jaurès in the original text.

testimony demonstrated his selflessness and generosity, but he had to be brought down by whatever means necessary.

On the 23 Nivôse, year II (January 12, 1794), his accusers were summoned before the criminal police tribunal to make depositions against Roux concerning the *coup d'état* at his section. And on 25 Nivôse, the tribunal, upon the findings of national agent Citizen Jacquelet, declared itself incompetent because of the seriousness of the acts imputed to Roux. It transferred him to the Revolutionary Tribunal and ordered that Roux be returned to Bicêtre Prison to await judgment.

Roux, upon hearing this decision, stabbed himself three times. His courage had reached its breaking point. Covered in blood, he was transported to a neighboring room. The judges halted the hearing and asked him what had caused him to commit an act "condemned by all laws." He answered that he had been led to it by the horrible insults and accusations of his persecutors. He said "that he scorned the life of the here and now, and that in another life a happy fate awaited the friends of liberty."

Up to the bitter end we find in him this mix of Christian exaltation and revolutionary fervor.

He recommended an orphan he had taken in to the tribunal and his fellow citizens; before ending his career, he asked to have the red bonnet put on his head and to receive from the president the kiss of peace and fraternity, which the president immediately gave him.

This was the end of a noble and strangely tormented soul. He did not immediately succumb to his wounds. He was transported to the infirmary at Bicêtre, but Fouquier-Tinville[12] was informed that he was attempting "to exhaust his strength" and allow himself to die in order to escape judgment. Roux stabbed himself again, and this time, having wounded his lung, he did die. The autopsy report of 1 Ventôse noted deep wounds. And so, Robespierre and Hébert had won out over Jacques Roux, but the Commune's persecution was the more direct cause.

However narrow Jacques Roux's social doctrine was, it was an attempt to systematize popular grievances and demands and was not without influence on the Revolution's economic and financial policies. Instead of considering

---

12   Antoine Fouquier-Tinville (1746–95)—the driving force of the Revolutionary Tribunal, he was the legal soul of the Terror, and guillotined after the fall of Robespierre.

adhering to what was serious and bold in his ideas, Hébertism thought only of crushing the man who embodied this doctrine with extraordinary stubbornness and a hope that he carried beyond death. Hébert and the Commune were unforgiving.

New Social Tendencies

It was at this point that socialist tendencies began to become a distinct element in Chaumette's thought. In the great revolutionary fever of 1793, in those months of September and October when the Revolution made an immense effort to free France from treason and civil war, and the people from distress and hunger; when it was necessary to rely on the proletarians to hold back the Girondin-supporting bourgeoisie and to force the big merchants to observe the maximum, Chaumette sensed that the socialization of industry, substituting the Nation for selfish and counter-revolutionary manufacturers, might be the ultimate solution, or in any case an unavoidable expedient for ensuring salvation. There is great historical interest in noting these collectivist moments of revolutionary thought and action. Chaumette was angered by the resistance to the maximum, whose application the city government of Paris had organized with due haste, and addressed the issue when he spoke at the October 14, 1793 sitting of the Commune.

Difficulties are being experienced in the execution of the law fixing the prices of food and merchandise of primary necessity. The cupidity of certain merchants and the bad faith of speculators have found supporters. Among the merchants of Paris some have evaded the law, claiming they weren't included in it; others have argued over omissions and errors that slipped into the tariff the city government devised in execution of the law. The time spent writing the law was too short for it to be perfect. Finally, some merchants shared out their merchandise among their relatives and friends, and when we present ourselves at their homes they say they have nothing.

I'm not going to speak of the small retailers; I will only attack the big merchants, the bankers and silent partners, those bloodsuckers of the people who have always based their happiness on the people's misfortune. We remember that in 1789 and the following years all of these men were involved in a variety of business affairs, but with whom? With foreigners. It is known that it was they who caused the fall of the *assignat* [Chaumette clumsily reproduces here Fabre d'Églantine's thesis],[13] and that they grew wealthy through speculation on paper money.

What have they done since the Revolution made their fortunes? They have withdrawn from commerce and threatened the people with shortages. But if they have gold and *assignats*, the Republic has something more precious still: it has the people's muscles. It is muscles and not gold that are needed to make the factories and manufactories function. So if these individuals abandon the factories the Republic will seize them and requisition the raw materials. They must know that whenever it wants to the Republic can reduce to mud and cinders the gold and *assignats* that are in their hands. Let the giant of the people crush mercantile speculation!

It is true that this is nothing but a threat presented as a last resort. Chaumette doesn't seem to understand that even under normal conditions implementing national and republican control of the forces of production would be superior to private exploitation. He foresees the organization of industry as a public service through doing away with private ownership.

But ideas don't lose their value when they spring up from force of circumstances rather than from systematic thought; in fact, their direct revolutionary significance is heightened by this. And Chaumette's statement wasn't simply an outgrowth of the sitting: he gave his idea detailed form. He requested that a commission be established for various purposes, but particularly

... to write a petition to the National Convention that will fix its attention on raw materials and the factories; that it be asked to requisition them by pronouncing penalties against those owners or manufacturers who

---

13   This comment is by Jaurès.

leave them inactive; and that it even place them at the disposal of the Republic, which is not lacking in arms to set them working.

This is probably the first official proposal for the nationalization of industry ever made. But this idea wasn't born only in Paris. It appears that all over France, wherever sans-culotte workers suffered from the *moderantisme* and federalism of the bosses, the idea occurred to them that the Nation could become a big industrialist, a big manufacturer, whose interests and ideas would combine with the interests and ideas of the sans-culottes. And at the same sitting of the Commune,

… a deputation of members of the Directorate of the *Dèpartement* of the Nièvre reported. The orator, after having given the most extensive and satisfactory details concerning the political situation of that *dèpartement*, painted a picture of that *dèpartement*, precious thanks to its products, its mines and its forests, all of which would be of the greatest utility to the Republic if it exploited them for its own account.

16

The Terror and Fall of Robespierre

(The Terror is installed, and extends in two directions, against the right and the former ruling class, but also against the left, the Hébertists and the Enragés. *As Jaurès viewed it, from Paris, which was not at the heart of the civil war, "there should come counsels of measure, of wisdom and humanity. But Hébertism insisted on fanning the flames." Jaurès wrote of their activities:*

> *The central idea was to appear to be taking up Marat's policies. This is why Marat's heart was displayed at the Cordelier Club like a relic ... They said that true revolutionaries should renounce any other name than that of "Maratists." And in March 1794, "Maratist" meant two things at the Cordeliers: first, be rid of the enemies of the Revolution quickly and violently, and second, the prisons must be purged of aristocrats, moderates, of Girondins, and suspects of all kinds ... And (and this too was Marat's idea) in order for these actions not to be carried out blindly, in order that the ignorant rage of the people not allow counter-revolutionaries to escape or go awry and attack patriots, the operation had to be led from above by a revolutionary delegate with temporary but dictatorial powers.*

And so, the left plotted a coup d'état *in March 1794. The plot discovered, Hébert and his followers, and the others of the left, like the radical former noble Anacharsis Cloots, were arrested and guillotined on March 24.*

Then it was Danton's turn:

> *[Robespierre] was only able to receive revolutionary assent in his fight against Hébert by reassuring the fervid revolutionaries against any tendency toward* modérantisme. *He was only able to bring around the Committee of Public Safety and the Committee of General Security by openly promising in his*

speech on February 5 and through Saint-Just's speech of 8 Ventôse, to strike the Dantonist faction.

But if Hébert and his followers really had tried to raise the people up, there was nothing that Danton could directly be accused of: "Since there were no material proofs of open and flagrant guilt against Danton and his friends as there were against Hébertism, in order to accuse them it was necessary to falsify their pasts, slander their entire lives. Danton had to be turned into a royalist, a sell-out, a traitor." Danton and Camille Desmoulins are arrested on the night of March 29–30, 1794 and guillotined April 5.
Jaurès wrote of these internal bloodbaths:

What is frightful and sad is not that all these revolutionaries, fighters for the same cause, killed each other. When they entered the fight they accepted the possibility of death from the start. It was the arbitrator between them, and the parties that fought over the leadership of the Revolution had no time to work out other solutions. At a moment when so much was occurring in so short a time, where minutes counted as centuries, death alone answered to the impatience of men and the rapidity of events. It's hard to see what other proceeding the factions could have resorted to in order to settle their differences ...
The Revolution wasn't weakened by the shedding of revolutionary blood, but by the divergences in ideas and the conflicts of conscience that rendered the surgical intervention of the executioner inevitable.
It wasn't by the decapitation of all these great men, but rather by their antagonism that the Revolution gave way to dictatorship. Let us suppose that Vergniaud, Danton, Hébert, and Robespierre survived. Had their dispute lasted Bonaparte would have burst on the scene and would have used them against each other until he reconciled them in front of the firing squad. In guillotining each other the leaders of the Revolution simply spared the future military dictator the odium of their bloody execution. The effect of these successive amputations was less that of suppressing great individual abilities than that of gradually killing the people's confidence in the Revolution and in themselves. How could it have created new leaders when Samson[1] showing

---

1   The public executioner.

them from the scaffold the pallid heads of the revolutionaries, demonstrated to them that they'd been duped? Each of these existences that was torn from the earth carried with it a portion of the roots of the Revolution.

The rule of the Jacobins and the Committee of Public Safety still had many good works left to it: the imposition of a maximum price of staple goods (a central idea of the Enragés*), the further sale of national lands, the establishing of a thriving industry to support the military, and pushing a democratic ideal heretofore unknown. And so, Jaurès says, "In the spring of 1794 the bloody battles of the Revolution didn't seem to have damaged its military élan, its economic activity, or its prodigious intellectual and moral strength, which it placed at the service of a lofty ideal."*

But even so, "the Jacobins and Robespierre had entered their final stage . . . .")

The Political Problem

When the Hébertist and Dantonist heads had fallen; when a few days later, in a sinister second liquidation, those accused of fomenting the prison plot—Chaumette, Gobel, Arthur Dillon, Hébert's widow and the unfortunate Lucile [Desmoulins]—already dead to herself after Camille's death—climbed the scaffold in their turn; when this cartload of people had emptied its heads into the basket; when Hébertism and Dantonism as factions were nothing but a memory, Robespierre and the Revolution faced the decisive test.

Nothing stood in Robespierre's way, but what was he going to do?

The Revolution was no longer threatened either by a demagogic organization that would have drowned it in an abject and ferocious anarchy, or by a half-hearted conspiracy of the indulgent who, by their impatient and hostile policies seemed to surrender the repentant Revolution to the revived boldness of its enemies. What was the Revolution going to do?

The opposing forces of demagogy and *moderantisme,* between which Robespierre balanced his policies, had fallen; he now had to find his equilibrium within himself, in his own ideas, in his own policies.

The extreme tension in all the revolutionary springs, in all the forces of life and death could not persist. The Terror couldn't be the normal system of ruling, and war couldn't continue indefinitely. The maximum wasn't a law that would be forever appropriate for a society based on private property and private production. Finally, the quasi-dictatorship of the Committee of Public Safety could not be permanent. Now that there was no longer any Hébertist party to sustain the tension of the springs of terrorism, now that there was no longer a Dantonist party to relax revolutionary energy so abruptly that the Revolution risked collapsing, one policy was possible, and one alone.

The Revolution, while inspiring fear in its enemies, in conspirators and traitors, in tyrants and their armies, had to prepare the nation's return to normal life. It was necessary to loudly proclaim that revolutionary France, heroically stubborn in defending its independence and pride against the entire universe, and having already waged military campaigns that demonstrated its genius, was resolved to achieve ultimate victory and was prepared to make peace with any government that would recognize, without reservations, the Republic and the French nation's right to liberty. It was necessary that it announce that as soon as peace was possible, the *assignats* would be removed from circulation and that a vigorous system of taxation would finally allow the Revolution to stop devouring the substance of the future. With the *assignat* either completely removed from circulation, or its value maintained at par through a partial removal, the crisis in prices would come to an end and the economic terrorism of laws regulating merchandise and supplies would gradually be brought to an end, as would political terrorism.

As soon as these policies, proclaimed and adopted by the Committee of Public Safety, by the Convention, by the popular societies, and by the revolutionary nation, would be implemented and accepted; as soon as the new victories it was certain to achieve allowed it to feel secure of its future possibilities, the Committee of Public Safety should then have asked the Convention if the moment had not come to put an end to the revolutionary government and to apply the Constitution.

How can anyone doubt that the country, its resounding victories giving it hope for a peace vigorously defended against any counter-revolutionary attacks from within and without, but also having been that the revolutionary regime would not continue indefinitely, would have chosen an assembly won over to the new order?

Yes, this optimistic and confident policy was possible in Germinal and Floréal of Year II (1794) after the crushing of the extremist and opposition factions; after the defeat of the rebels of Lyon, Marseilles, Toulon, and the Vendée; after the victories at Hondschoote, Wattignies, and Alsace; after the re-establishing of the *assignat* virtually at par; and after the immense and glorious efforts of a Committee of Public Safety that was invested with immense prestige. The almost criminal error of the Dantonists was compromising this policy at the moment of its appearance. They compromised it by turning it into a means of intrigue against the Committee of Public Safety, which alone could implement it. They compromised this policy by making it look like a disavowal and a *mea culpa*.

But now the triumphant revolutionary government could affirm this policy by normalizing it. It could proclaim it, not as a final disavowal of the Revolution, but as the fruit of its victories. This policy was possible, but more importantly, it was necessary.

Outside of it, there was nothing but the anxiety of an exhausted people before whom all doors were closed. The continuation of the war, devouring the country's resources, gave rise to new forms of discontent and prepared the way for new reactionary forces. And the Terror, after having crushed the actually existing factions, frantically pursued vague will-o'-the-wisps and incoherent plots. A frighteningly diffuse menace shrouded all of life, and the Revolution, like an angered blind man, struck out at itself to the point that it wore itself out.

A policy of revolutionary calming, practiced not against the Revolution but for it, not against the revolutionaries but for them, was the only way out. I see that it was necessary and I believe that it was possible. But I add that it was infinitely difficult. When a revolution has been forced to fight against the universe in order to defend itself; when in order to protect itself during a crisis it has created a political regime as violent and paradoxical as the Terror, an economic regime as violent and paradoxical as the *assignat* and the maximum; when it has given rise to a monumental unleashing of energy and thrown 1,400,000 men—almost the entire ardent soul of the country—into war, it is difficult for it to moderate and defend itself without weakening itself. The Revolution bore the original sin of war in its soul and its flesh, and it remained deformed by it.

How could it wholeheartedly carry out a war for liberty that was necessary and sacred while at the same time anchoring its policies and tactics in the uncertain hypothesis of peace? How could it announce that a normalized Revolution would immediately withdraw the *assignats* from circulation while at the same time reserving the right to issue them again should the prolongation of the conflict with Europe force it to? If they fail to inform the public of the desired goal, it will understand nothing of the policies of the Committee of Public Safety and will take its seemingly contradictory attitudes—dictated for some by concern for the immediate threat, for others by calculations based on long-term possibilities—for incompetence and treason. If they are told of this in advance, how can their enthusiasm be maintained, which, in great crises, is a vital necessity. How could the armies, which were beginning to feel an enthusiasm that was sublime but was already dangerous, maintain their vigor and élan if a policy of peace were to suddenly limit the boundless dreams of combat, danger, and glory that are the source of pleasure for both revolutionary patriotism and the secret calculations of ambition? Even if it could be foreseen that the maximum and the policy of requisition and taxation would end when the war was terminated or scaled back and the circulation of the *assignat* reduced, the *assignat* couldn't be immediately abolished, and as long as the policy remained in place, it would develop in keeping with its own logic, and the very difficulties it ran up against forced it to be pushed ever further.

Now the citizens were clamoring against the unfortunate and at times harmful effects of the unequal application of the maximum based on regions and industries. There were some who sold at the maximum and bought at competitive prices, which is an intolerable system. The maximum had to be applied everywhere with the same rigor or it should not have been applied at all. But for it to be applied everywhere with precision and rigor would it not have been safest to constitute, under the watchful eye of the Nation and the Commune, vast storehouses to which producers would bring all their goods and where distribution would take place in accordance with the law and at prices fixed by it?

This is precisely what was demanded by the Jacobin Society of Montereau. And one of Robespierre's closest friends, his childhood friend in Arras, the very man who warned him of Joseph Lebon's[2] cruelties, Antoine Buissart, wrote to him that commerce should be confided to the *communes*. How would it be possible to return to the regime of free circulation and free markets when it is impossible to abolish the law of the maximum overnight and when the latter, by its very functioning, hinted at systems even more all-encompassing?

The political and economic problems to be resolved were extraordinarily difficult, and were perhaps even superhuman. I mean by this that not only were they beyond the strength of an individual, but they were also beyond the strength of a nation to resolve. The application of calculus to moral forces, which according to Condorcet was the supreme progress of science, had not yet been realized, and no one knew if it was possible to regulate the enthusiasm and passion of an entire people without diminishing these sentiments or how the transition from the revolutionary to the normal state could be carried out. And so it is not surprising that immediately after crushing the factions that worsened but also masked the problems, Robespierre and his friends were gripped by hesitation and apprehension.

Saint-Just's Plans and Robespierre's Policies

Peace and the re-establishing of normal economic relations were Saint-Just's and Robespierre's secret hope and policy, but either they didn't dare openly formulate it, or they didn't know how to bend events and men in that direction. The intrepid Saint-Just knew that the Republic couldn't live on Terror; that it didn't bring out the necessary virtues, and that in lasting so long it had ceased to strike fear in vice and crime. He knew that the regime of the *assignats* and the maximum could not indefinitely continue, but in

---

2　Joseph Lebon (1765–95)—as mayor of Arras, he carried out a severe Reign of Terror against the aristocracy and enemies of the Revolution, though he was also accused of being in the pay of the counter-revolution. He was executed for "abuse of power."

the notes he wrote for his own use, in which he wrote of the need for great changes, he spoke of the need to temporize and be prudent. At times he seemed to expect the very excess of evil to be a remedy. After the removal of the Hébertists and the Dantonists, when all that he had to do was harvest the Revolution's victory, he wrote:

> The Revolution is frozen; principles have lost their force. All that is left are the red bonnets donned by intrigue. The exercise of the Terror had dulled crime, just as strong liquors do to the palate. It is doubtless not yet time to do good. The individual good we do is a palliative. We must wait for a general evil that is so great that public opinion feels the need for measures capable of doing good. That which produces the general good is always terrifying and appears bizarre when it is begun too early.

Speaking of commodities, he denounced the country's systems of the *assignat* and taxation as foreign inventions:

> From vicissitude to vicissitude the foreigners led us to these extremities. They also suggest a remedy. The original idea for taxation came from without, brought by the Baron de Batz. It would have led to famine. In Europe it is generally recognized today that it was hoped that famine would incite popular wrath and destroy the Convention and that the dissolving of the Convention was counted on in order to tear apart and dismember France. The circulation of commodities is necessary wherever everyone does not have property or primary goods. *Commodities don't circulate where taxes are levied* [underlined emphasis by Saint-Just]. The *assignats* must be taken out of circulation by taxing all those who have guided affairs and worked in the pay of the public treasury.

But it is precisely apropos of these ideas that Saint-Just reminds himself of the law of prudence, which calls for waiting and allowing ideas to mature:

> We would have presented the hemlock to whoever would have said these things eight months ago, but we have grown wise through experiencing

misfortune. May this example teach us not to mistreat stern men who tell us the truth.

Good people should not be reduced to justifying themselves for working for the public good in the face of the sophistries of crime. It's a fine thing to say that they will die for the fatherland, but they shouldn't die; rather they should live and the laws should support them. They should be sheltered from the vengeance of the foreigner. *I thus advise* [underlined emphasis again by Saint-Just] all those who want the good to wait for the right moment to do it in order to avoid the notoriety that is obtained by doing it too soon.

All of these words poorly conceal immense difficulties.

However great he may have been, Robespierre was lacking in the qualities required to solve all these problems. To be sure, for months he had learned to assume the most direct and terrible responsibilities. Since May 31, he seemed to have renounced speaking in a roundabout and allusive fashion. He now headed straight for the goal, straight at the enemy. But it should be noted that it was only when his preferred system was attacked that Robespierre revealed what he wanted and completely committed himself. After May 31, he saw that the authority of the Committee of Public Safety and the Convention were the salvation of the Revolution, and he fought courageously against every intrigue that threatened the Committee and the Convention. He feared that Hébertism would discredit and destroy the Republic and attacked Hébertism head on. But as soon as there were no enemies, as soon as the lack of precise attacks against him no longer forced him to have precise answers, he returned to his vague and wily habits.

When, after the elimination of Hébertism and Dantonism, he was truly the master of policy and was responsible for events, there was only one means to govern and rally the people around him, and that was to clearly say where he wanted to lead the Revolution. But he failed to do so, and at his side the proud and courageous Saint-Just, as if he had renounced defying death, counseled silence and temporization, which was fatal, for it gave rise to wide-spread uncertainty. Even more, after the great and bloody purges of Germinal, Robespierre's duty was to reassure the revolutionaries around him. The factions had been smashed and there was no reason to attack individuals, even if they were connected to these factions, even if they had carried out the most detestable policies. Robespierre knew this, and he limited sacrifices as much as he could. He had saved the 73 Girondins; he had opposed including Boulanger, Pache, and Hanriot in the outlawing of the Hébertists; he hadn't laid a finger on Carrier,[3] despite the horror he felt for the crimes in Nantes; he hadn't spoken out at the Committee of Public Safety against Collot d'Herbois.[4] But it wasn't enough not to strike these men; they had to be given confidence in the future. They had to be given the impression, and even the certainty, that their excesses would be imputed to the revolutionary fever, and that once this fever had fallen they would not be made to pay for the perhaps inevitable violence of the evil days. In addition, the fears of those like Tallien[5] in Bordeaux who, with his beautiful female companion Cabarrus, had surrendered to the attractions of power and pleasure, had to be taken into consideration, these people who saw in the oft-repeated words of virtue and morality a threat to their very lives.

So Robespierre was obliged either to condemn himself to a policy of perpetual gallows or to announce—and carry out—a large-scale revolutionary amnesty for all the aberrations of the Terror, for its sensual as well as its murderous frenzies. Then all the revolutionary energies that had momentarily been either over-stimulated by violent fanaticism or corrupted by a passionate and lascivious intoxication could hope for a place in the new, calmer, purer, more stable, revolutionary order.

Finally, the more powerful Robespierre was, the more important it was for him to show consideration for the self-esteem of his colleagues on the Committee of Public Safety and the Committee of General Security, to include them in all his ideas and acts. How could he calm, pacify, and

---

3   Jean-Baptiste Carrier (1756–94)—left-wing member of the convention, most famous for the fierce repression he carried out in Nantes during the rebellion in the Vendée. He was guillotined for his actions there after the fall of Robespierre.

4   Jean-Marie Collot d'Herbois (1749–96)—Jacobin deputy who, despite carrying out fierce repression of counter-revolutionaries in Lyon and being a member of the Committee of Public Safety, was later an opponent of Robespierre and participated in the latter's downfall. He was deported to Guyana after the 9 Thermidor; he died during his deportation.

5   Jean-Lambert Tallien (1767–1820)—defender of the September Massacres, he was a participant in the events in May and June 1792. Responsible for harsh repression in Bourdeaux while sent there on mission, he was a key player in the downfall of Robespierre.

organize the Revolution without the collaboration of the Committee of Public Safety? And how could he win over fanatics like Billaud-Varenne and hysterical and compromised declaimers like Collot d'Herbois to a broader policy if he didn't demonstrate confidence, frankness, and cordiality? Robespierre wasn't able to earn the confidence of those around him. Over the course of the bitter struggle, when he had had to assume so many bloody responsibilities, his pride had grown even greater. He had exclaimed in August 1793, "The Revolution is lost if a man doesn't emerge."

He had emerged, but having been forced to strike out on all sides and to deal out death, he had acquired a haughty melancholy. He was not made for those cordial conversations that were the absolute condition for the success of his policies. His dignity, his pride, and his pure love for the Revolution had suffered from the horrific violence that had dishonored the revolutionary government and he wasn't able to forget them. He detested the violence all the more because, not having been able to prevent it, he appeared to be in solidarity with it, and deep in his heart he sought a way to break with it in the eyes of history. This was a deplorable temptation inspired by pride and virtue. He despairingly remembered everything when he should have forgotten much, and sometimes those he scorned and hated saw on his face the disturbing reflection of a profound thought.

Finally, and this is the frightful cost of the gallows, for months death had so regularly been the final expedient, the ultimate solution, that it became entirely too familiar a choice whenever there arose a problem too troubling or too great to be solved. Death would either defeat the evil and corrupted men who sullied the Revolution or it would open to the virtuous the shelter of immortality they aspired to. Robespierre and Saint-Just sometimes felt a disquiet that resembled remorse. Was it possible? Vergniaud was dead, and dead by their hands? Desmoulins was dead, and dead by their hands? And quietly, in those hours of trouble, they would offer themselves up to death in order to absolve themselves for having so often appealed to it against comrades in the struggle, against friends.

Saint-Just wanted to live; he understood that the politics of death was the negation of the Revolution itself, one that that even the most illustrious shades wouldn't defend. And yet, how haunted he was by the ghosts of those whom he had sent to the gallows with a simple wave of his hand. And what a poignant mixture of melancholy and pride in the lines he wrote after Danton's death: "I had the touching idea that the memory of a friend of humanity must one day be cherished. For *the man forced to isolate himself from the world and from himself drops his anchor in the future, and, holds posterity, which is innocent of the evils of the present, to his heart.*"

It was Saint-Just himself who underlined these words, this appeal from a man already uprooted from life:

God, protector of innocence and truth, since you led me among the evil it was certainly in order to unmask them.

Our policies had depended on the idea that no one would dare attack famous men imprisoned in a grand illusion. I left all these weaknesses behind: in the entire universe the only thing I love is truth, and I have spoken it.

The times are difficult only for those who retreat before the tomb. I ask for the tomb as a blessing granted by providence so I will no longer be witness to the crimes plotted against my fatherland and humanity.

To be sure it is a small thing to leave a life that is unhappy, one in which one is condemned to vegetate, the accomplice or the impotent witness to crime.

I scorn the dust I am made of and which speaks to you. Let them persecute and kill that dust. But I defy them to wrest from me the independent life I have seized for myself in time and the heavens.

His words reveal a somber and sterilizing exaltation. These men's eyes were fascinated by the gates of death that they had so often opened for others. And at a time when they should have given the Revolution confidence in the goodness of life and calmed a people obsessed with bloody memories, they thought only of their own graves.

The Cult of the Supreme Being

In the meanwhile, Robespierre couldn't remain in this suspended state. The Revolution, France, and Europe awaited a word, a signal from him, but his first great act was a great mistake. In Floréal, he proposed and, after a long, eloquent speech, had the Convention adopt, the official recognition of the Supreme Being and the immortality of the soul. This was indeed a decisive political mistake. Not that these deist assertions shocked the reason of most Frenchmen: atheists and materialists were rare. Those who, like Danton, were to say before the Revolutionary Tribunal: "The void shall soon be my home" thought it politic to speak of God. It is also true that materialist pantheism was able to accommodate and interpret the word "God." The most deist among them, men like Laveaux, the former editor of the *Journal de la Montagne*, more or less confounded God with "the order of nature," and the Convention itself had decreed a Festival of the Supreme Being and Nature. Perhaps if at that time there had existed a clearly expressed and fully conscious form of socialism, it would have objected that the God external and superior to the world invoked by Robespierre to accomplish and ensure human justice negated human solidarity in the here-and-now. It rendered justice to each person individually, and all these separate souls, all these spirits whose destinies were fulfilled outside of humanity, diminished human society, since it was outside and above it that they found happiness and right. But communism hadn't yet found its form or fashioned a metaphysics of the world.

In addition, those who, like Condorcet, wanted no other Elysium than one created by reason were only a tiny and negligible minority. For many, the great revolutionary crisis had stirred the love of immortal life. The Christians, who'd been submerged by the indifference that dominated the century, rediscovered the ardor of their faith during these trials. How many of those in the tumbrils taking them to the gallows sought out in the crowd the non-juring priest who had promised them a sign of eternal reconciliation? The revolutionaries as well, into whom Rousseau had insinuated, like a vague moral reverie, the idea of immortality, now loved it with all the frenzy of those whose lives were in danger. The gallows filled the city with the glow of immortality. In their last words and final despairing writings, the Girondins attested to their faith in God and the immortal soul, and from his prison cell Camille Desmoulins asked Lucile to send him Plato's book on the immortality of the soul. To many of those exalted by misfortune, by heroism and glory, immortality seemed the sublime meeting place of the heroes of the centuries: Charlotte Corday, with the serenity of the ancients, said that she was going to join on the Elysian Fields those in all countries and all times who had died for freedom and the Fatherland. The Christian paradise seemed to have been eclipsed, like a dark, intermediate zone, by the great light of immortal glory that shone from ancient Rome and modern France. The Elysian Fields were a glowing avenue, continuous and serene, that went from Decius to Charlotte Corday, bypassing the centuries of the Middle Ages.

Saint-Just, in his pained and superb cry quoted above, seemed to confuse the immortality of the spirit and the immortality of glory: "... the independent life I gave myself *in the centuries and in the heavens.*"

The Convention's decree was not an abdication, but rather a display of the pride of reason and liberty. It made it appear that God's official recognition by Revolutionary France added to God's luster. And when Saint-Just speaks in his *Institutions* of the eternal, one would think he is making even God's judgment subject to the decrees of revolutionary thought:

The French people recognize the Supreme Being and the immortality of the soul ... The immortal soul of those who died for the Fatherland; of those who were good citizens, who cherished their father and mother and never abandoned them, lies within the breast of the Eternal.

More than God, it is the Revolution that separates the good from the evil for all eternity, and heaven is nothing but an invisible Pantheon where God resides but whose keys are held by the Revolution. And it opens the doors to those whose brows it has marked with an immortal sign.

So if Robespierre's act was dangerous and evil it's not because there was a violent contradiction between the deist formulas it imposed on the spirit of the French people and the French people themselves. It was not this, but rather that in organizing a Festival of the Supreme Being, by promulgating a philosophical dogma and organizing a kind of religion, he appeared to be seeking new powers for himself. He was, in fact, the head of the civil power. It appeared that he sought to become the leader of a religious power, and this gave rise to mistrust. In addition, the priests, ever alert for any ambiguity that could serve their purposes, went about saying that this Supreme Being was, after all, nothing but the God of Christianity. They saw the Festival of the Supreme Being as a transition towards the official glorification of Jesus. As a result, Robespierre revived counter-revolutionary hopes more than the *Vieux Cordelier*[6] had. Finally, Robespierre, after having crushed Hébertism as a faction, seemed to be taking posthumous revenge on the Hébertist spirit, which constituted a terrible threat for the survivors.

The Committee of Public Safety had allowed this to go on. But neither Billaud-Varenne, nor Collot d'Herbois, nor even Barère had approved this movement, which was marked with Robespierre's personal religious ideas. Robespierre hadn't dared directly confront the issues. He hadn't said to the thousands of men who had faith in him, "This is the road down which the Revolution must go." No; he prepared the easing of the Revolution by turning people's minds towards ideas he considered great. He wanted to calm the revolutionary fever by taking a religious and moral detour. But this was a deep and dark road, and Robespierre isolated himself, set himself apart, at the very moment when he should have been conciliatory, when he should have called all revolutionary forces—with their mixture of good and bad—to his side.

This was when people grew embittered and turned away from him, and the yeast of worry and mistrust once again fermented within the Revolution. On a beautiful day in Prairial, Robespierre, president of the Convention, led the cortege that bore to God the Revolution's official recognition. The joy that shone from his face was short-lived. Some murmurings, some outbursts from the deputies warned him of the burgeoning hatred and fear. He marched slightly ahead of the Convention: "There goes the dictator! He wants to attract the people's attention to himself alone! It's not enough for him to be king; he wants to be God!"

Suddenly the abyss opened. He had to strike again. Blood had to be spilled again. Yes, Robespierre wanted to strike. He wanted to act before his enemies, whose only wish was to act before he did. And death would circulate anew in this closed circuit of mistrust and terror.

---

6   Newspaper edited by Camille Desmoulins.

The Law of Prairial and the Great Terror

But this time Robespierre, as if in a fever, wanted to bring everything to a close. He wanted to hasten the march of revolutionary justice and free it of any hindrances to its delivering the blows that were required. In the first instance, the prisons were too full, and Robespierre could no longer open their gates, not even through the Justice Committee that he'd set up in opposition to Camille Desmoulins' Pardons Committee. His inopportune Festival of the Supreme Being had revived the hopes of counter-revolutionaries and the suspicions of the fanaticized revolutionaries. He had to attack the counter-revolution in order to have the strength to attack the revolutionaries who threatened him, that is, what was left of Hébertism and perhaps a segment of the Committee of Public Safety. And so, with a sinister monotony, the see-saw with Hébertists and Dantonists on opposite seats of the same board was repeated. But this time he needed a more frighteningly ambiguous murder weapon.

When there were still parties, they could be attacked by use of general but still precise definitions. Every party represents a tendency, has characteristics that the revolutionary judge can take note of. But once factions have been smashed, once the revolutionary power has nothing to fear but individual hatreds, loose groupings, and obscure and fleeting intrigues, then the law of death must be as formless as the feared conspiracy.

Robespierre, because of his weakness in the aftermath of his victory over the Hébertists and Dantonism, because of the mistrust he had awakened by his clumsy deist initiative, was forced to kill again. And he had to kill—at the same time and with the same law—a horrifying mixture of counter-revolutionaries, suspects held in the prisons, and men like Carrier, Fouché, and Barras, whom he feared and who feared him.

In his final speech during Thermidor, he would say something that serves as the key to those dark days: "The fall of the factions liberated all vices." He meant by this that the revolutionary power, of which he was the highest representative, was no longer threatened by political systems, but by the dispersed intrigues of egoism, envy, and fear. The law of death needed to be able to seep into this wide variety of hearts. And in order for it to adapt to all forms, it had to be formless, be an ambiguous specter that one day would recruit its victims in the prisons, on the Mountain of the Convention, and at the Committee of Public Safety.

This was the Law of Prairial. It can be summed up by saying that it created vague crimes, dispensed the accuser of providing any proof, and deprived the accused of any means of defense:

The Revolutionary Tribunal is established to punish the enemies of the people.

The enemies of the people are those who seek to destroy public liberty either by force or by ruse.

The enemies of the people are those who provoked the re-establishment of the monarchy or sought to demean or dissolve the National Convention and the revolutionary and republican government of which it is the center;

Those in the command of forts and armies and any other military function who betrayed the Republic;

Those who sought to prevent the provisioning of Paris or caused famine in the Republic;

Those who assisted the projects of the enemies of France, either by favoring the retreat and the impunity granted conspirators and the aristocracy; or by corrupting the elected representatives of the people; or by abusing the principles of the Revolution, or the laws and measures of the government through false and perfidious applications of them;

Those who misled the people or the representatives of the people in order to induce them to undertake measures contrary to the interest of liberty;

Those who seek to inspire discouragement in order to favor the undertakings of the tyrannies leagued against the Republic;

Those who spread false news in order to divide and trouble the people;

Those who seek to lead public opinion astray and to prevent the education of the people, to deprave morals, and to corrupt the public conscience.

Truly, with such vague crimes there was not a man in France, counter-revolutionary or revolutionary, who wasn't threatened by the law of 22 Prairial. And what summary procedures! What a terrible punishment!

The punishment for all crimes falling under the jurisdiction of the Revolutionary Tribunal is death.

The proof necessary to condemn the enemies of the people is any kind of document, either material or moral, either verbal or written, which would naturally gain the assent of any fair and reasonable person. The rule governing judgment is the conscience of the jurors enlightened by the love of the Fatherland. Their goal: the triumph of the Republic and the destruction of its enemies. The procedure: the simple methods that good sense indicates are needed to arrive at the knowledge of truth in the forms determined by the law.

If there exist either material or moral proofs independent of testimonial proofs, no witnesses shall be heard unless this formality appears necessary in order to uncover accomplices or for other major considerations of public interest.

The law grants slandered patriots patriotic jurors as their defenders. It grants none to conspirators.

And so, no witnesses, except witnesses for the prosecution; no defenders; no discussion: nothing but summary execution. This law of Prairial is like a fantastic knife that appears everywhere, glides like a shadow, and suddenly, when it touches the vertebrae of the neck, becomes murderously rigid.

From this point and however one might view the matter, Robespierre was lost. This law demonstrates that he was no longer capable of confronting the immensity of the problems and events, and that the void left by the disappearance of his enemies had caused him to lose his way. In all likelihood, when he proposed and imposed this atrocious law on the Committee of Public Safety it was with the hope and the thought of bringing things to a quick conclusion. No discussions, nothing that recalled the scenes of the trial of the Dantonists: silent, rapid, and oppressive death. Robespierre thought that after a few weeks of this regime, which would freeze with fright all the enemies of the Revolution, he would have so totally eliminated all those he called "fake revolutionaries" that he would finally be able to introduce a normal regime.

The excesses of the Terror were to have led to the abolition of the Terror. Robespierre dreamed of intensifying terrorism, of concentrating it into a few terrifying and unforgettable weeks in order to have the strength and the right to put an end to it. If the Terror were to be diluted or prolonged, there was a risk of permanently enervating the Revolution. Let all the horror be crammed into a few days. O Death, sinister craftsman, hurry, do your work in haste. Don't rest either by day or by night. And when your horrible task is completed, you will be placed on permanent leave.

This was a mad dream. Instead of playing this desperate card at the risk of seeming the dupe, Robespierre should have demonstrated confidence in the survivors of the factions he'd smashed. Even if he were to succeed or appear to succeed; even if he managed to simultaneously strike the counter-revolutionary and suspect prisoners and those revolutionaries who offended or disgusted him, it would only have been a temporary solution: it would have been necessary to start over the next day. A policy of confidence, the only one that could have saved the Revolutionary government after the elimination of organized Hébertism and Dantonism, became even more difficult after the period of frantic executions. New suspicions would have arisen, provoking new rigorous measures. But there was a strong possibility that this risky and horrific operation would not succeed. It had hardly been implemented before it united against Robespierre a coalition of all who had reason for worry or fear. The counter-revolutionaries, the suspects, and the moderates, become the bloody ransom for future and uncertain schemes for clemency, immediately tied the name of Robespierre to the system of the Terror. In their eyes he became the man of the Law of Prairial.

The Girondins and their friends who he had saved wondered if he hadn't done so calculatedly and if they weren't going to be sacrificed to new calculations, while hanging over the Dantonists was the threat of "morality."

All the representatives on mission who according to Robespierre, had "abused revolutionary principles" and compromised the Convention by their cruelties or disorganization, Tallien, Barras, Carrier, and Fouché, read on Robespierre's face—however inscrutable it might have been—

their death sentence. They instinctively found their means of defense: Robespierre was headed towards dictatorship, or rather he already exercised it. At the Festival of the Supreme Being, low yet audible voices had murmured as he passed: "There are still Brutuses." The Law of Prairial had not received the whole-hearted consent of the entire Committee of Public Safety: Robespierre had written it with Couthon and Saint-Just, and the others had simply gone along with it. Billaud-Varenne and Collot d'Herbois began to take fright, the latter for his safety, the former for his share of power and at Robespierre's primacy. The Convention passed the law, but added a reservation that cancelled out the use Robespierre had hoped for: the Convention decreed that it alone could proceed to the arrest of its members. Robespierre couldn't strike the rapid and decisive blows he'd contemplated.

The same distrust could be found in the Committee of General Security, whose police bureau, created by Robespierre and annexed by him to the Committee of Public Safety, had offended many. Robespierre felt himself caught in a web of hostility, and the terrible law he counted on for the final liquidation of the Terror was paralyzed and deformed.

At that point he adopted a change in tactics and feigned loss of interest in it. Now the law could no longer touch the main guilty parties, those seated in the Convention. Now that it couldn't with certainty and at the moment chosen by Robespierre purge the Revolution of Carrier, Fouché, Bourdon de l'Oise, Tallien, and Barras, it was nothing but an imbecilic machine for pointless killing. It was better to leave the responsibility for its functioning to those who had thwarted its political value.

For its part the Revolutionary Tribunal, as if it too wanted to escape its frightful responsibility by taking on the appearance of an automaton, interpreted the law of Prairial as a law of mechanical murder. It was simply a question of killing as many people as possible. On a daily basis the accused filled several rows of seats and were sent off with barely a word; heads fell by the hundreds. This was the great Terror, which caused more victims in the few weeks between 22 Prairial and the 9 Thermidor[7] than the revolutionary regime had between March 1793 and 22 Prairial of the year II. The guillotine was the subject of appalling intrigue. In order to make

---

7   That is, June 10–July 27, 1794.

it clear that it wasn't his machine, that it wasn't his law, Robespierre didn't intervene or moderate its use. The public prosecutor, Fouquier-Tinville, and the juries, affecting not to see that the law had lost a large part of what, for Robespierre, had been its *raison d'être*, saw to it that it functioned at full steam. Many consoled themselves with the thought that it rendered Robespierre odious without making him any stronger. And Robespierre couldn't say, "You know full well that the there's no point to this law since it can no longer punish the wretches taking refuge in the Convention." No, he couldn't say this; he couldn't disavow the mangled machine that killed in his name. His enemies didn't let a single occasion pass that might compromise him or do him harm. They made much noise concerning the petition of a zealot of the Supreme Being, who demanded that the name of god not be profaned by oaths.

Was the Inquisition to be reborn? Yes, an Inquisition and a dictatorship, and Robespierre, as Saint-Just said, was going to be accused of "having Sulla's phalanxes march before God."[8]

A crackpot, a madwoman, Catherine Théot, connected to the Benedictine Dom Gerle, announced the advent of a mystical era during which Robespierre would be the savior of men. The Committee of General Security carried out an inquest concerning this absurd affair, inflated its importance, and Robespierre had a hard time saving the prophetess from the gallows.

Was the Incorruptible preparing his tyranny by corrupting the minds of the simple with religious fanaticism? Barère cynically praised the Law of Prairial, perhaps to court Robespierre, perhaps in order to increase the all-embracing Terror with fright-inducing comments. He said with a calculated and heinous joviality, "It is only the dead who never return."

Billaud-Varenne and Collot d'Herbois either sulked or, at the stormy sittings of the Committee of Public Safety, attacked Robespierre. Barère remained silent; Saint-Just was with the army; Carnot and Prieur cloistered themselves in their military specialty. Lindet dealt with virtually nothing but staple goods, and it should be recalled that he had refused

---

8   Lucius Cornelius Sulla Felix (138 BCE–78 BCE)—Roman general and statesman who twice had his armies march on Rome and who revived the title of Dictator. While in office he carried out important constitutional reforms.

to sign Danton's death sentence, saying, "I'm here to feed patriots, not to kill them."

Isolated and embittered, from early Messidor,[9] Robespierre refused to appear at the Committee of Public Safety. Or at least he ceased to assume his share of activity and responsibility. Why does M. Hamel insist on denying this? He cites in vain a few Committee decrees signed by Robespierre in these final weeks. This signifies nothing but the execution of a mechanical task.

But political deliberations were suspended, as Saint-Just himself declared in his speech of 9 Thermidor. Robespierre, no longer able to count on the Law of Prairial, feigned lack of interest in it. No longer the master of the government, he left the responsibility for governing to others. Instead, he prepared his revenge. He was going to attempt by other means to cut off the heads that he couldn't obtain through the Law of Prairial. He assured himself of the ever-closer cooperation of the Jacobins, who were still fervently behind him. It was through him and him alone that they saw democracy and the Revolution sovereign and organized. In the Commune, national agent Payan had replaced Chaumette, and Pache and Mayor Fleuriot were totally devoted to him. Hanriot, who commanded the National Guard, was also in his pocket. Would he use the power of the people to force the Convention's hand, to wrest the indictment from it against those he wanted to destroy and which only they had the right to issue? No. Robespierre still counted on the force of his words, on his moral authority, on all those things that backstair intrigues had undermined but hadn't destroyed. At the Jacobin Club, he took the initiative against Fouché. He attacked him for his materialist and atheist policies in the Nièvre; and as if to mix all grievances together and provide a guarantee to the revolutionaries, he also accused Fouché of having mistreated the most ardent democrats of Lyon, the friends of Chalier.[10] Fouché refused to accept combat on the battleground of the Jacobin Club. Surprised by the first attack and invited to explain himself at a later sitting, he didn't

---

9   That is, mid-June.

10   Marie-Joseph Chalier (1747–93)—leader of the sans-culottes of Lyon, he was guillotined for his revolutionary activities there and became one of the great martyrs of the revolutionary cause.

appear, instead weaving together the threads of the conspiracy against Robespierre. That night he went to warn the members of the Convention he knew to be—or believed to be, or wanted to believe to be—threatened. Lists of the proscribed, an addition to the everyday by fear and intrigue, circulated. Perhaps the Convention, made courageous by its great fear, would strike first.

And it was precisely during the period when Robespierre seemed to have become indifferent to the Committee of Public Safety that the army achieved its most brilliant victories. The Army of the Sambre-et-Meuse under the command of Jourdan, with Kléber and Marceau as lieutenants, had accelerated its march. On 7 Messidor it took Charleroi; on 8 Messidor, after a long and glorious combat, it dislodged the Austrians from the battlefield of Fleurus and forced their retreat. On 22 Messidor it made its triumphant entry into Brussels. With each new victory it became more difficult for Robespierre to strike at the Committee of Public Safety. This is why Barère would later say, "The victories fell on Robespierre like Furies." The moment of crisis had arrived.

The 9 Thermidor

In his dreams, Robespierre goes to Ermenonville and walks alongside Rousseau. He will ask the primordial innocence of his visions and ideas for the strength to follow the bloody road to its end. And on 8 Thermidor he took the fight to the Convention. He complained that it was originally the Committee of Public Safety that was accused of dictatorship and tyranny, and that this accusation had gradually become focused on him alone. He complained that in order to eliminate him the claim was being made that he was planning to lead the Convention to destroy itself, to surrender itself piecemeal. He affirmed that these fears were vain; that the "rogues" were few in number and he asked if the Republic, which only virtue could save, would be sacrificed to this handful of rogues.

Would all the difficulties come to an end if the Convention were to surrender a few more heads to him? What would his policies be the next day? And would the barely disguised threat contained in the speech against Cambon[11] suffice to make new financial and economic policies possible?

Robespierre didn't name these few "rogues," and so the threat, which he had wanted to limit, because vague, became immense. Every single member of the Convention felt himself to be under the blade. And again, once this "handful of rogues" would have been brought down, what assurance did the Convention have that the next day and the day after Robespierre would not ask for new batches of victims?

I don't know why Buchez and Roux[12] say that the most important mistake in Robespierre's speech was that it was nothing but the preface to the speech Saint-Just wanted to give the following day, and which announced that the Committee of Public Safety would hand its powers over to the Convention. This was Saint-Just's final tactical move, partially setting himself apart from Robespierre. Nothing allows us to say that this was what Robespierre had in mind. In all likelihood, he was not ready to dissolve the revolutionary government and enter the Convention, where so much anger, rancor, and fear were fermenting, disarmed. And if the vagueness of his speech of 8 Thermidor was a mortal error, it was also an inevitable one. Given the road he had chosen Robespierre couldn't say, "This is what the final step will be." He had condemned himself to forever reserving the possibility of striking again.

Nevertheless, Robespierre's prestige had not yet been totally squandered and his speech was applauded. But Charlier, Cambon, Amar, and Billaud-Varenne (who had been expelled from the Jacobin Club the day before), and Panis opposed its being sent to the *départements*. Charlier wanted to force Robespierre to name names: "When someone brags of having the courage of virtue he must have the courage of truth. Name those you accuse."

If Robespierre were to name them, however few they were, given that they represented all tendencies of the Convention the whole of the Convention would feel itself threatened. But if he didn't dare name them

---

11   Robespierre had given a violent speech attacking Pierre-Joseph Cambon, president of the Convention's Finance Committee, for economic policies that hurt the middle class and the poor.

12   Authors of the multi-volume *Histoire Parlémantaire de la Révolutions Française*.

then what solution could he hope for? He remained silent. In a way, Bréard put an end to his shaky dictatorship with a phrase that re-established the power of the Convention: "This is an important issue that must be judged by the Convention itself."

And the Convention decided that the speech wouldn't be sent to the *départements*. Robespierre had tried to exert his moral force, but it hadn't been enough to tame the revolt of the threatened members of the Convention. He was finished. At the Jacobins that night, after having read the speech he'd given at the Convention, he said: "This is my last will and testament."

Saint-Just, recalled from the army during the tragic night of 8–9 Thermidor, was appealed to by Robespierre's enemies, the fraction of the Committee of Public Safety led by Billaud-Varenne. Saint-Just didn't want to betray Robespierre, but he sought a deal. He recognized that Robespierre was wrong to stay away for so long from the meetings of the Committee of Public Safety, but he accused Billaud-Varenne and Collot d'Herbois of having sought—in the absence of an embittered Robespierre, of Saint-Just delegated to the armies, of Jean Bon Saint-André still on the coast, of the ill Couthon—to take control of the revolutionary government. His plan seems to have been to change the members of the Committee of Public Safety, to expand it in order to do away with its *esprit de coterie*, and by doing so revive the power of the Convention. But the moment had passed for striking these kinds of bargains, which would have reassured no one. Who would dominate the renewed or enlarged Committee of Public Safety? And who would wield the axe?

On 9 Thermidor, Saint-Just was only able to deliver the first lines of his speech. The battle between Robespierre and his enemies had begun. Billaud-Varenne and Tallien led the fight.

As soon as Saint-Just alluded to his controversies with Billaud-Varenne, saying "The confidence of the two committees honored me, but last night someone struck at my heart … ." Billaud-Varenne violently interrupted him and seized the tribune:

Know, Citizens, he exclaimed, that yesterday the president of the Revolutionary Tribunal openly proposed to the Jacobins to drive all the impure from the Convention, that is, all those they want to sacrifice. But the people are here, and the patriots will know how to die to defend freedom. (*"Yes, yes" shouted a large number of members.*)

Billaud-Varenne continued: "An abyss has opened beneath our feet: we must not hesitate to either fill it with our corpses or to triumph over the traitors."

Robespierre climbed the tribune to respond, but the cries of "Down with the tyrant! Down with the tyrant!" drowned him out. This was the watchword worked out during the night-time meetings organized by Fouché. Tallien leapt up alongside Robespierre:

I imposed silence on myself until now because someone close to the tyrant of France had informed me that he'd drawn up a proscription list. I didn't want to cast any recriminations, but I saw yesterday's meeting of the Jacobins and I trembled for the Fatherland. I saw the army of a new Cromwell being formed, and I armed myself with a dagger to pierce his breast if the National Convention lacked the courage to indict him.

But more than anything else, Robespierre's enemies wanted to smash his outside support. Tallien demanded the arrest of Hanriot and that the Convention remain in permanent session "until the sword of the law has saved the Revolution." All that was left was the arrest of Robespierre. But it appears that the Convention hesitated before this decisive act. Would it not be striking at the Revolution itself?

Tallien convinced the Convention and led it to act by elevating the glory and the impersonal force of the Revolution over that of individuals. He denounced

… this man who, in the Committee of Public Safety, should have been the defender of the oppressed; who should have been at his post but abandoned it for four decades.[13] And when did he do this? When the Army of the North was causing his colleagues great concern. He

---

13   Ten-day weeks that were part of the revolutionary calendar.

abandoned it in order to slander the Committee, and it was they who saved the Fatherland. (*Loud applause.*)

Tallien, having granted the Committees all the benefits of victory, placed the responsibility for the Terror on Robespierre: "It was while Robespierre was charged with general policy that the acts of oppression of individuals were committed."

"That's not true," shouted Robespierre.

He climbed the first steps of the tribune and, no longer able to make himself heard above the tumult, he appealed to the patriots of the Mountain. They no longer knew him: it was the moment of abandonment, and they turned their heads away. And as if to oppose one coalition against another coalition Robespierre exclaimed, addressing the entire Convention: "It is to you pure men that I address myself, and not to the brigands." What is this? Will a guillotine maneuvered by one man be charged with knowing which men are pure and which are brigands?

The storm blew stronger. Robespierre, on the verge of sinking, called out to Collot d'Herbois, who was presiding and assisting in the shipwreck: "President of the assassins: will you give me the floor?"

But the Dantonist Thuriot had taken Collot's place in the chair. After the pitiful ghost of Hébert it was Danton's great one that presided. And it was Danton who said to Robespierre, "You'll have the floor when it's your turn."

But would Danton really have said this? Robespierre's voice cracked and grew hoarse. Garnier de l'Aube shouted: "You're being suffocated by Danton's blood."

And in a last attempt to speak, he said: "And so it is Danton you want to avenge. Cowards! Why didn't you defend him?"

In this final cry I believe I hear despair mixed with regret. It was the little-known Louchet who spoke the decisive words: "I demand the indictment of Robespierre." The arrest was decided, not only of Robespierre, but of Saint-Just and Couthon; Robespierre the Younger and Lebas asked that they too be tried along with their great friend.

The Convention, moved but determined to put an end to all this, acceded to their request. All of them went up to the bar and were handed over to bailiffs, who were hesitant about laying hands on men who just a few minutes before represented the government of the triumphant Revolution.

Was it from fear or because of a secret watchword that the jailers refused to receive these fearsome prisoners? The latter went to the *Hôtel de Ville*, and on Barère's motion they were immediately declared outlaws. Would they resist this decree by force? Supported by the Commune, the Jacobins, and the National Guard, would Robespierre attempt to do violence to the Convention? Many of his friends pressed him to act.

After some hesitation, he refused to do so. It was no longer a May 31 or a June 2 that was being asked of him. The Convention, in decreeing his arrest, in declaring him an outlaw, had committed itself against him. It was the entire Convention that he had to smash. But in the name of what principle? By virtue of what right? And what would he do on the morrow? He would be nothing but a dictator lost in the void who would soon be devoured by the armies; a civil sub-Cromwell at the mercy of the first military adventurer claiming to undo the *coup d'état*. He waited. In the meanwhile, Barras and Léonard Bourdon, in the name of the Convention, crisscrossed the streets of Paris, haranguing the citizens, appealing to them against the "tyrant," against the "conspirators." And all those worn down by the extreme tension of affairs and who hoped for calm from the fall of the great man; all those who after so many bloody wounds were still moved by the prestige of the Convention and the word of the law, rallied to them. They brought several sections along with them and invaded the *Hôtel de Ville*. A gendarme shattered Robespierre's jaw with a pistol shot; Couthon was seriously wounded by a saber blow; Lebas shot himself in the head. Saint-Just, proud and stoic, remained unshakeable and silent beneath the insults.

The blood-soaked Robespierre was transported to the Committee of Public Safety and there, laid out on a table, wiping his cruel wound with his handkerchief, indifferent to the cowardly insults being shouted at him, he reflected as he awaited death. Perhaps he saw it as a liberator. It delivered him from problems that had defeated his spirit and from responsibilities beyond human capability. It also delivered him from the anguish he felt for the punishment of Danton and Camille Desmoulins. Since he was dying for the Revolution, hadn't he had the right to deliver blows for it?

At noon on 10 Thermidor, the outlaws were transferred to the Conciergerie by order of Billaud-Varenne. The itinerary of their final voyage was meant to make them resemble all those they had themselves sent to their deaths. At 4:00 p.m., they were taken to the gallows. Women danced behind the tumbrils and insulted Robespierre. He smiled sadly and doubtless forgave them. He had faith in justice and the future. As they passed, a child smeared blood on the door of the Duplay house.[14] Robespierre turned his head away, and not a tear fell from his eyes. He hadn't closed his heart to suffering; rather he had tamed it in service to the Revolution and the Fatherland.

---

14 Robespierre's residence.

17
How Should We Judge the Revolutionaries?

A historian is always allowed to oppose hypotheses to fate. He is allowed to point out the errors of men and parties and to imagine that without these errors events would have followed another course. I have spoken of Robespierre's immense services after May 31, organizing the revolutionary power, saving France from civil war, anarchy, and defeat. I have also spoken of how, after the crushing of Hébertism and Dantonism, he was struck with doubt, blindness, and distraction.

But what must never be forgotten when judging these men is that the problems fate imposed on them were formidable and probably beyond human strength. Perhaps it wasn't possible for one generation alone to bring down the *ancien régime*, create new laws and rights, raise an enlightened and proud people from the depths of ignorance, poverty, and misery, fight against an international league of tyrants and slaves, and to put all passions and forces to use in this combat while at the same time ensuring the evolution of the fevered, exhausted country towards normal order and well-ordered freedom. The France of the Revolution required a century, countless trials, backslidings into monarchy, reawakenings of the Republic, invasions, dismemberments, *coups d'état*, and civil wars before it finally arrived at the organization of the Republic, at the establishing of equal liberty through universal suffrage. The great workers of revolution and democracy who labored and fought more than a century ago are not accountable to us for a labor that required several generations to be accomplished. To judge them as if they should have brought the drama to a close, as if history was not going to continue after them, is both childish and unjust. Their work was necessarily limited, but it was great. They affirmed the idea of democracy to its fullest extent. They provided the world with the first example of a great country governing and saving itself through the power of the entire people. They gave the Revolution the magnificent prestige of the idea and the indispensable prestige of victory. And they gave France and the world so prodigious an impetus towards freedom that, despite reaction and eclipses, the new rights they established took definitive possession of history.

Democracy and Socialism

Socialism proclaims and rests on these new rights. It is a democratic party to the highest degree since it wants to organize the sovereignty of all in both the economic and political spheres. And it bases the new society on the rights of the human person, since it wants to grant every individual the concrete means of development that alone will permit him to fully realize himself.

I wrote this long history of the Revolution up till the 9 Thermidor in the midst of struggle, a struggle against the enemies of socialism, the Republic, and democracy. A struggle as well among the socialists themselves over the best methods of action and combat. And the further I advanced under the crossfire of that battle, the stronger was my conviction that democracy is a great conquest for the proletariat.

It is at one and the same time a forceful means of action and the form in accordance with which economic and political relations should be ordered. This was the source of the passionate joy I felt when I saw the molten metal of socialism that flowed from the Revolution and democracy as if from a furnace.

In an important sense—in the sense Babeuf meant it when he invoked it in speaking of Robespierre—we are the party of democracy and the Revolution. But we haven't shackled and frozen it. We don't claim to have fixed human society in the economic and social formulae that prevailed between 1789 and 1795 and which responded to living and economic conditions that are no more. The bourgeois democratic parties too often limit themselves to picking out a few fragments of cooled-off lava from the foot of the volcano, to scooping up some extinguished ash from around the blaze. Instead of this, the burning metal must be poured into new molds.

The problem of property is no longer posed, can no longer be posed, as it was in 1789 or 1793. Private property was then proclaimed to be both the form and the guarantee of human individuality. Given the existence of large-scale capitalist industry, the socialist association of producers and the common and collective property of the means and methods of labor have become the conditions for universal liberation. Strong class action by the proletariat is needed in order to wrest the Revolution and democracy from all that is now outdated and retrograde in the bourgeois world view.

"Class" and not "sect," for the proletariat must organize all of life, and it can only organize democracy and life by involving itself in them. The action must be grand and free and carried out under the discipline of a clear ideal. A democratic politics and a class politics: these are the two non-contradictory terms the proletarian force moves between, and which history one day will merge in the unity of social democracy.

In this way socialism is attached to the Revolution without being chained to it. And this is why we have traced the heroic efforts of revolutionary democracy with a free mind and a fervent heart.

I pass to the hands of our friends the torch whose flames have been swirled about by the storm winds and which half-consumed itself in tragically lighting up the world. A tormented but immortal flame which despotism and counter-revolutionaries will strive mightily to extinguish and which, ever-revived, will expand into an ardent socialist hope. It was in the murky atmosphere of Thermidor that the light of the revolution would now have to struggle.

Index